Georges Perrot, Charles Chipiez

History of Art in Sardinia, Judaea, Syria, and Asia Minor

Georges Perrot, Charles Chipiez

History of Art in Sardinia, Judaea, Syria, and Asia Minor

ISBN/EAN: 9783744752404

Printed in Europe, USA, Canada, Australia, Japan

Cover: Foto ©Thomas Meinert / pixelio.de

More available books at **www.hansebooks.com**

HISTORY OF ART IN SARDINIA AND JUDÆA.

HISTORY OF
Art in Sardinia, Judæa, Syria, and Asia Minor.

FROM THE FRENCH

OF

GEORGES PERROT,

PROFESSOR IN THE FACULTY OF LETTERS, PARIS; MEMBER OF THE INSTITUTE,

AND

CHARLES CHIPIEZ.

ILLUSTRATED WITH FOUR HUNDRED AND SIX ENGRAVINGS, AND
EIGHT STEEL AND COLOURED PLATES.

IN TWO VOLUMES.—VOL. II.

TRANSLATED AND EDITED BY

I. GONINO.

London: CHAPMAN AND HALL, Limited.

New York: A. C. ARMSTRONG AND SON.

1890.

CONTENTS.

THE HITTITES.

NORTHERN SYRIA AND CAPPADOCIA.

CHAPTER I.

THE HISTORY AND THE WRITING OF THE HITTITES.

CHAPTER II.

NORTHERN SYRIA—EASTERN HITTITES.

CHAPTER III.

ASIA MINOR—WESTERN HITTITES.

CHAPTER IV.

ARTISTIC MONUMENTS OF THE WESTERN HITTITES.

CHAPTER V.

LIST OF ILLUSTRATIONS.

PLATE.

A HISTORY OF ART IN SARDINIA AND JUDÆA.

THE HITTITES.

NORTHERN SYRIA AND CAPPADOCIA.

CHAPTER I.

THE HISTORY AND THE WRITING OF THE HITTITES.

§ 1.—*How Oriental Civilization spread Westward by Overland Routes.*

THE Phœnicians were not the only people which in remote ages acted as intermediate agents between the East and the West, or, to speak more accurately, between the older civilized races of the Euphrates and the Nile valleys on the one side, and on the other the as yet savage tribes of the islands and the countries bordering on the Ægean. The germs of culture deposited in the sister peninsulas of Greece and Italy, which were to blossom out with so much vigour, far removed from the hot zones where they had first come to maturity, were not wholly due to the ubiquitous light crafts of the Sidonians. The social habits engendered by polished life, with the handicrafts, the processes, and the needs they involved, were likewise propagated by overland routes, wherever their diffusion was not arrested by impassable arid wastes, the ungenial climate of denuded uplands and high mountain ranges covered with snow during part of the year, as towards the east and north. No such obstacles existed to the westward of Mesopotamia, and

the north-west of Syria, where from the Euphrates to the foot of
the Amanus, the land is almost everywhere open to cultivation,
and in some places, around Damascus, for instance, it may be
ranked among the most fertile in the world.   These plains were,
doubtless, occupied in very early days by pastoral tribes that
found here abundant grass to graze their flocks, the smallest
amount of manual labour ensuring comparative ease, almost
wealth, for the overflowing of the rivers and winter rains have
deposited everywhere a layer of rich soil.   The Amanus, notwithstanding its steep rocky sides, and even the snowy-peaked Taurus,
have at all times been crossed by numerous passes.   Beyond the
defiles of the Amanus are not forbidding parallel ranges, as in
Kurdistan, which must be successively scaled, but the broad plain
of Cilicia ; and as soon as the narrow gorges of the Taurus are
got over, plateaux covered with vegetation are seen everywhere,
presenting an agreeable contrast with the naked aspect of the
mountains around, dotted here and there with habitations which
testify to the improved conditions of nature.   Valleys, as so many
roads prepared by nature, intersect these gently undulating
plateaux towards the west, yielding easy ascent for the circulating
of man and ideas.

Owing to this happy combination of circumstances, a civilizing
stream must ever have flowed from northern Syria to the mouth
of the Hermus and the Mæander, a stream which, although remote
from its head source, had sufficient vitality to cross the Ægean
without being confounded with its azure waters, causing its shores
to blossom forth wherever they were kissed by its flood.   Comparative philology, archæology, and numismatics, have enabled
modern historians to remove the landmarks of civilization thousands of years further back than was formerly done by the sole
light of classic writers.   In the early art of Greece, especially
Ionia, where native genius first showed itself, were certain elements
which it was vaguely felt could not be derived from a Phœnician
source, and which indicated that other influences had been at work
in bringing about this development.   The question, who was the
people that had been instrumental in effecting this progress, was
not easily answered ; for it was evident that this borrowed art was
much older than the Eastern empire, which by the conquest of
Persia, had extended its limits to the Euxine, the Propontis, and
the Ægean.   On the other hand, it was well known that the

distance from the great river to the Mæander had never been
crossed by the Chaldees and Assyrians, who, at the time of their
greatest prosperity, had not ventured beyond the Halys and the
Taurus.   Trade and its acting influence on the manners and ideas
of nationalities were adduced to explain these importations.
Caravans, it was urged, had included in the bales which they
brought to Sinope, Miletus, and Ephesus, these peculiar types and
plastic forms, which the Ionians with their marvellous facility had
used to so splendid a purpose.

Trade had no doubt its share in this movement ; but, however
active we may imagine it, it will not account for the many-sided
discoveries upon which the attention and acumen of archæologists
have been directed of late.   The vast plain which stretches from
the Euphrates to the coast, on which rose the first Ionian cities
known to the world, cannot be considered as a mere open waste.
This is so far from being the case, that the vast region divided by
the Taurus in two unequal parts, everywhere bears traces of independent and original development.   Thus, in the valley of the
Orontes, and the central plateau of Asia Minor, are monuments
resembling in some of their details those of Mesopotamia, yet
preserving a character of their own.   This is evidenced in the
outline of their figures, and more particularly in their hieroglyphs,
which are distinct from Chaldæan writing, and seem to have been
used from the Euphrates to the Hermus and Mæander, whilst
we have positive proof that they were known east and west
of the Taurus range, until they were replaced by the Phœnician
alphabet.

The dress, weapons, and religious symbols figured on these
bas-reliefs, side by side with inscribed characters, point to rites
and customs as peculiar and distinct as the actual hieroglyphs.
We cannot imagine that the people to whom they belong were
content to act the subordinate part of conveyers and agents during
the lapse of a thousand years.   It is undeniable that certain
elements of their art were borrowed from Egypt and Mesopotamia, but these they elaborated and transformed to a certain
extent by personal effort, giving them the impress of their own
individuality.

The question that presents itself to the historian, is to know
which of the races interposing between Babylon and Miletus may
be credited with sufficient inventive genius, to have led this

secondary movement and created the monuments that we propose to describe and classify in the next chapter. We shall call to our aid recent discoveries which have thrown floods of light upon this obscure question, the importance to which, in France at least, has not been justly apprehended.

§ 2.—*Recent Discoveries in Northern Syria.*

In 1812, the celebrated traveller Burckhardt was in Syria hard at work learning Arabic, preparatory to visiting Mecca in the guise of a pilgrim. Whilst at Hamath, now Hamah, he noticed a stone embedded in the angle of the wall of a house, " with signs and figures which were certainly hieroglyph, but different from the Egyptian."[1] His work was read at the time by every one who felt interested in Syria, and wished to know something of her past and present condition. But, curious enough, nobody seems to have noticed the words just quoted, and no subsequent explorer tried to rediscover the monument. Indeed, so little was known about the place that only a few years ago (1865) *Murray's Hand-book* declared, " There are no antiquities at Hamath."[2]

In 1870, Mr. J. Augustus Johnson, Consul-General U.S. at Damascus, and the Rev. S. Jessup, of the Syrian Mission, visited Hamath, and during their short stay heard of the stone seen by Burckhardt, and of other inscriptions of the same nature. Their attempt to obtain a copy was frustrated by the fanaticism of the natives, which is perhaps nowhere so rampant as in this part of Syria, and which obliged them to desist. The consul dared not repeat the experiment, and was fain to be content with such copies as could be obtained from a " native artist," as he somewhat pompously styles him, and these he forthwith despatched to Damascus. The following year (July, 1871), he published a fac-simile of one of the inscriptions—that seen by Burckhardt—in the *First Statement of the Palestine Exploration Society*. The copy, though imperfect, did much to awaken public interest to the inscriptions, and had the happy effect of stimulating others, who presently succeeded.

In 1871, the English Palestine Exploration Society sent out Mr.

[1] Burckhardt, *Travels in Syria*, p. 164.
[2] *Handbook for Syria*, tom. ii. p. 588, 1868.

Tyrwhitt Drake, the joint author of *Unexplored Syria*, as their representative, with instructions to make copies of the stones. His perfect knowledge of the country and of the Arabs was invaluable in dealing with them.   After a good deal of manœuvring, he contrived to take a photograph and copy of the most important text; but it soon became known, and the other stones had to be abandoned, for fear of a general uproar.   Captain Burton, then British consul at Damascus, also visited Hamath.   He managed to see all the monuments, noting carefully their position and size; but he too was obliged to be content with copies made by a Greek, Kostantin-el-Khuri by name.   These he published, in ten sheets, in *Unexplored Syria*, at the same time warning the public that, in places, "the imagination of the 'painter' had run wild with him."   His attempt to purchase one of the stones was unsuccessful, owing to the greed of the owner of the house in which the stone was embedded, who began by asking a hundred napoleons. Further negotiations led to no better result, for Levantine dealers began to barter for the monuments, in the hope of selling them in Europe at enormous profit.   Fears began to be entertained lest these stones, which had lain forgotten and been held of no account for so many ages, but which had suddenly acquired a fabulous value and importance in the eyes of the natives, since they had seen them coveted by those who were supposed to know, should share the fate of the Moabite tablet.   Nor were these apprehensions ill-founded, for in 1872 Messrs. Smith and Drake, in their visit to Aleppo, lit upon a basalt slab similarly engraved, of which they made an indifferent copy; the following year, wishing to obtain a proper cast, they discovered that the stone had been broken up by the natives.   At this juncture, an opportunity, which was promptly accepted, offered itself to Dr. W. Wright, of the English Mission at Damascus, to visit Hamath.   The results of this expedition were presently published in book form, entitled *The Empire of the Hittites*, from which we shall freely borrow in the sequel of these pages.[1]

During his residence at Damascus he had become acquainted with the Governor-General of Syria, a post then filled by Subhi Pasha, of Greek extraction, a man of rare intelligence and integrity

---

[1] Second edition, Nisbet and Co., 1886, 1 vol. in 8vo, xxxiii.–246 pages, and 26 plates; with decipherment of Hittite inscriptions by Professor Sayce, a map by Sir C. Wilson, and a complete set of Hittite inscriptions revised by Mr. W. H. Rylands.

His fine collection of coins and engraved gems—subsequently sold to England—had made him known to Western scholars, with some of whom he was in correspondence. He at once recognized the importance of the inscribed stones, and, unwilling that his country should be deprived of them, he telegraphed to the Sultan to have them securely deposited in the museum at Constantinople. The Waly's offer to Dr. Wright to accompany him on a journey of inspection included Mr. W. Kirby Green, British consul at Damascus. Hamath stood on the list of places that were to be visited. Here the two Europeans lost no time in discovering the locality of the inscribed stones. They next persuaded the pasha to have them taken to the serai—governor's palace—that they might have leisure to take good casts of them undisturbed. The removal of these peculiar monuments produced a great commotion among the green and white turbans of the place. The next day, a deputation, consisting of all the more influential members of the Moslem community, waited on the Waly to urge a restoration of the stones. The account of this interview and the final discomfiture of the ulemas should be read in Dr. Wright's graphic narrative, where he recounts by what skilful management—a combination of good-humour and firm policy—Subhi Pasha not only succeeded in quelling the disturbance, but sent away the deputation satisfied and comforted.

The Hamah stones, five in number,[1] are far away the most important monuments of this class that have as yet been discovered. Messrs. Wright and Green, to guard against accidents, of frequent occurrence among Turkish officials, took two sets of casts in plaster of Paris ; one was sent to the Government for the British Museum and the other to the Palestine Fund, where everybody may study them, their excellence making them as good as the actual originals.[2]

The copy that had been made of the Aleppo inscription, although very imperfect, served to prove that similar characters were not confined to Hamath, but were to be found in other parts of the country.[3] Soon after (1874 and 1875), Mr. Skene, British consul

[1] See Salomon Reinach, *Catalogue du Musée Impérial* [Constantinople] *d'Antiquités*, p. 83, 1882.

[2] The Plates I–V., "Hamath Inscriptions," in Dr. Wright's book, were reproduced from the casts sent to England.

[3] These copies were reproduced in Plates V., VI., VII., in Dr. Wright's *Empire*.

at Aleppo, and George Smith, in the same year, visited some ruins on the right bank of the Euphrates, marked in the map about six hours below the village of Birejik, which they identified as being the site of ancient Garga-mish, Carchemish, so often figured on Egyptian and Assyrian monuments as commanding the minor stream of the great river. The ruins had been described by Maundrell and Pococke and noticed by other travellers, but none of them had suspected that the *tell*, "mound," called by the Arabs Kala'at Jerablus, covered the remains of the ancient capital of the Hittites. Some authorities derive Jerablus, or Jerabis, from Hierapolis, "holy city," and Kala'at, Kala'ah, "fortress," "high." Curious to say, this is the exact meaning it bears with the Arabs.[1]

A temple to Ashtoreth stood here during the Roman sway, described by Lucian as one of the finest and most frequented in this part of the world. Hierapolis rose on the ruins of the older city, destroyed by the Assyrians, and, like its predecessor, acquired great importance and became a flourishing place under the Seleucidæ. Here Mr. Skene and George Smith, at a short interval from each other, were shown fragments of the ancient wall of the citadel, still commanding an elevation of more than thirty metres above the bed of the river, with several well-cut shafts of columns and large blocks of basalt, where, side by side with sculptures which recalled those of Assyria, were inscriptions akin to those at Hamath. In his third and fatal journey, George Smith wrote from Jerablus to the trustees of the British Museum, pointing out the importance of properly exploring the site. They immediately procured a firman from Constantinople, empowering him to begin excavations at once; but it never reached him, for he died of fever in a few days at Aleppo, where he had gone to wait for it. Mr. Skene had been transferred to some other post, hence his successor, Mr. Henderson, was entrusted to conduct the diggings. The "finds" were duly despatched to the British Museum, where I saw them in 1880; those that were too heavy for transport or of minor interest were left behind.[2]

Simultaneously with the discoveries at Jerabis, attention was drawn to another monument, first copied by Major Fisher, and

---

[1] It is possible that during the Roman rule there was here a stronghold to protect the great Syrian temple and keep in check the Parthians, and afterwards the Sassanides, who occupied the country east of the river.

[2] They are figured in *The Empire of the Hittites*, Plates VIII. and XIII.

subsequently by the Rev. E. J. Davis, from whose drawing a plate was published in 1876 in the *Transactions of the Biblical and Archæological Society*. It was found at Ibreez, or Ibris, in ancient Lycaonia, near Kuleth Boghaz, the Cilician gates of classic times. The bas-relief, rock-cut, consists of two figures, a king, or god, and his worshipper, with hieroglyphs, many of which were identical with those on the Hamath, Aleppo, and Jerabis stones.[1] This monument is interesting, inasmuch as it shows that the peculiar system of characters first noticed at Hamath extended over a far greater area than had at first been supposed ; traces being found throughout central Asia Minor, and about the mouth of rivers that carry their waters to the Ægean. Other rock-cut sculptures were noticed at Boghaz Keui, in the uplands formerly known as Pteria, and at Eyuk, both east of the Halys ; whilst near Smyrna the "Nymphi warrior, the pseudo Sesostris, and the so-called Niobe," had been described. In 1882, a German mission, headed by Dr. Puchstein, visited the vast tract that lies between the Euphrates and the Pyramus. They discovered monuments with figures of the type always seen side by side with hieroglyphs that have been called Hamathite ; but from the very meagre official report that was issued, we cannot determine their real character.[2] Recently too at Merash, ancient Germanicia, on the Pyramus in Cilicia, a lion was found built in the wall of a castle, entirely covered with characters resembling those at Hamath and Aleppo.[3]

These signs were not only used in monumental inscriptions on the mountain side, or on the massive foundations of temples and palaces, but were likewise introduced in political and commercial transactions ; with this difference, that the type became smaller and more cursive, as may be ascertained in all public collections where numerous clay seals or casts are preserved. Hundreds of similar seals were found by Sir H. Layard in the archive room of Sennacherib's palace at Kujunjik ;[4] and others are also reported from Asia Minor.[5] Finally, Sorlin-Dorigny presented cylinders to

[1] *Loc. cit.*, Plates XXVI., XXVII , p. 162.

[2] *Berichte über eine Ruse im Kurdistan.* Otto Puchstein (*Sitzungsberichte* der Academie, Berlin, 1882, p. 845, and following).

[3] This lion is now in the museum at Constantinople.—Editor.

[4] Wright, *The Empire.*

[5] We have published a whole series in the *Revue Archéologique*, tom. xliv. p. 333, under the title, "Sceaux Hittites en terre cuite appartenant à M. G. Schlumberger."

the Louvre of peculiar make, wherein ideographs and figures recall those at Hamath.

Our space forbids giving more than a few specimens of these inscriptions, but those who should wish to study the whole series will find them in the *Transactions of the Biblical and Archæological Society*, where they have been admirably reproduced, with notes by the secretary, Mr. Rylands. The woodcuts published in

FIG. 254.—Hittite Hieroglyph. Actual size. St. Elme Gautier.

Dr. Wright's work were copied from these, thus completing and supplementing the letterpress. A primary fact to be deduced in regard to these ideographs, signs, and figures, is that they were of native invention, different from Egyptian hieratic writing, and in many instances with a physiognomy of their own. As far back as Rosellini,[1] and, after him, all the Egyptologists who visited the

They were drawn by Mr. Rylands for the Biblical and Archæological Society, and reproduced by Mr. Wright, Plates XVI., XVII.

[1] Rosellini's view is quoted by Kiepert in his paper upon the Nymphi monument, tom. i., *Archæologische Zeitung*, pp. 33, and following. Consult also MASPERO, *Histoire Ancienne des Peuples a'Orient*, 4ᵉ edit. p. 247.

pseudo Sesostris,[1] on examination of the characters carved in relief
between the head and the spear, which at one time were supposed
to be a royal cartouche, were unanimous in declaring them unlike
the hieroglyphs of Egypt. To-day, when inscribed monuments of
this class abound, affording ample scope from which their distinct
manipulation and outline can be traced, it is hard to realize that
they should ever have been confounded with Egyptian writing,
which is decidedly finer and more realistic than the ruder Hamathite characters. The hieroglyphs which are now generally called
"Hittite," whether in Northern Syria or Asia Minor, with two
exceptions, are carved in relief; a disposition which has only been
noticed in the oldest known Egyptian monuments. What is a
rare occurrence at Memphis, forms the rule at Carchemish,
Kadesh, Eyuk, and
Boghaz-Keui. On
looking at them, we
feel that they were
traced by a sturdy
race more accus-
tomed to handle the
spear than the point
of the graver, and
that when they
carved these charac-
ters they were still
at the stage when
art had not been
conventionalized by
long practice, and
that time was not
given them to pro-
gress beyond a real-
istic rendering of
nature. Hence some
of these images, despite awkward manipulation, bear a lifelike

Fig. 255.—Hittite hieroglyph. Actual size, St. Elme Gautier.

[1] Herodotus, ii. 106. We published an article as far back as 1866, to demonstrate
that the rock-cut figure in the Karabel Pass was not of Assyrian nor yet of Egyptian
origin, but the result of an art peculiar to Asia Minor ("Le Bas-relief de Nymphi,
d'après de nouveaux renseignements," *Revue Archéologique*, tom. xiii.). This article
was reproduced in our *Mémoires d'Archéologie, d'Épigraphie et d'Histoire*, in 8°.
Didier, 1875.

FIG. 256.—Hittite inscription, Jerabis. WRIGHT, *The Empire*, Plate X.

resemblance to the objects they represent, such as is never seen on the monuments of Egypt. Note, for instance, the two conies, figured among a number of other characters to the right of the Merash lion (Figs. 254, 255).[1] Could anything be conceived more truthful than the action of the two timid creatures, which seem to have been surprised by a sportsman; one has already taken to flight, whilst the other is preparing to follow its companion. We could almost imagine that the artist had chalked them down as he came upon them by the woodside. This faithful portraiture applies to the human form as well as the heads of animals; the former is generally placed at the commencement of the inscription, with one arm raised to his mouth, as if to emphasize his words, or prepare us for what is to follow. Rough though the art may be, it is so instinct with truth and sincerity, that we are never puzzled as to the intention of the artist (Fig. 256). These inscriptions, about four inches apart, are carved within horizontal lines, also in relief, except where only two or three signs occur. Some occupy the whole division, whilst the smaller are ranged in two or more rows, so as to fill up the whole space. This arrangement, irregular in detail, produces uniformity of outline, and is more satisfactory to the eye than the haphazard disposition of Egyptian hieroglyphs.

As scholars began to transcribe and collate these texts, found on so many points widely apart from each other, they naturally inquired who were the people that had traced these mysterious characters. As so often happens, when a problem of unusual interest engages the attention of the learned, persons in different parts of the globe came almost simultaneously to the same conclusion. To Professor Sayce, however, must be assigned the merit of having perceived it plainly and clearly from the outset, and of having invested the subject with an amount of verisimilitude as to be almost equivalent to certainty.[2] Archibald H. Sayce,

---

[1] Our attention was called to a cast of this charming monument in the Trocadéro, from which our draughtsman, through the kindness of Dr. Hamy, made the spirited drawing of the woodcuts (Figs. 254, 255).

[2] On the bearing of Professor Sayce's works, see our article in the *Revue des Deux Mondes*, 15 Juillet, 1886, entitled "Une Civilisation Retrouvée. Les Hétéens, leur écriture, et leur art." *The Principles of Comparative Philology*, more than any other of Professor Sayce's works, helped to make his name known on the Continent. It has been translated into French by Ernest Jovy, with a preface by Michel Bréal, in 12, 1884, Delagrave. It was owing to this work that he was nominated Assistant-Professor to the Oriental Chair, illustrated by Max Müller. Professor Sayce is the

M.A., Fellow of Queen's, Deputy-Professor of Comparative Philology of All Souls, Oxford, stands in the foremost rank among the progressive men of our time. To the wide range of inquiry which recent discoveries have added to the domain of science, he brings a mind singularly receptive, and of Attic rather than Anglo-Saxon vivacity. The origin and decipherment of the inscribed characters in Northern Syria and Asia Minor seem to have had peculiar fascination for him. For nearly a decade, he has done more, with his ready pen, than any other man, to substantiate and popularize the theory which identifies the Kheta (Hittites), with these ideographs. Their name is of as frequent occurrence in the epic of the Theban poet, Pentaur, as Ramses, the hero he celebrates : the beloved of Ammon, whose fabulous courage and invincibility far outweigh those of the Homeric champion.[1]

author of a work on Semitic philology; and at one time ran a pretty close race on the study of Assyriology with our lamented Stanislas Guyard. At first, he was solely concerned in trying to decipher the obscure language represented by the cuneiform inscriptions. He soon enlarged the circle of his researches at Van, in Armenia, but during his frequent visits to the East, whither he was obliged to repair for the sake of his health, he has followed with keen interest all the explorations that have been made during the last fifteen years in Egypt, Syria, Cyprus, Asia Minor, Argolid, and other localities in Greece. The results of his investigations have appeared in numerous articles published by learned societies and leading English reviews. The chief of his publications are : "A Forgotten Empire in Asia Minor" (*Fraser's Magazine*,* August, 1888) ; "The Monuments of the Hittites," with capital map, plates, and figures (*Bibl. and Archæ. Soc.*, vol. vii. pp. 248–293) ; "The Bilingual Hittite and Cuneiform Inscription of Tarkondemos," with plate, *loc. cit.*, pp. 294–308. *The Proceedings of the Biblical and Archæological Society* contain sundry notes from his pen, brimful of facts and ideas, which, even when we cannot endorse them, are always suggestive. The result of his journeys and researches were published in 1883, under the title, *The Ancient Empires of the East. Herodotus I.*, III., with notes, introductions, and appendices, in 8°, London, Macmillan. In his introduction, he seems to us to do scant justice to the father of history ; the best part of the work, however, is an appendix, which, besides chronological tables, contains a substantial and brilliant *résumé* of the history of Eastern empires brought up to date.

[1] Long extracts from Pentaur's poem will be found in MM. Maspero and Lenormant's *Ancient Histories*. In this part of our work we have adopted M. Maspero's transcriptions of names of peoples and cities. Literal translations of Pentaur's poem may be seen in *Records of the Past*, ii. 61 ; and in Brugsch's, *Egypt under the Pharaohs*, ii. 56.

---

* *Fraser's Magazine* ceased to exist in 1888, and its successor, *Longman's*, has no such paper during that year.—Editor.

§ 3.—*The History of the Hittites from Biblical, Egyptian, and Assyrian Documents.*

The recitals of battles and the bulletins of victories which may be seen on the walls of Theban temples and the palaces at Nineveh, were the instances that led us to infer the place which the warlike race variously called Kheta, Khati, and Khatti, whose history we are about to summarise, had occupied for centuries in the Eastern world, so far at least as translations made by Egyptologists and Assyriologists of the various texts will enable us to reconstitute it. But long before these had been deciphered we read their name in the Old Testament, where they appear as Hitti, *pl.* Hittim; Bene-Heth, son of Heth ; whilst in the Septuagint we find the variants Χετ, Χεττίν, Χεττίη, Χεταῖοι, whence the French *Héttéens*. The initial letter is the Hebrew ח, *ch*, always pronounced with an aspirate guttural sound, and the double τ is a strong terminal dental.　These, it will be seen, are the same, whether we find them in Hebrew texts, Egyptian or Assyrian inscriptions.　The vowels, it is well known, have but a relative importance in those languages, and were seldom noted in writing ; hence some degree of uncertainty must always exist as to their full value.

The power of the Hittites was already on the wane when the Hebrews crossed the Jordan.　They had ceased to occupy advanced outposts in the south, and had concentrated their forces towards northern Syria, where their cities were far beyond the farthest limits ever attained by the Israelites under David and Solomon to render a conflict between the two races possible. Hence it is, that in the Bible their name occurs as though from hearsay rather than personal knowledge.　But, however meagre our information from this source may be, it coincides in a marvellous manner with Assyrian and Egyptian inscriptions.　Aided by these, mere biblical allusions become rich in suggestive meaning, and enable us to read aright many a passage that had been obscure and a dead letter in reference to the Hittites, who at one time made their influence felt almost over the whole of Syria. Thus, in Genesis (x. 15, 16), they head the list of the sons of Canaan, coming immediately after Sidon.　When Abraham came to Hebron as a wanderer, he found the Hittites among the settled and peaceful inhabitants of the country ; clearly evidenced by the purchase of the field with the cave of Machpelah (*Gen.* xxiii. 3–18 ; xxv. 9). Again, after the death of Moses, the Lord spake to Joshua to assure Him of the fulfilment of His promise, saying : " From the wilderness and this Lebanon, even unto the great river [Euphrates] all the land of the Hittites, and unto the great sea [Mediterranean] towards the going down of the sun, shall oe yours" (i. 4). When the spies sent to reconnoitre the land return to Moses, they describe the Hittites, together with the Amorites and the Jebusites, as "dwelling in the mountains " (*Numb.* xiii. 29, 30). A little later, when the Hebrews had crossed Jordan, they figure among the Canaanite tribes banded together to oppose the invaders (*Josh.* ix. 1).[1] About this time, the growing power of Egypt, under the Theban dynasty, obliged the Hittites to fall back northwards ; but under the degenerated Pharaohs of this race, Upper Egypt fell, whilst Lower Egypt rose in wealth and in importance with the new kings of Tanis and Bubastis. The rival parties were too busy at home striving for mastery to think of foreign conquests. During these years the Hebrews had gradually defeated the Canaanites, and gained possession of a large part of the country. Under David and Solomon they made their power felt from the Great River to the Nile, and such of the Hittites as had remained in the country were reduced to a servile condition, for we find them among the press-gangs employed in the building of the temple, together with the Amorites, the Jebusites, the Hivites, and the Perizzites, whom the Israelites had failed to destroy.[2]

After that time, no more reference is made in Hebrew writers to Hittites lingering in the Land of Promise. On the other hand, there are allusions to independent tribes occupying the country east and west of the Orontes, which can have been no other than Hittites. Evidence of their friendly relations with the Jewish empire may still be traced ; some of their princes owned allegiance and were among David's vassals.[3] Solomon numbered among his

---

[1] Under the early Judges the Hittites are enumerated with the other Canaanite tribes amidst which the Israelites found a footing (*Judg.* iii. 5).

[2] Reference to these tribes is indeed found in *Ezek.* xvi. 3, where the prophet rebukes Jerusalem for her pride : "Thus says the Lord unto Jerusalem, Thy birth and thy nativity is of the land of Canaan ; thy father was an Amorite, and thy mother an Hittite." But all the passage proves is that the names of Amorite and Hittite were still used as terms of reproach, synonymous with heathen in general parlance.

[3] This is deducible from a passage in 2 *Sam.* xxiv. 5–7, relating to the mission entrusted to Joab and his staff to number the people of Israel. "And when they

foreign wives daughters of the Hittites, Moabites, Ammonites, Edomites, and Sidonians (1 *Kings* xi. 1).   He brought up horses and chariots out of Egypt for the kings of the Hittites and those of the city of Aram (1 *Kings* v. 29).   We read that the Syrians whilst besieging Samaria fled panic-stricken, because the Lord caused the noise of chariots and horses to be heard in their camp (2 *Kings* vii. 6).   The inference to be deduced from this passage is that their might, like that of Egypt, lay in the number of their chariots, coinciding with what we know of them from Assyrian and Egyptian monuments, where they are represented fighting from cars.   To Egyptian and Assyrian paintings and sculptures we are indebted for our main information concerning the Hittites ; whom Jewish writers only mention in ignorant wonder, as of shadows vaguely perceived in the blueish distance of an almost boundless horizon.

The Kheta first appear in the history of Egypt under Manetho I. (eighteenth dynasty) ; from that date until Ramses III. they constantly figure on the mural paintings along with the Khar and the Ruten.   At the outset, they are scarcely distinguished from other Syrian tribes ; but a little later, they are described as a warlike, powerful race—sometimes indeed as the " vile enemy from Kadesh" —fiercely disputing the possession of Syria with the Egyptians. The name of this place was first brought into notice by the labours of Champollion.   In the great battlefield pictures of Egypt, Kadesh is represented as a fortress situated south of Hamath on Orontes, surrounded on all sides by water, so as to form an island, two bridges and causeways connecting it with the mainland.   A double wall encircled it, between which was a deep ditch or channel fed by the river.[1]

passed over Jordan, they pitched in Aroer, on the right side of the city that lieth in the midst of the river of Gad, and towards Jazer : then they came to Gilead, and to the land of Tahtim-Hodshi," or Hodsi. Tahtim-Hodshi has not been identified, but the Abbé Vigoureux is of opinion that the proper reading may be restored from some manuscripts of the Seventy, where we read : καὶ ἦλθον εἰς Γαλαὰδ καὶ εἰς γῆν Χεττίμ Χάδης : "And they came to Gilead and to the land of the Hittites of Kadesh." The Hebrew text has Hahitim, not Tahtim ; the slight difference between the *thau* and the *he* causes them to be frequently confused in the manuscripts (*Les Hétéens de la Bible dans la Revue des Questions Historiques*, tom. xxxi. pp. 58–120).

[1] This may be inferred from the picture in the temple of Ipsamboul, which portrays the battle fought by Ramses (ROSELLINI, *Monumenti Storici*, Plate CX. ; LEPSIUS, *Denkmæler*, Pt. III., Plate CLXIV.).   There can be no doubt about the identification of this city, for its name, " Kadesh," is carved on the wall. This detail,

The sculptures and paintings at Thebes and Ipsamboul, recording the battles fought by Ramses II. around Kadesh, show the
Orontes in the upper compartment. It surrounds the walls of the
fortress on three sides, widening out at one point, the outflow being
to the right of the picture (Fig. 257).

Kadesh has disappeared without leaving a trace, its very site
being a matter of dispute. It was rebuilt about two hours from
the river by the Greeks, who gave it the name of Emesa, now
Homs, but the lake formed by a dam at its north end still exists,
and on its banks must be sought the remains of the Hittite citadel.
The American traveller, Robinson, was the first who noticed this
lake, the excavation of which local tradition ascribes to Alexander
the Great, and which in Egyptian sculptures, commemorating this
great battle, is represented as close to the fortress. Owing to the
persistency of popular custom, not unusual in the East, the old
name of Kadesh, now Kades, still survives in the lake which was
once its chief defence. The island, topped by a tell, or mound, is
to the south,[1] and, were it explored, would doubtless disclose the
walls so often stormed by the Egyptians. Conder, on the contrary,
would recognize Tell Neby Mendeh as the site of Kadesh, which,
though much shrunk from its former size, has still an elevation of
60 m , and is situated 5500 m. south of the lake (Fig. 258).[2] The

omitted in Rosellini, is reproduced in Lepsius' drawing, which we have copied in our
woodcut taken from Rosellini's admirable sketch.

[1] Major Conder mentions the island now called Tell-el-Baheirah, and the lake
mound.

[2] *Ibid., Quarterly Statements, Palestine Exploration Fund,* pp. 163–175, 1881 ;
Heth and Moab, chap. i. I can scarcely conceive how he can refuse to acknowledge
that the "widening of the river" under the walls of Kadesh looks for all the world
like a lake. Excavations he thinks would be productive of the happiest results, the
ground around Neby Mendeh being strewn with pottery and chips that fell from
slabs cut out of calcareous stone and basalt. The natives, he states, apply the name
of Kades to foundation walls, which may be seen on the southern slope of the tell
on a level with the ground, whilst they restrict the name of Neby Mendeh to its
summit, occupied by a mosque. Mr. Tomkins, in the *Quarterly Statements,* p. 47,
1882, combats this view, and places Kadesh in the centre of the lake, about half a
mile each way from the mainland.

The conclusion reached by M. Ary Renan, who visited Northern Syria in 1886,
with regard to the moot site of ancient Kades, is in accord with Major Conder's
hypothesis. He argues that the islet identified by Robinson as covering the ruins
of Kadesh is so small as to have scarcely yielded sufficient space for a tower,
excluding therefore the possibility of having been the site of an important place,
such as the capital of the Hittites must have been ; moreover, no accumulation of
débris is to be seen on its narrow surface, such as we should expect around a great

Fig. 257.— View of Kadesh. After Egyptian monuments.

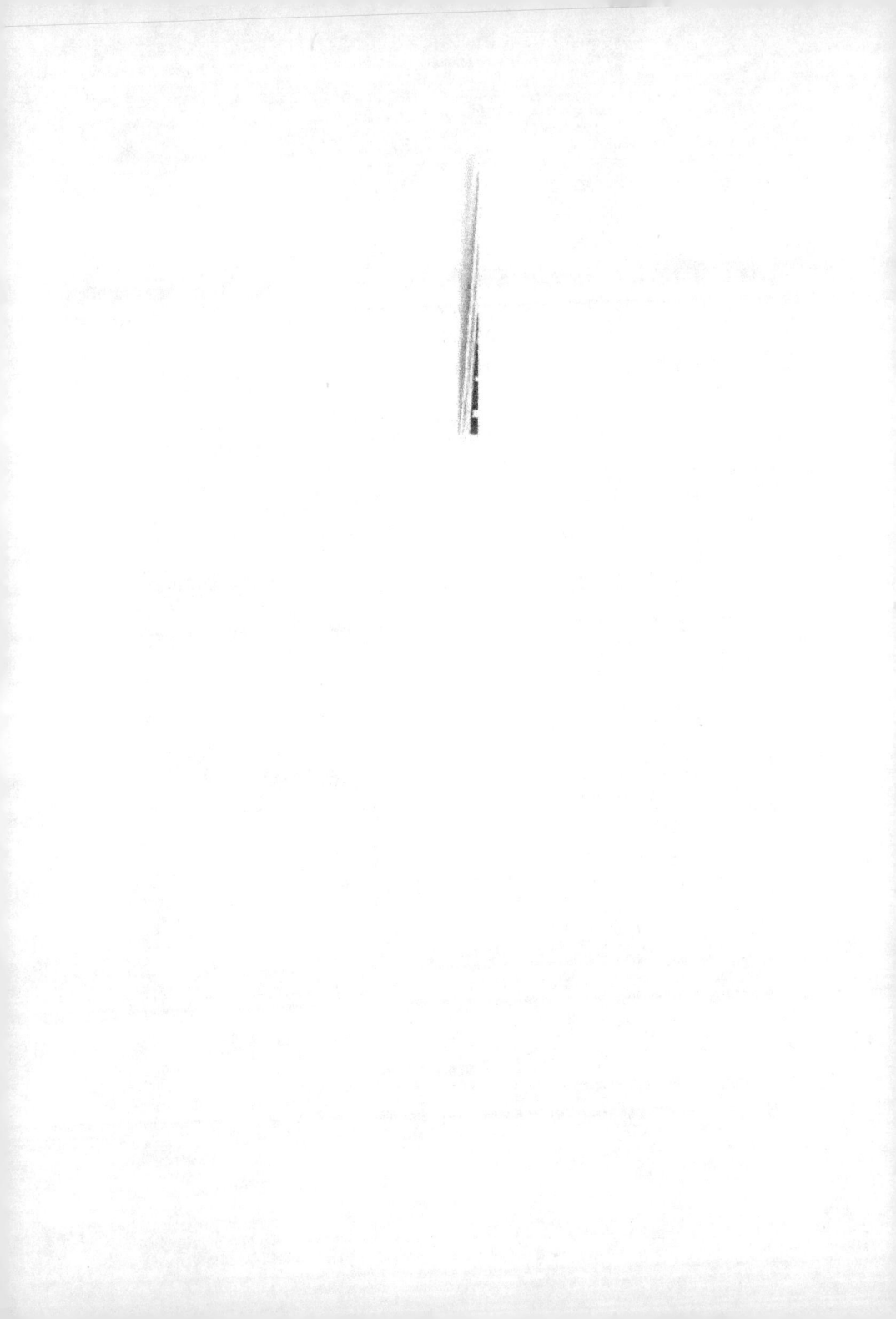

natives, according to Robinson, do not apparently know the reason why the lake is called Kades. Whatever may be the truth, the question is one easy of solution, for the two sites are very little way from each other. We know now that Robinson was not misled by mispronunciation or a sound imperfectly heard. Before him, Abul Fedah had mentioned the lake, which he calls Kedes, and which he considered owed its existence to the hand of man.[1]

Thothmes III. is the first Pharaoh whose line of march is known to us, but the route followed by the Egyptian armies for five hundred years, from Thothmes I., must always have been along the coast held by the Phœnicians and the

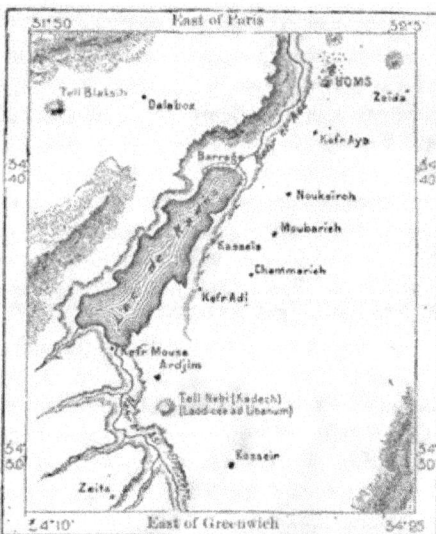

FIG. 258.—Lake of Kadesh. After Conder.

Philistines. At Megiddo, Thothmes III. encountered the King of Kadesh and with him all the Syrian tribes, including the Phœnicians. The allies were defeated, and, leaving their chariots, took refuge within the walls of the city, unhindered by the enemy,

centre. On the other hand, the Tell Neby Mendeh fulfils the conditions requisite in a fortified place. It rises about 60 m. above the level of the surrounding plain, and its base is sufficiently large to support the village on its slopes. It could be easily surrounded by water, for it is comprised in an angle formed by the Orontes and an arm on its right bank which joins the river a little below. The low ground around the hill is soft and marshy, and a dam would turn it in no time into a lake. Thus was obtained the Lake Homs, which is nothing but a shallow sheet of water, and probably not so old as recounted by local tradition, if we are to rely on a passage of the Talmud, cited by Neubaur, which runs thus : "Why should not the waters of Homs be numbered among the seas? Because they were due to the union of several rivers by the Emperor Diocletian" (*Geography of the Talmud*, p. 24).

[1] Upon Upper Syria, consult the *Mémoires* of l'Abbé Vigoureux, from which we have freely borrowed.

intent upon the rich plunder. Pharaoh tried to storm the place, but lack of war-engines obliged him to raise the siege and graciously to pardon the kings, soothing his pride with laying waste the country that lay before him. The effect of each successive expedition was to drive the confederates further north. In his sixth campaign, some years later, the Egyptian Pharaoh seems to have found no resistance in his onward progress until he reached Kadesh, behind whose walls a small remnant that had not lost all discipline were entrenched. Here they hoped to keep the Egyptians at bay, but the place had to surrender before the reinforcements which they expected enabled them to accept battle. The allies were dispersed, and the Egyptians, flushed with their victory and loaded with spoils, easily captured Hamath, Aleppo, Patina, and Batnæ, whence only a short march divided them from Carchemish on the Euphrates.

A tombal inscription, put up to one of the generals that fell in this siege, records, *inter alia*, the stratagems resorted to by the besieged to retard the fall of the city into the hands of the enemy. The Hittites figure among those that were obliged to pay tribute, consisting of precious stones, gold, silver, cattle, chariots, and even men, native and negro, who were sold as slaves or enlisted in the Egyptian ranks.

Syria enjoyed a respite during the last Pharaohs of this dynasty. Ramses I., founder of the nineteenth dynasty, again led his forces across the isthmus, when, doubtless to ensure possession of the southern provinces, he concluded a defensive and offensive treaty with Sapalil, king of the Hittites, on equal terms. It was broken by the latter, and hostilities began afresh under Seti, successor of Ramses. The chief episodes of this campaign are carved in the great hall at Karnac. Seti is represented with long processions of the tribes he has subdued ; the Hittite warriors, generally three in one chariot, are distinguished by lighter complexions from their swarthy Semite confederates. That no mistake, however, should occur as to their identity, the sculptor was careful to write, " This is the perverse race of the Kheta, whom the king has destroyed."

But such official boasting and contemptuous epithets, applied to the Hittites, were scarcely borne out by actual events. Seti was obliged to enter into an alliance with Maura-Sira, son and successor of Sapalil, which was maintained during the life of the former. The Hittites were now at the height of their power ; their influence was felt over the whole of the neighbouring populations; they occupied the Naharaim, "land of the two rivers" (the Orontes and Euphrates), and formed an almost impassable barrier against the Pharaohs on their line of march against Mesopotamia.   From this date, the frontiers of Egypt, even under the most warlike princes, did not extend beyond Orontes, Palestine, and Phœnicia.   In their former conflicts with Egypt, the Hittites could only reckon on the support of adjoining tribes; but in the time of Ramses II., they were able to summon to their help the Masu or Mysians, the Dardani of the Troad, with their towns, Iluna or Ilion, and Pidasa or Pidasus, as well as the Lycians or Leka, the Carians or Akerit, and the Colchians; in a word, Phœnicia, Syria, Asia Minor and Chaldæa, were brought together to oppose, and certainly in the hope to plunder, the mighty host of the Egyptians.   If the Kheta were able to show so bold a front, it was no doubt due to the fact that they had used the opportunities afforded them during the long intervals of peace to consolidate their power in Asia Minor.   It is uncertain, however, whether we are to consider these auxiliaries as vassals of Kheta-Sira, the new king of Kadesh, or tribes, many of whom may have been bound to the chief commander by no stronger tie than the hope of plunder, caring little to quit themselves as soldiers, so that they carried away goodly spoils.   This supposition would account for the Hittites having been so easily routed, the actual number that stood the brunt of a pitched battle having, in all probability, always been very small.

Even allowing for Egyptian exaggeration, to increase the importance of the victory, there is reason to suppose that the allied forces far outnumbered those of their opponents.   One of the confederates alone was able to bring into the field 18,000 men, that fought in regular ranks, and 2500 war chariots fell to the Egyptians.   The advantages of undivided counsels and better discipline told in favour of Ramses.   At first, the odds were against the young Pharaoh, who with but a small following had marched far in advance of his army, when he was surrounded and had almost fallen into the hands of the Kheta.   In his distress, he called upon his father, Amu-Ra, reminding him of the temples he had built in his honour, of the altars ever a-smoke with the fat of victims, beseeching him to deliver him from the vile Kheta.   Amu-Ra heard his prayer, and sent astray the darts of the enemy, i.e. he was joined by his army, and the Syrians were obliged to fall back, whilst the second day their lines were forced at all points and completely broken.   The account of the more than heroic courage displayed by Ramses on this occasion must be received with a large grain of salt or rather *salinus*.   He is represented rushing single-handed among the serrated ranks of the Kheta, and to have hewn them down : " I was alone," he declares ; " none of you stood by me when I was surrounded by thousands of chariots; but, with the help of Ammon, I destroyed them all " (Fig. 259).

Then Kheta-Sira, after twenty years of struggle with Ramses, concluded a treaty of peace upon equal terms with the Egyptian king.   A marriage with the daughter of the Hittite prince contributed no doubt to the maintenance of friendship between the two nations, Kheta-Sira soon after conducting his daughter to Egypt, to be present at the celebration of her marriage, which took place in the thirty-fourth year of Ramses' reign (Fig. 260).   The astonishment of the population at the strange dress and different cast of countenance of the Kheta gave way to feelings of gratitude when they beheld their late bitter foe turned into a friend and staunch ally of their monarch.   The treaty was maintained by his successor, Menephtah II.; but his feeble successors were obliged to relinquish Syria, or at least only to retain the southern provinces. A stela, recording the alliance entered into between Ramses and Kheta-Sira, was discovered by Champollion on the outer wall of the temple at Karnac.   From it we learn—albeit some lines have disappeared—that the treaty was offensive and defensive, it provided for the extradition of criminals and deserters, and may be considered as the earliest diplomatic document that has come down to us.[1]

The natural boundaries of Egypt, which keep her separated from the rest of the world, cannot but have had a large share in moulding the character of her inhabitants, which were as sharply divided by castes as though oceans and sandy wastes had interposed, rendering them little prone to stretch out the hand of fellowship or to assimilate with aliens.   Hence it came to pass that the hold of Egypt upon Syria was precarious and loose at best; for the moment the back of the conqueror was turned the

---

[1] A translation of this treaty by De Rougé may be read in Egger's work entitled, *Études historiques sur les traités publics chez les Grecs et les Romains*, pp. 243-252, 1886, in-8°. See also *Records of the Past*, vol. iv. p. 27, containing a translation by MR. GOODWIN.—EDITOR.

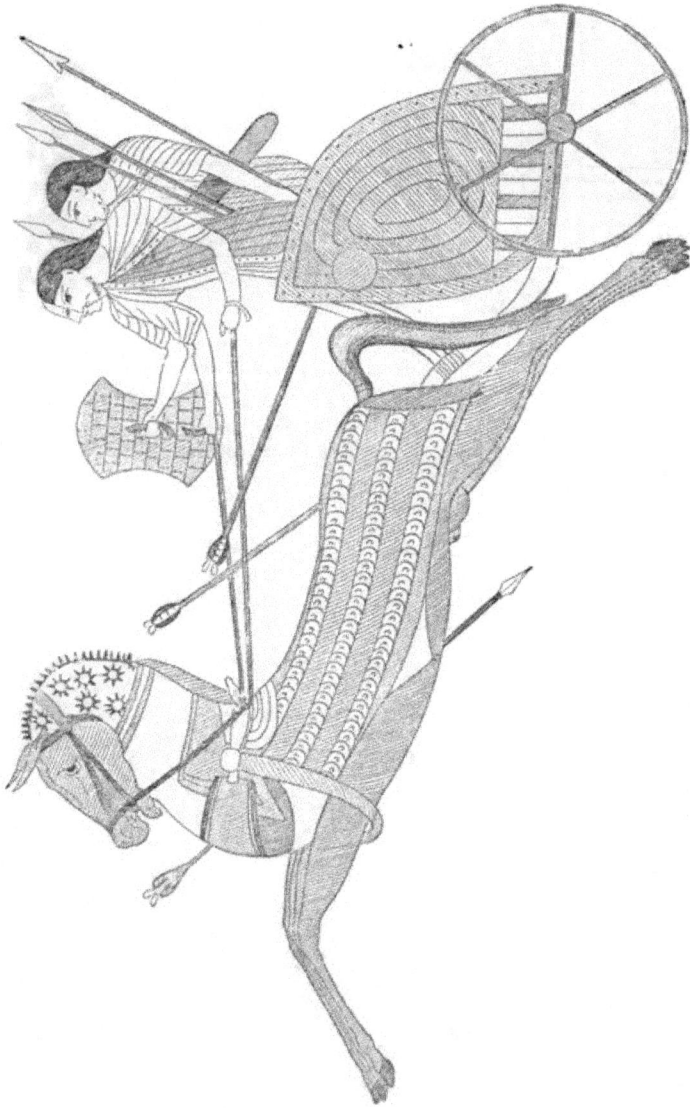

FIG. 259.—Hittite Chariot. ROSELLINI, *Monumenti*, Plate CIII.

storm-bell was sounded, and the whole country rose up in arms, as it did in our times against Mehemet Ali and Ibrahim Pasha.

A new confederacy was formed, consisting chiefly of tribes from Asia Minor, of which the Kheta, from some unexplained reason, had not the leadership. As usual, all were eager for plunder, and they advanced as far as Pelusa on the very borders of Egypt, where Ramses III., the last great Pharaoh, awaited them. Once again superior discipline and organization triumphed over mere barbarous numbers; the invading hordes were repulsed, and Ramses entered Syria as a conqueror. But, threatened at home by a rising on the Libyan frontier, he was obliged to renounce the fruit of his victory and his intended march upon Kadesh, contenting himself with the allegiance of Phœnicia and Philistia. Henceforth Egypt ceased to concern herself about what might happen beyond the mountains of Judæa.

At first sight, it seems as if the withdrawal of Egypt from Syria should have been the Hittites' opportunity; but whatever desire they may have had to possess themselves of the provinces lately vacated by the Pharaohs was checked by the growing ascendency of Assyria. The balance of power so long wielded by Egypt had migrated to the regions watered by the two great rivers of Western Asia; and the first place to be attacked was undoubtedly Carchemish on the Euphrates, where the river is fordable during the best part of the year. It was not to be expected that the kings of Kaláh and Nineveh would neglect to occupy a point that offered so many advantages. In fact, Tiglath-Pileser, towards the end of the twelfth century A.C., moved through the upper part of Syria, and reached

FIG. 260.—King Khitisar. LEPSIUS, *Denkmæler*, iii., Plate CLXVI.

the Mediterranean near Arad. We cannot determine whether he crossed the river at Carchemish, and consequently stormed the place ; but we know that his grandson was routed here by the Khetas for attempting it. Then ensued a long interval of peace, which lasted two hundred years ; but towards 877 A.C. they were again invaded, by Assur-nat-sirpal, who overran the whole country washed by the Orontes and the Euphrates. Either through selfishness or stupid jealousy of each other, they did not unite in opposing the invaders; so that whatever chance they might have had as a body was lost, and Assur-nat-sirpal easily defeated them in detail. Sangara, the king of Carchemish, was compelled to open the gates of his city and to pay tribute, and Phœnicia, uncovered in her rear, submitted to the conqueror. The provinces wrested by Assur-nat-sirpal were retained by his no less fortunate son, Shalmanezer II. The only opposition which he encountered was from Benhadad, the able ruler of Damascus, who had gathered around him Samaritans, Arabs, and Egyptian mercenaries, together with 10,000 foot from Hamath, doubtless Hittites. Here a battle was fought, and, owing to the overwhelming numbers of the Assyrians, irretrievably lost (854). A century later, Damascus was captured, and the population transported to Mesopotamia.

The Hittites, however, had lost their former importance long before the final overthrow of Damascus. The "abasement of Great Hamath" is alluded to in Jewish writings ; and Pisiris, the king of Carchemish, figures in Assyrian inscriptions among the vassals paying tribute. With the death of Tiglath-Pileser and the advent of Sargon, a mere youth, Pisiris had deemed the moment favourable for throwing off the yoke under which he groaned, but to no purpose. Carchemish was taken, himself loaded with chains and removed, with the population, beyond the Euphrates, whilst the old Hittite capital was colonized by Assyrians (717). The fall of Carchemish is recorded in Isaiah (x. 9, 11), in the following words : "*Is* not Calno as Carchemish ? is not Hamath as Arpad ? is not Samaria as Damascus ? . . . Shall I not, as I have done unto Samaria, and her idols," etc. ?

Carchemish did not disappear ; thanks to the natural advantages of its position, in Semitic hands it again became the centre of trade between Eastern and Western Asia. The "mina of Carchemish" was the current money with merchants throughout Asia Minor, and became the standard according to which coins were subsequently struck. The people, however, that had founded and defended it to the last had no hand in its new prosperity; and, with Pisiris, the name of the Hittites disappears from history.

§ 4.—*The Writing of the Hittites.*

Were the warlike energetic tribes, whose political existence thus came to an end, the inventors of the system of signs which have been called "Hamathite," from Hamath, once the very centre of their power? It cannot be demonstrated with absolute certainty, but many instances lead to that conclusion. In the first place, there was no other people at that time in Syria that could have united all the tribes of western Asia under one command, implying aptitude for organization such as can only exist in a settled condition of life. On the other hand, the data we possess do not carry us back beyond the fifteenth and sixteenth centuries, when we find them in full possession of the country, able to withstand Egypt in her might, and contend with Assyria, not always to the latter's advantage. Can any one point to any people in that part of the world that could have played the part ascribed to them under the kings of Kadesh and Carchemish? If possession constitutes the nine points of the law, we have strong overwhelming evidence to go to the jury.

Egyptian inscriptions tell us that Hittite princes had scribes who accompanied them in their campaigns, to record their deeds. Among the notable Khetas killed in the battle of Kades were the chief eunuch, the arm-bearer, and Khalepsar, the "writer of books," who was, doubtless, the official chronicler.[1] Fifteen years later, another scribe, Khirpasar, drew up the treaty which was to establish a lasting peace between Khitisar and Ramses, the conditional clauses having previously been discussed and settled between the two princes. Ambassadors were sent to Egypt bearing with them the text of the treaty engraved upon a silver plate, to have it ratified by Ramses. This has disappeared, but a copy, in the form of an oblong stela, with a top ring as if for the purpose of suspension, is to be seen on the wall of the temple of this king at Karnac (Fig. 261). Though not formally specified, the context scarcely allows room for doubt but that the treaty was couched

---

[1] The figure of Khalepsar, with legend denoting his business in life, will be found in LEPSIUS, *Denkmäler*, Pt. III., Plate CLXV It is in the middle of the penult compartment, under the body of Ramses' horse.

in the Kheta language and hieroglyphs, since it contained the enumeration of Hittite gods, male and female, whose names and attributes no Egyptian was likely to know.   This stela, albeit much defaced, allowed us to read the following words : " The

central figure of this silver tablet represents the image of the god Sutekh embracing the image of the great king of the land of Kheta," with an inscription around the figure : " This is the [figure] of the god Sutekh, the king of heaven and [earth]." What a

FIG. 261.
Stela bearing the Treaty.

piece of luck for the learned world were Egyptian explorers some day to light upon this silver tablet, which in that dry soil would doubtless have preserved images and text intact.   Differences would only exist in the formulas relating to the deities of the two nations, but these, with the evidence at our disposal, would be easily distinguished, whilst the actual treaty being precisely the same in the twin documents—like the Rosetta stone— would constitute a bilingual text, and furnish us with the key to the decipherment of all the other Hittite monuments.

FIG. 262.—Silver Boss of Tarkondemos.
WRIGHT, *The Empire*, p. 65.

If this may seem too much to expect, even in an age that has seen so many wonders, we may point to Assyria, where, in the palace of Sargon, gold and silver leaf, recording a dedication in fine characters, was found by M. Place, and is now in the Louvre.[1] If Egypt should have another such surprise in store for us, bare justice would require that Professor Sayce should be the fortunate discoverer, for no one so fully deserves to be the Champollion of the Kheta language. A bilingual inscription has already opened the way ; but, unfortunately, it is too short to allow of much progress being made. The history of this remarkable object is briefly as follows :

Some twenty-seven years ago, the British Museum was offered a convex silver plate, something like the skin of half a small orange (Fig. 262).[2] The concave surface was occupied by a figure representing a warrior standing erect in the middle, holding a spear in

[1] *Ninive et l'Assyrie*, tom. iii. pp. 303–306, and tom. iii. Plate LXXVII.
[2] Its diameter is o m. 045 c.

his left hand, with symbols on each side of it, which one could
see were unlike any characters hitherto known. A border, with
letters similarly incised, surrounded the boss. The singular
appearance of these hieroglyphs roused suspicions of the genuineness of the piece, and caused it to be refused ; not before, however,
M. Ready had taken an impression by electrotype. This copy
lay forgotten in a drawer of the museum, when Professor Sayce
happened to read an article, bearing on this very plate, by the late
Dr. Mordtmann, who was inclined to identify the lettering of the
border with the Vannic cuneiform inscriptions. What specially
struck Professor Sayce was the curious fact that the "obelisks"
on the plate were stated to resemble the peculiar shafts of rock
which are seen in the volcanic district of Cæsarea, in Cappadocia,
whilst the central figure was characteristic of Hittite art. The
professor could not rest until he had procured a copy of this
interesting silver boss, which seemed to come to him as the
realization of his long-cherished hopes, confirming what had been
mere guess-work. In a letter to the *Academy*, he asked if any
of its readers were acquainted with the localization of the original.
Replies soon came, first from Mr. B. V. Head, of the British
Museum, informing him that an electrotype fac-simile had been in
the Museum for the last twenty years, enclosing at the same time
a cast of it. This was followed by M. Fr. Lenormant, who also
sent a fac-simile of the one he had taken from the original in 1860,
when he had found it in the possession of M. Alexander Iovanoff,
the well-known numismatist at Constantinople, who had obtained
it at Smyrna. The collection of M. Iovanoff has been dispersed,
but the impressions we have agree in every particular, and for
the purposes of science are as good as the original itself.

The disappearance of these "curios" from public investigation
has been adduced in proof of the spuriousness of the silver tablet ;
but, to our mind, the suspicion is hardly justified. To have created
the type of the figure and the ideographs about it in 1860, *i.e.*
long before the Hamath inscriptions had been transliterated and
Hittite hieroglyphs were known to exist, we must suppose the
forger to have been endowed with supernatural power, a theory
too absurd to be discussed.

Professor Sayce being satisfied with the perfect agreement of the
casts he had obtained, found no difficulty in reading the legend :
"Tarik-timme [or dimme], king of the country of Ermé." The

existence of this king was unsuspected, but not the name, which is mentioned as that of a leading man of Cilicia who lived at the beginning of our era. In its subject form, Ταρκονδεμος is met with on numerous coins, as well as in Plutarch; and we read of a Ταρκοδιμάτος, Bishop of Ægæ in Cilicia.[1] The frequent occurrence of this name in a province which was so thoroughly Greek at the time we are treating, may have been due to ancestral reminiscence; perhaps of a benevolent prince, whose graciousness lingered in the place that had witnessed his good deeds. However this may be, Ermé, the country over which Tarik-timme is supposed to have ruled, has been identified with Arima of the Greek geographers. Assyriologists are at one with Professor Sayce in the rendering of the legend around the border, and in referring the characters to the age of Sargon.[2]

The first question that arises, when we try to decipher the inner hieroglyphs with the aid of the cuneiform inscription, is whether they are the exact reproduction one of the other. In the present state of our knowledge, it would be rash to give a categorical answer; but to judge from other bilingual inscriptions, such a correspondence between the two legends, if not certain, is at least probable. The relative number of hieroglyphs in the twin legends tends to confirm this view; for if there are nine cuneiform letters, and only six in the other, this is easily explained from the fact that the Hittite writing was not so far advanced in phonetic values as the cuneiform; a whole word, or group of words, being expressed by a single character, such as Tarik-timme; whereas in the Assyrian hieroglyphs we should find the name divided into syllables: Tar-rik-tim-me-sar-mat-Er-me-e, the long e being noted by extra cuneiform lettering. As to the words sar, "king," mat, "country," they are figured by an almost identical ideograph in all systems akin to that under discussion.

If similarity between the Assyrian and Hittite text be admitted, we have six characters at least of which the values cannot be contested. For the rest, we shall not follow the ingenious line of argument by which Professor Sayce tries to establish the values of

---

[1] Theodoret, Hist. Ecclésiastique, p. 539.

[2] See Sayce's, The Bilingual Hittite and Cuneiform Inscription of Tarkondemos. M. Theo. Pinches proposes a different interpretation for Ermé (Wright, The Empire, p. 220), whilst concurring with Professor Sayce in the reading of the proper name and kingly title.

other thirty hieroglyphics, which to some may not always appear well founded.[1] In all fairness, however, it should be stated that certain renderings are only tentative ; his method of going to work is always eminently suggestive, whilst the Cypriote syllabary most opportunely gave him the means to check and prove his theorem.

The curious complicated outline observable in some of the letters which occur on the older Cypriote inscriptions, coins, and contract-tablets had long puzzled scholars, but without being able to offer a solution for them. The late George Smith, by analogy of other bilingual scripts, was the first to surmise, and finally to establish, that such characters were remnants of an older syllabary, or rather the survival of an extremely ancient mode of picture-writing, which was connected with the Æolian group of dialects, and that in conservative Cyprus they had been preserved down to the first Ptolemies, along with the ordinary Greek writing. The older alphabet consisted of about sixty signs, of which five were vowels (α, ε, ι, ο, υ), and twelve consonants (κ, τ, χ, μ, ν, λ, ρ, F, j, σ, ξ, ζ), most of these being capable of assuming a different form before each different vowel, for instance, κα, κο, κε, κι, κυ. In all probability j, ξ, and ζ, had fewer signs. There were seemingly no aspirates, at least they were not noted in writing. The fact of the ruder Cypriote alphabet having been retained side by side with the simpler Phœnician was due—as already stated—to the conservative spirit which obtained in a country separated by the ocean from the rest of the world. The primitive syllabary was looked upon with reverence as an ancestral relic ; it became the hieratic writing made use of in all public deeds. Like Egypt, Cyprus was proud to own a system of hieroglyphics.[2]

The Cypriote system of writing was at first supposed to have been derived from the Assyrian characters introduced into the island in the age of Sargon ; but the hypothesis was overthrown by comparison of the various inscriptions where this peculiar mode of epigraphy occurs. Thus legends in Cypriote letters were found in the lowest strata, seemingly of great antiquity, by Dr. Schliemann, in his excavations at Hissarlik ;[3] and the alphabets of Caria,

---

[1] WRIGHT, *The Empire*, ch. xi.

[2] On Cypriote writing, consult *Hist. of Art*, tom. iii. pp. 493, 494, 496, Figs. 347, 348.

[3] *Ilios.* J. Murray, London, 1884. In Appendix III., Professor Sayce draws the

Lycia, Pisidia, Pamphylia, and other localities, preserved a considerable number of the characters of the old syllabary, in order to express sounds not provided for by the Phœnician.   All these instances put together enable us to look back upon a time when the primitive ideographs represented by the Hamathite inscribed characters were common to the whole peninsula; if they were preserved in their complete homogeneous state in Cyprus alone, they yet left deep traces in localities where they had once reigned supreme, until they were finally superseded by the Phœnician alphabet.   But the latter had started on its voyage round the world ages before the conquests of Sargon and Assur-nat-sirpal had made Assyrian influence felt in the basin of the Mediterranean.

Setting aside therefore comparison of the different modes of writing, it is not likely that the Asianic alphabet, as Professor Sayce calls it, waited to constitute itself until Assyria, already in possession of a cuneiform syllabary, came in contact with the various populations of Asia Minor.   The characters adopted by these to suit their different dialects, had come to them from Northern Syria, or perhaps Cappadocia, whence they gradually spread.   But in course of time they were found too unwieldy for the purposes of trade and daily life, and as a natural consequence underwent complete change.   The date in which these profound modifications took place stretched over a long period, and cannot now be ascertained; but, could we do so, such a procedure would exceed the narrow limits we have prefixed to ourselves.   This much is certain, they coincide with Hittite preponderance in those pristine days when their battle-cry was heard from the Orontes to the Hermus and the Mæander.

The Cypriote alphabet, with only sixty characters representing a syllable each, is but a much-reduced copy of the Hittite, which according to Professor Sayce has about 125 distinct signs.   In the Hamathite inscriptions a considerable number of ideographs were preserved, bearing witness to the primitive age when they were rude representations of the actual objects.   They did not pass into later syllabaries, which only received phonetic signs with pretty much the values they had in the original writing.

conclusion that the inscriptions found at Hissarlik represent an earlier system of writing than the Cypriote syllabary, and that it was derived straight from Hittite hieroglyphics, which did not pass on to Cyprus until long elaboration had simplified the form and reduced the number of the signs.   A *résumé* of this paper will be found in an appendix to *Comparative Philology*, entitled " Asianic Syllabary."

At the outset, it seems as if comparison of the Cypriote characters, the values of which are nearly all known, would enable us
to make out the value of the original Hittite pattern.   But great
difficulty is encoun-
tered in restoring
the perfect initial
form, with any de-
gree of certainty
or even verisimili-
tude, from the late
abridged sign. The
primitive outline is
still to be traced in
a certain number
of hieroglyphs, as
will be seen in the
annexed table by
Professor Sayce
(Fig. 263).   The
idea of juxtaposing

HITTITE	CYPRIOTE
o‖o o‖o *i e*	)'(*yi*
⇡ *ka ku*	⇧ *ka*
te to	木 人 F *to*
me, mo	▯ ⊕ *mo*
se	Υ Ψ *se*
si	*si*
ti di	↑ *ti di*
u	*o*

FIG. 263.—Comparative Table of Hittite and Cypriote Hieroglyphs.

certain Hittite cha-
racters of which he had endeavoured to determine the values,
and which he thought denoted voices or consonants followed
by a vowel, along with eight corresponding Cypriote signs, was
suggested to him by Dr. Isaac Taylor, and the result was as
unexpected as it was satisfactory.   With the exception of "se"
and "u," which are open to criticism, the resemblance was so
close in each case as to be almost identical (see fig.).[1]   In a word,
the Cypriote syllabary bears the same relation to the sculptures of
Asia Minor and the Hamathite inscriptions, as the Egyptian
demotic and hieratic modes of writing do to the monumental
hieroglyphics on pylons and sepulchres.

It is needless to dwell upon the importance of the "Hittite Question," or remind the reader that to deal with it under all its aspects
would involve a whole volume.   Excellent and reliable though
Dr. Wright's work may be, it can lay no claim to originality, and
is but a compilation, leaving many things unsaid.   Thus, to name
but one, no attempt is made clearly to define the art of the
Hittites, who excelled in the portraiture of the human and animal

[1] WRIGHT, *The Empire*, p. 178.

form. These characteristics of their art, together with their peculiar mode of writing, they carried to all the peoples subjected to them. Northern Syria, being the nearest country, received them in their primitive form, abundantly proved by the frequent recurrence of living images on all its monuments.

The alphabets therefore derived from Hittite hieroglyphics, once used over so vast an area, must of necessity exhibit similarity of manipulation in some of the outlines of the figures and characters. This should be particularly noticeable in those syllabaries which belong to the early style, before the action of Greek art was felt in the interior of the peninsula; such as Hamath, Carchemish, and the towns generally of Northern Syria. Hence, a special, a vital interest attaches to the rare fragments which have been and may be discovered in that part of the world; they alone can reveal to us the character and real value of the pictorial art of a nation whose history we have summarized in this chapter. The largest number of Hittite inscriptions are met with east of the Halys, in the Naharaim and Cappadocia. In the latter are the best-preserved and, in size at least, most important monuments, not excepting the districts washed by the Orontes and Euphrates rivers. The Hittites do not seem to have made a long stay west of the Halys, at any rate inscriptions here are insignificant and exceedingly rare, albeit characterized by the same stamp of originality which is distinctive of all Hittite art. We will proceed to give a table, as complete as possible, of such monuments as were recovered in the very centre of Hittite power, together with a circumstantial description of rock-cut and other sculptures in Cappadocia, which it was our fortune to examine in place; illustrating the result of our excavations—we fear not so complete as we should have desired—by careful and reliable representations of them, so that those who devote their energies to this subject may have ample scope to form a just estimate of the whole series of documents.

CHAPTER II.

§ 1.—*Boundaries and Character of the Country occupied by the Hittites.*

THE vast region once under Hittite sway seems carved out by nature to hold an important place in the history of man. The length of line of its coast is protracted far inland by numerous arms of the sea, the most important, perhaps, being the Cilician bay to the north-east of the Mediterranean. Here, amidst unhealthy lagoons, rises Alexandretta or "small Alexandria," with a cross communication of three highways; one leading to Constantinople by an oblique cut across Asia Minor, the second coasting the sea to Arabia and Egypt, whilst the third takes the caravans to the Orontes, following its banks for awhile, until at the height of Antioch it strikes out to meet the Euphrates at the long curve it describes towards the Mediterranean above Issus Bay, as though for the very purpose of irrigating this part of Syria.[1] Were we to take the whole line of country which extends between Alexandretta and the delta, it would be impossible to name a spot to equal the solitude and dreariness of the small flat level which begins at Alexandretta and stretches to the foot of the Amanus range, or an area of the same dimensions where the presence of man is so rarely seen. Notwithstanding its many disadvantages, its deadly climate, which renders the place unfit for human habitation during six months in the year—notwithstanding its lack of roads and insecure harbour, through the eternal fitness of things, Alexandretta is destined, sooner or later, to draw to itself the tide of human activity. Even now the number of camels that yearly travel between it and Aleppo averages 10,000;

---

[1] RECLUS, *Nouvelle Géographie*, tom. ix. pp. 766, 767.

whilst the returns for 1882 showed that merchandise to the value
of £1,280,000 was shipped from its small port.[1]   Here, railway
engineers place the terminus of the line which is to connect the
coast with the Euphrates Valley, over the same route now taken
by caravans.   But instead of painfully climbing the Amanus up
the Beilan Pass, the supposed classic "Syrian Gates," 700 m. high,
a short tunnel will land passengers in a few minutes on the other

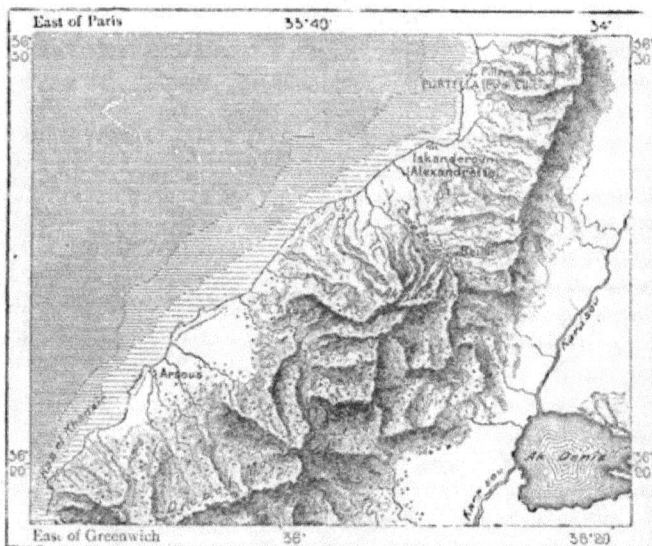

FIG. 264.—The Defiles of the Amanus Range. From RECLUS.

side (Fig. 264).   Other roads, traces of which were recently noticed
by travellers, ran from the valley of the Orontes, over the mountains to the coast.[2]   If to the south the way is obstructed by the
formidable escarpments of Cape Ras-el-Khanzir, or wild boar's
tusk, no such difficulties are encountered on the north side, the
pass called "Little Gates" or Jonas's Pillars, affording easy access to
the sea by a road which crosses the plain washed by the Pyramus
and the Saros (Fig. 265).   Cilicia is thus a natural dependency of
Northern Syria; its rich loamy soil, which only requires the hand

[1] RECLUS, loc. cit. p. 759.
[2] MARMIER, "Les Routes de l'Amanus" (Gazette Archéologique, pp. 40, 50. 1884).

of the husbandman to become one of the most fertile districts in
the world, is bound on the west and north by the almost perpendicular rocks of the Taurus range, which will always secure its
happy possessor against foreign inroads.

The battle of Nazib, in 1836, gave Syria and Mesopotamia to
Mehemet Ali; his son Ibrahim, conscious of the importance of
Kulek-Boghaz, the "Cilician gates" of the ancients, had it fortified
and guarded.   It is the only pass to which pieces of artillery can
be brought from the coast.   Behind the walls of this stronghold,
its garrison was secured against attacks from the Turkomans in

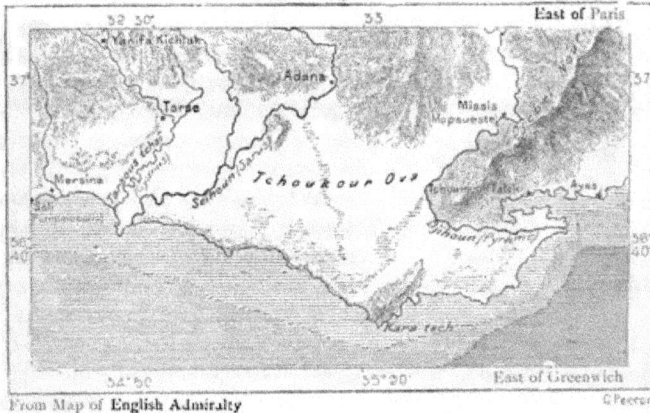

From Map of **English Admiralty**   C Perron

From 0 to 25 m.   From 25 to 50.   From 50 and beyond.

FIG. 265.—Plain of Cilicia. From RECLUS.

their raids on the central plateau ; but as soon as they retired the
garrison, to keep its prestige, would sally forth with great bravado,
frightening the inhabitants into passive quietude.   The political
and military frontier of Syria therefore is not Issus Bay, but the
Taurus range, which, having no passes through which the enemy
can pour down their forces, opposes an impassable barrier, which
can be held by a handful of men.

A glance at the map will show the soundness of our view,
corroborated by historical facts.   It is well known that Syrian
centres contended with Egypt for the palm of antiquity, and that
their language, art, and religion, outwardly at least, were unin-

fluenced by Greece until Alexander. A tradition, still current at
the end of the old era, declared Heracles the founder of Tarsus; [1]
a supposed older tradition, soothing to the national pride, named
Samdam, the Asiatic Heracles, as its real builder; [2] again, a third
maintained that it was erected by Sarda-nat-sirpal; [3] finally, a later
account, with pretensions to historical truth, stated that it was
raised by Sennacherib and enclosed on the pattern of Babylon. [4]
Whatever the truth may be, Assyrian inscriptions tell us that
Cilicia was among the provinces conquered by the kings of
Babylon; and in one of them Shalmaneser III. boasts of having
taken Tarzi. [5]   Perhaps no other city of equal size exceeds the
number of coins that were struck in its name, bearing witness to
the intimate relations that existed for centuries between it and the
countries east and south of the Amanus mountains. [6]   Aramæan
legends do not disappear from the
coins of Tarsus until the Seleucidæ,
and occur far more frequently than
Greek legends in the two centuries
preceding that era. [7]   During the whole
archaic period the ornament on these
pieces is of a decidedly Asiatic character—a character preserved to a certain
extent even under Roman rule; when,

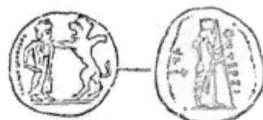

Fig. 266.—Silver Coin of Tarsus.
Waddington.   *Mélanges*, 1861,
p. 80, Plate V., Fig. 7.

if the style and make had nothing to distinguish them from countless other contemporary objects of the same class, the subjects, as a
rule, were still those dear to the Phœnician artist.   The stirring
incidents of the chase were replaced by more peaceful occupations;
instead of the traditional hero, holding a sword which he is about
to plunge into the side of the animal (Fig. 266), a local deity is
figured.   But even he has undergone modification to suit the taste
of the time.   In early days—as on the bas-reliefs of Cappadocia—
the god with high headdress, and bow or quivers slung behind
his back, or holding a double-headed axe in one hand and a scourge
in the other, stood erect on the back of some fabulous animal,

[1] Nonnos, *Dionysiaques*, xli. 85.
[2] Dion Chrysostom, xxxiii. tom. ii. pp. 1, 23.   Reiske's edition.
[3] Ammien Marcellin, xiv. 8.   *Samdam*, signifies "strong," "powerful."
[4] Cléarque de Soli, quoted by Athenius, xii. p. 599.
[5] Eusebius, *Chron.* p. 25.   Mai's edition, after Abydinus.
[6] Menant, *Annales des Rois d'Assyrie*, p. 101.
[7] See *Hist. of Art*, tom. iii. Fig. 285, showing a Tarsus coin.

chimæra, or horned lion, and had preserved much of the warlike aspect of heroic times (Fig. 267).[1]   Later he is given a more dignified mien, and is seated upon a throne, like Jupiter Olympian, with whom he would be easily confounded, but for the clustering grapes and ears of corn carried in his hand.[2]   But although he has followed the whims of fashion in his outward appearance, were we to enter his temple we should find that the rites in his honour had preserved much of their pristine character, when he was worshipped as Tarsi-Baal, closely related to the Baalim of Tyre and Sidon.   This equally applies to the coins of Cilicia;[3] thus when we wished to illustrate the type of Phœnician deities of this era, we quoted the coins of Mallos, a maritime city north-west of Issus Bay.[4]   The climate and pro-ductions of Cilicia are those of Syria rather than Asia Minor; two rivers, the Saros (Sihoun) and the Pyramos (Jihoun), leave on the plains fringing their banks a soil as rich as that of the Nile, needing little or no labour from the husbandman. It is protected from northern blasts by the Taurus range, whose rocky sides, reflecting the sun's rays, are as a huge hothouse, yielding almost tropical fruit as fine as any in the delta, which together with the cotton grown on the broad level below, are shipped off from Mersina, the port of Tarsus, and find a ready sale in the European markets.

FIG.   267. — Bronze Coin   of   Tarsus. LAJARD,   Atlas, Plate IV., Fig. 9.

Here we might expect to meet with many a fragment of Hittite civilization, for we read that Khitisar, in his journey to Egypt, was accompanied by the prince of Khidi, evidently a Cilician chief (the name spelt kidi, khodi, κητις, is applied by Ptolemy to the maritime portion of Cilicia, which faces the north coast of Cyprus),[5] were it not that Cilician

[1] FR. LENORMANT identifies the figure seen on the coins of Tarsus with Adar Samdam, "the strong" "the powerful," the Assyrian deity (*Essai de Commentaire sur les Fragments Cosmogoniques de Bérose*, p. 112).

[2] See HEUZEY's "Les Fragments de Tarse au Musée du Louvre," Fig. 2 (*Gazette des Beaux-Arts*, November, 1876).

[3] Κιλικία πεδία, the Cilicia campestris of the Romans.

[4] *Hist. of Art*, tom. iii. p. 418, Figs. 288, 298.

[5] It is possible that the name of Cataonia, a southern province of Cappadocia, may have the same origin (MASPERO, *Hist. Ancienne*, p. 216, note 1).

cities, being placed on the high-road of the invader, were oftener pillaged and destroyed than those of northern Syria, less open to aggressions from sea pirates. Then, too, the material used for building was the calcareous stone of the country, which, lacking the hardness of basalt found in the valley of the Orontes, when exposed to the disintegrating action of the elements, is apt to crumble away; thus inscriptions or bas-reliefs worked on its surface were obliterated.

If we except coins, which, being of metal, are not open to this objection, and the lintel of a door, which seems to have preserved some Hittite characters, the only old monument is an enormous ruin, near Tarsus, now called Deunuk-tach; all the other remains, whether architectural or sculptured, date from the Roman occupation.

Hence Cilicia, although for ages among the petty kingdoms of the Hittite confederacy, has preserved no monuments of this early period. Our only chance of finding specimens of Hittite art is in the volcanic region of northern Syria, notably the Naharaim, including Comagena and its capital Samosata.[1] Here a stela was discovered bearing the distinctive impress of Hittite civilization. It represents a female figure, now almost disappeared, save a bit of her long garment and feet shod with boots which have the ends turned up, with Hittite characters on the edge of the slab.[2] Other stone documents have been recovered at Merash in the upper valley of the Pyramus. Owing to its position, which lies outside the main road, we do not hear of its existence until we find it on the Roman itineraries. But should a chance stone suddenly turn up with its old Hittite name, there would be no difficulty in identifying it among the fortresses figured on Assyrian and Egyptian inscriptions that were captured after the battles fought at Kadesh and Carchemish. The only remains that have been found are rudely sculptured lions, which probably belong to the Hittite era—at any rate they are inscribed all over with characters

---

[1] The birthplace of Lucian.—Editor.

[2] I am indebted to Dr. Otto Puchstein for a drawing of this stela, the result of whose exploration in Asia Minor and Northern Syria first appeared in the *Sitzungsberichte* of the Berlin University, for 1882, p. 845, under the title, " Bericht über eine Reise in Kurdistan." A more detailed account was published in 1887, by Dietrich Reimer of Berlin, in 1 vol. in 8°, with atlas illustrative of the more valuable and best-preserved monuments. The work is divided into two parts. In the first, Herr Humann relates a journey undertaken to Angora for the purpose of taking casts of the " Index rerum gestarum divi Augusti," reproduced in the atlas.

peculiar to Hamath and Jerabis.   These lions, three in number,
stood formerly in the outer wall, frequently damaged in the wars
of Byzantium and the Caliphs.   Its last restoration took place in
the Middle Ages, when the Arab builder used two of these stout
archaic figures to ornament the top of the doorway (Fig. 268).[1]

FIG. 268.—Lion built in the wall of the Citadel of Merash.

Sculptures akin to the Merash lions, to those of the Euphrates
and the Orontes valleys, have likewise been reported from
Albistan, on the south of the plain called Palanga Ova, north
of the Jihoun Pass.[2]

[1] I am indebted to Professor Sayce for the last and many of the woodcuts contained in this chapter—reproduced from photographs taken by Dr. Gwyther, who saw
the original in place in 1885.

[2] Our information is based upon a letter of Mr. J. H. Haynes, which he addressed
to us from Aintab, dated February 8, 1886, together with photographs of the two
Albistan lions taken the year before. Their mutilated state however renders them
valueless for the purpose of our publication.

§ 2.—*Architecture*.

We know almost nothing of the architecture of the Hittites, nor are we better acquainted with the forms of their tombs and temples; our scanty knowledge being confined to the nature of the fortresses they raised to defend their cities and the decoration resorted to for the houses of the great.

Owing to the difficulty of penetrating into Northern Syria, scarcely any excavations have been made. The few travellers that have crossed this region on horseback were fain to content themselves with cursorily noting as they went the remains of buildings seen above ground. The history of plastic art must await to be written until the day when the pickaxe shall have attacked, and shafts shall have been sunk in the tells which are found in places here as they are in Mesopotamia. Until then our only evidence relates to civil architecture.

These tribes lived in constant conflict with their neighbours, who to the north and south threatened their liberties, or among themselves; the bone of contention being now a fat pasturage, now a conterminous bridge or pass. Such feuds between rival clans or sheikhs are even now laying waste Kurdistan, part of which was formally Hittite ground. In an unsettled state of society like this, the main concern of the people is to erect sturdy walls, behind which they can find shelter; nor, as we have seen, were the Hittites slow in availing themselves of every spot fortified by nature, which they further strengthened by artificial means.

The remains of the walls of Kadesh, if they still exist, are hidden in the mounds washed by the lake Homs or in the tell Neby; but Carchemish still preserves visible signs of its ancient wall and chief buildings.[1] The area of the fortified town did not exceed three kilometres in circuit. It was oblong in shape, and on the right bank of the Euphrates, which covered its side to the east and its width to the south. From this point extended suburbs, where

---

[1] Our information is borrowed from the *Times* (August 11, 1880) entitled "Carchemish, from a Correspondent." It is much to be regretted that the intelligent observer did not think fit to add a plan and drawings to indicate the materials and the character of the structures. As we are sending to the printer, we at length receive a number of the *Graphic* (December 11, 1880) which contains, if not all we should wish, sketches made on the spot by Mr. Chas. Boscawen. The Addenda to this volume will contain the most interesting; but, of course, as they were only used as illustrations by the paper, we cannot expect to find them strictly accurate.

the rich had their summer-houses, surrounded by pleasure-grounds and gardens, where traces of rills or canals have been found which bisected each other in every direction for the purpose of irrigation or drainage. On the north and north-west, where the enclosed city was unprotected by the Euphrates, a deep ditch or moat had been excavated to receive the flow of a small rill; whilst the side which skirted the country was fenced by a tall wall. Reference to Fig. 257, representing Kadesh, shows that both fortresses had a double wall, and that the interposing space was occupied by a broad ditch or moat always full of water.[1] The set-off of the wall is still apparent throughout; its height from the outside is from eight to ten metres. To the north-east of the enclosure is a mound, which rises about 15 m. above the city level, and more than 30 above the bed of the river, so that it can be seen at a great distance. A ravine cuts it in two parts; these doubtless formerly supported twin buildings, separated by the steep ravine, which was ascended by a ramp, thus constituting a strong citadel, which there is every reason to suppose was the royal palace.

To the north-west of the acropolis, Mr. Henderson discovered a long room or passage, whose walls were covered with bas-reliefs, as at Nineveh; the western wall, which is still intact, is 20 m. in height by 6 m. in breadth. It is no easy matter to fix the date of this building; bricks were certainly found with the name of Sargon incised upon them, from which it might be argued that the palace was erected under the Sargonides by the Assyrian governor residing here. On the other hand, two large sculptured tablets of stone found in place bear the unmistakable stamp of Hittite art, leading to the not improbable conclusion that the Assyrians found the building on their arrival, which they repaired or added to, to suit their individual taste or convenience.

With regard to the manipulation of the female deity figured on one of the slabs, and the worshipping priestess on the other, we can form no distinct idea except such as may be derived from verbal description, for the stones were found too heavy to be taken away, and no drawing or photograph was attempted to supply their place. It represents a winged Anath or Ashtoreth, full face and nude, her hands pointed to her breasts—a type, it will be seen, nearly identical with that so often encountered throughout the East, from Susiana to Cyprus, and the Western colonies of Phœnicia—a

---

[1] CONDER, loc. cit.

purely Eastern type in its widest signification.[1] The conical cap of this goddess suggests Hittite art, and seems to have been the national headdress, for we find it in Khitisar (Fig. 260), and with but slight modifications in nearly all the sculptures that may be attributed to this people.[2]

On the other hand, the Assyrian helmet sometimes so closely resembles the Hittite cap, that no judgment can be formed in the absence of the monument. This, by this time, has in all probability been broken up to make lime for a new structure; nor are basalt slabs much more safe in the destructive hands of the ignorant natives. Over the brook, now called Aïn-beddar, which once filled the ditch that protected the town, a mill has been erected, and the sculptured slabs which adorned palaces and walls long before the Thothmes and the Shalmanesers brought here their victorious armies, have been used as millstones by the miller delighted to find ready to hand blocks of the required size and thickness.

Many more slabs have shared a like fate; nevertheless, Birejik, Merash, and other places in North Syria still preserve a certain number. Their comparative thinness at once calls to mind the alabaster slabs that lined the inner walls of palaces and doorways in Assyria. The supposition that the Hittite builder used them in the same way is placed beyond doubt by M. Puchstein's discovery of a wall near Sinjirli so enriched. This wall, portions of which are still visible at the base of a tell, with traces of ancient buildings, formerly surrounded the whole mound. The longest series of sculptured slabs still exposed to view is to the left, for soon after it turns the angle to the right it disappears in the depths of the mound (Fig. 269).[3] The upper courses have disappeared, but it is highly probable that the wall was built throughout with unbaked bricks, as on the banks of the Tigris.[4] M. Puchstein also

---

[1] *Hist. of Art*, tom. ii. Figs. 16 and 228; tom. iii, Figs. 150, 321, 379, 380, 417.

[2] See Addenda, drawing of this figure.

[3] Sinjirli is five hours' walk south-west of Saktchégheuksou, which will be found between Mount Amanus and the Kurdagh in M. Puchstein's map. We hope that the learned doctor will carry out his intended plan of making excavations at both places, which cannot fail to be of great interest from a structural and even a decorative standpoint, even though the intrinsic value of the latter may be small.

[4] This, Dr. Puchstein writes, is the impression he received on viewing the rubbish accumulated at the base of the wall. But, aware how difficult it is to distinguish unbaked bricks, turned to their original mud, from the clay soil in which they are mixed, he does not care to commit himself to a decided opinion.

recovered a series of carved stones around a tell at Saktchégheuksou, three of these at least represent a hunting scene (Fig. 279), the details being carried on from slab to slab. They are now built in the wall of a modern house, and the question as to the place they once occupied in the building for which they were designed is satisfactorily met by reference to similar pictures in the monumental ruins at Khorsabad and Nimroud. The same observation applies to the nameless ruins near Albistan already alluded to, where two lions carved on huge slabs have been found. One is still standing, but the other lies on its side, probably at the very entrance where they were originally placed, like the winged bulls and

FIG. 269.—Sculptured Scenes at Sinjirli. From M. PUCHSTEIN.

lions of Assyrian palaces, one on each side of the doorway through which you passed to enter the private apartments of the sovereign.[1] The size of the lions, 2 m. high by 3½ m. from head to tail, confirms this hypothesis;[2] they were supposed to guard the entrance to the palace or town, even as in the present day the petty lord of a district in Turkey, whose castle generally commands a defile, is called Dere-bey, "guardian of the pass."

The modern Kurds, albeit less civilized than the Hittites in the time of Khitisar, of the Ramses, and the Thothmes, in some respects may be considered as their successors.   Like the earlier inhabitants, they love to erect strongholds at the entrance of a narrow gorge, or upon inaccessible summits, with walls thick enough to ensure their safety and guard them against sudden attacks. But the parallel ends here, for their prototypes did something more than provide the bare necessities of existence. Long usage with a certain degree of refinement of life, had stimulated them into elaborating an art of their own, or, if the term be deemed too ambitious, industrial productions.   Some of these, their citadels, for instance, bear witness to their skill in the science of self-defence. Their kings lived in houses, in which their images and that of their deities were sculptured, along with inscriptions that we cannot read as yet, but doubtless containing their names, the recital of their peaceful avocations and warlike deeds, mayhap their prayers and thanksgivings.

[1] *Hist. of Art*, tom. ii. p. 282.

[2] The measurement is only approximative, the scale having been obtained by photographing a man of the escort with one of the lions.   We have also the drawing of a still larger lion before us, sculptured on a slab 4 m. long by 2 m. 30 c. high, discovered by Haynes, the American traveller, at Aslan-tach, the "lion-stone," in the plain of Serug.   We do not reproduce the monument, because we think it posterior to Hittite art.   The execution, at once more skilful, but destitute of vigour and lightness of touch, is a later development, and betrays Assyrian origin.   Decidedly Assyrian is also the peculiar conventional mode of figuring the fore-paws of the animal, full face and in profile at the same time, a detail never seen on Hittite monuments.   Moreover, as far as our experience reaches, we have no reason to suppose that the tribes which made use of the Hittite writing ever crossed the Euphrates; and the Kurdish village, where the lion under notice was found, is on the right bank of the river, ten hours from Birejik, and twelve on the south-west of Urfa. M. Sterrett writes : " Some two hours and a half from Arslan Tachi, in Cataonia, the Wolfe Mission came upon a very archaic lion, which was forthwith photographed. At a place called Jegin, a short way west of Albistan, the Rev. H. Warden, of the American Mission, discovered a Hittite inscription, which covered the sides of a quadrangular stela, of which he made a careful copy."

Whether covered with hieroglyphs or bas-reliefs, there is every reason to suppose that the square basalt stones, discovered at Hamath, Aleppo, Birejik, Merash, and other localities, once belonged to princely dwellings, and that a few strokes of the pickaxe would bring to light many more of the same nature. At Homs alone, four mounds are said to exist, by travellers who descried them at some height above the surrounding level. Nor would the restoration of the monuments hidden in these tells be a difficult matter, for we may surely assume that they are closely allied to those already known.

On the other hand, the Deunuk-tach, to which reference has been made, is sufficiently high above ground to have enabled travellers to note its dimensions and structural character; from the fact, however, of its having been exposed, the outer facing and ornament are obliterated, and although attempts were made to uncover the wall buried under the accumulated rubbish, the problem is certainly unsolved, and mayhap will remain so.[1] As far as has been ascertained, the monument consists of a vast enclosure, surrounded by a wall 6 m. 50 c. deep, having a mean altitude of 7 to 8 m. describing a parallelogram of 87 m. long by 42 m. wide,

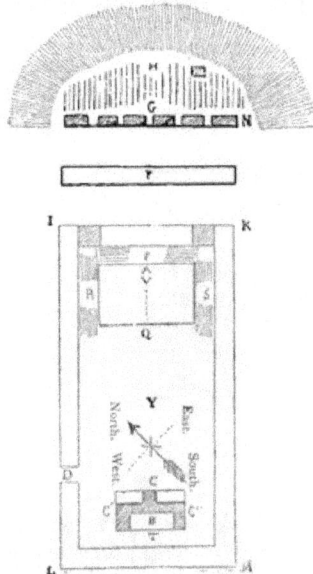

FIG. 270.—Plan of Deunuk-tach.
LANGLOIS, p. 267.

built of a kind of concrete of small pebbles and sand cemented together with lime into a hard compact mass, upon which the pick

---

[1] The etymology of *deunuk-tach*, "overthrown stone," is derived from the verb *deunmek*, "to return," "to turn over," from which the past participle *deunuk* is formed. The local epithet, "overthrown," seems singularly unfitting a monument where all the parts preserved are still in place. The appellation may, perhaps, be referable to an older state of the ruin, where accumulated blocks, or a prostrate statue of colossal size, formed a striking feature in the enclosure of which the substructures alone remain. The blocks and fragments of the statue may have been removed to build the modern town, and the old name adhered to the spot, although the reason for it had long ceased to exist.

of the miner strikes without producing the slightest effect (Fig.
270) I K L M.[1] The base of the wall shows larger stones apparently
used as foundations. Inside the court are two rectangular blocks
built with the same concrete as the enclosure wall and slightly
overtopping it (Fig. 270, A B). Either end of the court is occupied by one of these blocks, and a narrow space divides them from
the wall on both sides. This space (R P S), of which more anon,
is completely blocked up, but quite free at C′ C″ T. Reference to
Fig. 271 shows a deep regular cut on the upper face of this block,

FIG. 271.—Massive Block in the Courtyard, Deunuk-tach.

which does not occur in the other. To the south-east, towards the
top of the wall inside, are holes at stated intervals, which seem to
have been intended to receive the ends of the framing work.
This, we are told, is the only part of the wall where they exist.
The single entrance to the building (Fig. 270, D) did not occupy
the centre of the face in which it occurs (Fig. 272).

[1] Our description of this monument is taken from Langlois, *Voyage en Cilicie et
dans les Montagnes du Taurus, exécuté pendant les années*, pp. 85, 86, and 265–285,
1852, 1853. We have also borrowed his plan (Fig. 270), albeit exceedingly defective
and not drawn to scale, given in the text, but there was no other alternative. His
general view of Deunuk-tach is so confused that no good could come in reproducing
it. Hence we have preferred making use of two slight sketches most kindly placed
at our disposal by M. Maxime Colignon, who visited Tarsus with the Abbé Duchesne
in 1876, at the end of a journey in Asia Minor. Téxier, from some unknown reason,
brought no plan or drawing of this monument, and his observations add nothing to
what may be gathered in Langlois.

Without the court, facing the main block on the north-east, are twin walls (P and G on plan), which are parallel to the small

Fig. 272.—Doorway of Deunuk-tach.

side of the enclosure. These structures are of the same height as the walls of the great rectangle, and the rubbish accumu-

lated at this point leads to the supposition that there were here
covered halls adjoining the principal building.[1]   Behind the last
wall is a great heap of earth, rounding off in a semicircle as it
approaches the ground.

At the base of the large enclosure, as well as of the blocks
within it, was found a great quantity of fine-grained white marble
crumbled to pieces.   Some of these fragments, pounded very
small or pulverised, cover the upper part of the wall.   Here and
there are seen shallow cavities, apparently to receive tablets fitted
into the wall, which they divided into panels.   Now the whole
building looks like a huge rock cut with the chisel; but this
cannot have been the primitive aspect of the monument, and we
may reasonably suppose that every part was richly revêted in
order to disguise meanness of material.

If the excavations made here in 1836 by M. Gillert, then
French consul at Tarsus, yielded very poor results, they were

Fig. 273.—Bronze Coin, Tarsus.   Lajard,
Plate IV.

of service in demonstrating the
structural nature of the twin
blocks within the court.   A
gallery, 1 m. 80 c. high by 1 m.
50 c. wide, was with some
difficulty excavated more than
half-way through the depth of
the larger cube, as far as Q V,
but no hollows representing
chambers were encountered, it being full throughout.   A shaft at
Q V was then sunk, without bringing aught of any interest.   A
trench was next attempted between the blocks at Y; but, beyond
chips of white marble and fragments of so-called red Samian
pottery, the only object met with was a huge finger of white
marble, supposed to have belonged to a colossal statue, the remains of which are strewing the ground in great masses, and
which formerly graced the monument.

Such an hypothesis is borne out by countless imperial coins
struck at Tarsus, bearing on one side a rude structure, doubtless
one of the chief monuments of the city (Fig. 273).   As will be

---

[1] Langlois mentions "vaults;" but he uses architectural nomenclature in such
haphazard fashion, that it would be unsafe to rely upon a chance word, followed by
no passing allusion to his having lit upon keystones or fragments of the actual
vaults built of concrete.

seen, the lower portion of the building is a rectangle, resting upon a slightly projecting base, which in its turn serves as pedestal to a pyramid, terminating with a colossal bird, probably an eagle. Festoons are carried round the line which supports the pyramid. In the centre of this, over the pendentives, is a statue of a type already encountered on an older coin of the same city, *i.e.* a royal personage standing upon a horned lion (Fig. 267). The fact of the statue being figured with or without pedestal implies that it represented the principal hero or deity of the town, round which a whole cycle of traditions or myths had gathered. The place, too, it occupies in the sacred building, in view of the whole multitude come to Tarsus to participate in his public worship, further strengthens the theory. The monument and its conspicuous statue were symbolical, and reminded the inhabitants of their old creed and the Eastern origin of their town.

Whatever may have been the name of this divine being, he was the founder and tutelar deity of the place. In his honour quinquennial festivals were celebrated, and his effigy was borne round the city, followed by the whole population, and finally burnt upon an imposing funeral pile set up for the purpose.[1] These gorgeous pageants increased no doubt with the enormous prosperity of Tarsus under Greek and Roman rule, down to the beginning of our era. The singular rite of burning the effigy of the god was neither a Greek nor Roman invention, but of Eastern origin, and closely allied to the ceremonies that followed upon the death of Adonis, circumstantially described by ancient writers. Unfortunately we have no account of the special rites at Tarsus, beyond a passing allusion from a rhetor. Had he thought fit to give us the programme of the performance, we should certainly find that soon after the god had disappeared amidst devouring flames, his triumphal resurrection was witnessed with jubilant cries by his worshippers.

The main theme of all naturalistic religions is this eternal antithesis manifesting itself under different forms, according to the country and people, to express the striking succession of night and day, of spring and winter, of life and death. When the early Greeks first witnessed these peculiar rites, they thought they recognized their own Heracles in the dying god of Tarsus;[2]

[1] DION CHRYSOSTOM, *Orations*, xxxiii. tom. ii. p. 25. Reiske edition.
[2] *Loc. cit.*

but a later development of the myth, brought into fashion by
Clesias, who wrote about the fifth century B.C., declared Assur-
nat-sirpal the hero of this tragedy.[1]   The Greeks, with their
proneness to find a reason for everything, were not to be deterred
because lack of historical knowledge, notably in matters pertaining
to alien peoples, rendered them singularly unfit to explain subjects
which they saw enacted before them, but which they were wholly
incapable of apprehending, and willingly numbered the Baal of
Tarsus among their own revered gods.   It has been asked
whether the representation on the coins of Tarsus was not
intended for the funeral pile of the quinquennial festival (Fig. 273).
Ingenious though the conjecture may be, it seems more natural
to view it as the permanent pedestal upon which the statue was
set up, such as appears on older coins (Fig. 267).   The rude
portion of the monument, extant to this day, was far away a more
apposite symbol of the city than a scaffolding of resinous wood
temporarily raised in an open space to be destroyed.   Nor is this
a self-unsupported opinion ; the multitudinous coins of Byblos,
Paphos, and Eryx, published in a former volume, all bear the
impress of their chief sanctuary, which served to remind the
inhabitants of their old creed, connected with all their civic and
religious associations, and the envy of more modern neighbouring
centres.   Even granting the not improbable assumption that the
funeral scaffolding was a copy of the stone pedestal will not
invalidate our theory, since it is evident that the aim of the
engraver was to reproduce a sample of the original, held to be
coeval with the town, in regard to which no one could tell when
or by whom it had been founded.

All things taken together, we think that we shall not greatly
err in ranging the Deunuk-tach in the same category.   The
largest cube (A in plan) was the pedestal which supported the
statue of the god dressed as a warrior ; whilst the famous τύπος
λιθινός, bas-relief, which the companions of Alexander mistook
for the image of Sarda-nat-sirpal, whom they described snapping
his fingers in utter unconcern at his impending fate,[2] probably
covered block B — perhaps a royal stela — akin to those of
Assyria figuring monarchs in sacerdotal robes, the right arm
raised and thumb closed upon the forefinger, in sign of adora-

---

[1] Arrian, *Anabasi*, II. v. 1–5 ; cf. Strabo, XIV. v. 10.
[2] Aristobulus, cited by Athenius, xii. p. 530.   A. Arrian, *Anabasis*, II. v. 2.

tion.[1] Below the figure was an inscription written in Asianic characters, which the Greeks designated under the general term of Ἀσσύρια γράμματα, Assyrian letters. Was the legend in cuneiform writing, or signs derived from Hittite hieroglyphs, analogous to the Cypriote alphabet? To this question it is not easy to give an answer. For if the Assyrians did not acquire a firm footing in Cilicia, the stela of Sargon, discovered in Cyprus, is sufficient proof that even where their occupation of the country was of brief duration, they left behind them traces of their art and influence. On the other hand, the native tribes of these districts belonged for centuries to the Hittite confederacy; and the natural inference that presents itself is that during that time they adopted, like the other populations of the peninsula, a variant of the Asianic alphabet. However it may be, it is certain that the translation of the local Dry-as-Dust was purely imaginary, akin to the tales which the Egyptian interpreters at Sais and Memphis poured in Herodotus's willing ear. In no well-attested ancient epigraphy of Chaldæa or Assyria has there been found aught that even faintly resembles the gross epicurism expressed in the terminal wording of the so-called epitaph to Sarda-nat-sirpal.[2]

Whether Hittite or Assyrian, whether the image of a local prince or a Ninevite conqueror, the tablet has withstood the destructive changes which the hand of time wrought upon the city. The Greeks settled at Tarsus, ere long intermarried with the earlier population, and readily accepted a deity of such ancient date, with the rites and traditions attached to his name, interpreting them after their own egotistic fashion. Hence the tablet,

---

[1] HEUZEY, *Les Fragments de Tarse au Musée du Louvre.* Reference to Figs. 233 and 306, tom. ii., *Hist. of Art*, will give a capital idea of the style of this stela.

[2] We give the best-known version of this epitaph "I, Sarda-nat-sirpal, son of Anaxindaraxes, founded Tarsus and Anchiales on the same day. Stranger, eat, drink, make love, all else is nought." The dramatic ending of this monarch was of a nature to exercise the ingenuity and form the theme of later poets and moralists. An inscription to Sarda-nat-sirpal was also trumped up at Nineveh, supposed to have been discovered in a ruin in one of the temples, where his tomb was also shown. But the first European scholar who saw it found that, far from being an old Assyrian epigraph, it was written in Greek verse by Khœrilos, of Iassos. It runs thus: "I have reigned, and, so long as I beheld the light of day, I drank, I ate, I made love, recollecting the many vicissitudes and hardships of man, and how short is his span of life" (Amyntas, Fragment 2; also *Fragmenta Historicorum de rebus Alexandri*, collected by Müller, in *Biblio-Greco-Latine*, of Diderot, at the end of ARRIAN's *Anabasis*.

albeit no one could read its inscription—perhaps on that very
account invested with greater mysterious awe—was religiously
preserved throughout the Greek period. Its place, as of yore,
was in the sacred area surrounded by the great poliote deities ; its
image was precisely similar to that sculptured on the rocky sides
of Cappadocia, accompanied by mysterious Hittite hieroglyphs.

From Alexander to the beginning of our era the sanctuary was
doubtless often repaired and modified, in order to keep pace with
the fashion of the day. To this period must be assigned the
marble facing—a mode of enrichment unknown in primitive days.
Then, too, the archaic statue of Tars-Baal was in all probability
replaced by one of white marble (which the huge finger found in
the court seems to suggest) ; whilst preserving the traditional
posture, character, and attributes of the former, attested by countless contemporary medals, whether of the Seleucidæ or the Anto-
nines. We incline to think that the wall is older than this
restoration. Its four angles faced the cardinal points, a certain
indication of its having been erected before the Greek conquest ;
for such an arrangement is never found in Grecian temples,
whether in Hellas proper or in her colonies, whereas it is a
characteristic of the palaces and storied towers of Chaldæa and
Assyria.

Had the monument been due to Greek hands, the wall and the
cubes would have been built of stone in large square blocks almost
unhewn, as at Tirynthus, or in regular courses remarkable for
their beauty of joint. On the other hand, we know that the
Phœnicians, notably in Africa, made frequent use of these artificial
rocks.[1] Deunuk-tach, with its unsymmetric opening, its absence
of cella or colonnade, has nothing to remind us of a Greek building ;
if it had a porch, it was a mere shelter, placed along the inner
enclosure, as in the ma'abed at Amrit.[2] For the reasons adduced,
therefore, we must place this sanctuary before the action of
Hellenic genius was felt in Cilicia. The remains of this monument deserve to receive the attention of a specialist able to note
and take advantage of the slightest indication ; for, if we can fix
no certain date to it, we know that it was accounted very old when
the Macedonians entered Tarsus, and that it formed its chief
attraction in the time of Strabo and Dion Chrysostom. This was
due, no doubt, to its essentially Asiatic character, which was that

[1] *Hist. of Art*, tom. iii. pp. 363-365.   [2] *Ibid.*, p. 245, Figs. 39, 40.

of the Semitic haram. The twin pediments were a local feature, encountered also in its most elementary form in the rude stone enclosure of Moab, and in its most developed stage at Byblos, Paphos, and Jerusalem. Whether the sanctuary was due to Hittite, Assyrian, or Phœnician influence is a question shrouded in great obscurity. We can only say that the connexion between Phœnicia and the coast cities of Cilicia was intimate and lasted a long time. In the present day, Syrian merchants crowd the bazaars of Mersina, Adana, and Tarsus, and Arabic is as much the language of the country as Turkish. All that can be urged for Deunuk-tach, in the absence of an inscription, is that it was not a Grecian building; this is its chief claim for being classed with the too rare architectural monuments of Syria and Asia Minor.

In the same category should be placed a door, built of square stone blocks, here and there roughly cut, to the height of four metres. It was found on the road leading from Lamas, ancient Lamos, to Kannideli, which some identify with Neapolis of Isauria,[1] near the ruins of Aseli-Keui.[2] Symbols, of which a careful drawing is difficult to find, are engraved on the lintel. These, so far as can be made out from the very indifferent sketch at our disposal (Fig.

FIG. 274.—Doorway near Aseli-Keui. LANGLOIS, *Voyage en Cilicie*, p. 169.

274), recall Himathite hieroglyphs, albeit with slight differences in the form of caps, ploughshares, vases, etc., easily accounted for. To these may be added the peculiar sign in the legend of the Nymphi warrior, which has been taken for a caduceus and a pair

[1] LANGLOIS, *loc. cit.*, Pt. II. chap. iv.

[2] It is passing strange that Langlois, who first descried this monument, and who was quite aware of the importance of his discovery, should have given no map to guide future travellers to the ruins of Aseli-Keui and Kannideli, of which he only gives verbal descriptions. These localities do not figure in Kiepert's map. It is tantalizing to have to work on such poor materials, which a little care would have made satisfactory.

of pincers indifferently.[1] If ever the door is found again—and diligent search should be made for it to obtain a careful drawing, without which it is impossible to arrive at any satisfactory conclusion—excavations should be made around it to recover the building to which it formerly belonged.[2]

A pre-Hellenic origin should likewise be ascribed to the Direkli-tach, or colossal rock-cut menhir, 15 m. in height, 4 m. in breadth, and 12 m. in depth, which is still to be seen on the side of the ancient road which connected Tarsus with Pompeiopolis.[3] It was probably set up, like the rude stone monuments of Hebrew and other Syrian tribes, to commemorate some local event.[4]

If Hittite sculptures and inscriptions have been found in distant Lycaonia and Isauria, important discoveries may be looked for in the unexplored valleys of Cilicia, only a few hours' journey from the very centre of that civilization.

§ 3.—*Sculpture.*

Like Chaldæan and Assyrian sculptors, the artists of northern Syria did not progress beyond bas-reliefs. The only instance we have of a statue about natural size is a torso, found at Merash by Puchstein, who made a drawing of it. It is in a deplorable state ; the high relief of the front part has suffered most, and nothing but the mass remains. The back is in better preservation, showing that the figure was dressed and wore the long fringed shawl which served as mantle, and which we know, from the sculptured pictures of Mesopotamia. It has no inscription. But the lower portion of a statuette, whose feet are gone, is covered all over with engraved signs. Unfortunately, this part, 21 c. in height, is least calculated to indicate the posture and type of the figure. The fragment of a huge closed hand was also unearthed here, but the colossal statue to which it belonged was searched for in vain. From these remains it might be inferred that the Hittite artist was not ignorant of the processes of sculpture in the round boss ; nevertheless, not one of the lions which he was so fond of introducing everywhere in his compositions is wholly disengaged from the block on which he was cut. A very forcible outline forms the relief of the general figure ; whilst a certain amount of care is

---

[1] Wright, *The Empire*, Plate XVII.   [3] Langlois, *loc. cit.*, pp. 239, 253.
[2] *Ibid.*, pp. 239 and 253.   [4] *Hist. of Art*, tom. iv. pp. 342, 343.

bestowed upon some of the details—the paws, for instance, which, though adhering, stand out from the mass by their great salience of contour; special attention being given to the head, which is quite free.

FIG. 275.—The Merash Lion. Height, 88 c. WRIGHT, *The Empire*, Plate XXVII.

The Merash lion, with inscribed characters, may be taken as type of the figures which stood one on each side of a palatial entrance (Fig. 275). The inscription, it has been remarked, was only on one side, the other being left flat; hence, the assumption that it stood against a wall, and was faced by a second, both

as bases to pillars or columns; these in their turn supported a lintel
or penthouse. It is a disposition of frequent occurrence in Assyria,
one, too, which was revived with excellent effect by mediæval
builders to decorate the porches of cathedrals and important
buildings.[1] One line of the inscription runs along the backbone,
and then there is a slight ledge on the side and top, yielding a
convenient space for the superincumbent pillar.[2] One out of

FIG. 276.—Carving, Carchemish. St. Elme Gautier, from a photograph of Dr. Gwyther.

the two Merash lions was sent by Handi Bey to the museum at
Constantinople. Our woodcut (Fig. 268) shows it before it was
taken down from its exalted position.

These and other figures of the same class—the Albistan lions,
for example—stand midway between images worked in the round,
the highest degree of perfection reached in sculpture and bas-
reliefs, the handling of which offers fewer difficulties. Low reliefs,

---

[1] *Hist. of Art*, tom. ii. pp. 228, 229.

[2] It was Dr. Wright who pointed out the ledge on the lion's back. A side view
may be seen in Fig. 1. Plate XXVI., *Empire of the Hittites*. All these inscriptions
and drawings were reproduced from those published in *Trans. Soc. Bibl. Archæ.*,
vol. vii., made from the casts by the secretary, Mr. Rylands.—EDITOR.

properly so-called, are plentiful, making it all the more singular that up to the present time not a single rock-cut exemplar has been reported, whether at the entrance of a pass, or on those volcanic cones that rise in countless numbers from the ground between Mount Amanus and the Kurdagh. All those that are known were carved on slabs, mostly basalt, as at Hamath. Of these tablets, some are rectangular, and others irregularly cut; the former were evidently intended as lining to walls; whilst it is equally clear that the latter, narrowing towards the base, were fixed in the ground of a cemetery or other sacred enclosure. Such would be the stela at Samosata, where the stone was thinned out below the rough plinth, upon which rest the feet of the figure, to facilitate its entering the ground.

There is no lack of diversity in the themes treated by this art; national deities, as a matter of course, holding the first place : such would be the bearded winged personage on the sculptured slab at Gargamish, standing on the back of a crouching lion, with tiara and long robe drawn in at the waist (Fig. 276). Next comes a figure with precisely the same costume, but without wings, a sufficient indication that he belongs to the sublunary world—a king or priest—and holds in his left hand a sacred object he is about to offer; but the condition of the carving does not allow us to make out what. From the same place is another sculpture, unfortunately much worn. It represents a god, or genie, with four wings; one set raised and the other inclined to the ground. In his hand is carried a vase, or basket, akin to those on Ninevite monuments. But for the Hittite characters at the side and the square border of his robe, always rounded

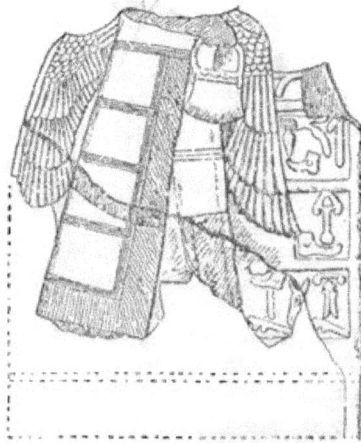

FIG. 277.—Carving at Carchemish. Basalt. Height, 76 c. British Museum.

at Calach and Nineveh, we might almost imagine that we had before us an Assyrian bas-relief. The figure on the next stela, from Birejik, where it was found built in the wall of a castle, is now in the British Museum, entitled " Monolith of a King " (Fig. 278). His attitude, the object he holds in his hand, doubtless a pomegranate, his gaze fixed on the patera in the other hand,

which is raised, suggest a worshipper standing before the deity, whose presence is announced by the solar disc over his head. The tall, very modern-looking hat will be noticed ; it is unique of its kind, and nothing like it has been seen in Chaldæa, Assyria, Cyprus, or Phœnicia.

The narrow dimensions of this stela call to mind the ancient monuments of Babylonia. It is without inscription,[1] and may with equal propriety be ascribed to Mesopotamia, whence it was carried off by a Hittite prince as a memento of some expedition or, conversely, have been set up here by Nebuchadnezzar or some other Chaldæan conqueror. In favour of this hypothesis is the fact that the tablet is basalt, the stone of the country. On the other hand, the absence of a cuneiform inscription renders it probable that the stela, being found on the very border of

FIG. 278.—Royal Stela.   British Museum.

Mesopotamia, was due to a Chaldæan, or a native craftsman instructed by the former.   This applies to a semi-column 1 m. 70 c. in height from Jerabis.   The characters inscribed on the curved face are remarkable for clearness and the peculiar shape of some

---

[1] It was first noticed by M. BADGER, and pictured by him in his work on the *Nestorians and their Ritual*, tom. i. p. 352, 1852.   Mr. Wright had misgivings in respect to this bas-relief, which he first reproduced from Professor SAYCE's *The Monuments of the Hittites*, but which does not figure in the second edition of *The Empire*.   Plate XX. gives the figure ; Plate X. the inscription.

of them. On the flat side, in a shallow niche, stands the full-face figure of a king or priest, cut in low relief. The head and shoulders are gone, but enough remains to show that he wore a richly embroidered costume. On the breast is a pectoral, with meanders and rosettes running round it, like the patterns on the monuments of Assyria. The border of the mantle, which alone remains, was of no less ornamental description. It is open in front, showing a closely plaited fine tunic, akin to that of early Greek statues. In his hand is carried some object, perhaps a sceptre ; but, whether priest or king, he was certainly an exalted personage, taken in his gala dress. On the fragment of another stone, also in the British Museum, is figured an officiating priest, whose attributes and details—the earrings, for example—are closely allied to those of the monuments of Nineveh.[1] Finally, a slab, likewise from Jerabis, represents a figure clad in a long robe reaching to the ankles, and shoes curled up at the end. In his left hand, which is outstretched, is held a sceptre by the middle, or, as some think, one or more arrows. The lines of the inscribed characters, in great part preserved, are high up on the stone and about the sides of the image.[2]

The sculptures that we have brought together are but the first instalments of a peculiarly interesting series, which, it is to be hoped, fresh discoveries will render complete at no distant date, and form a pendant to the royal stelas of Assyria, published by us in a former volume.[3] The day that shall unravel the mystery of Hittite hieroglyphs will also reveal the names of the kings who struggled with Seti and Ramses, with Shalmaneser and Sargon ; names that we only know from Theban and Ninevite inscriptions, but which a native Pentaur may have engraved along with his own version of the campaigns on the banks of the Orontes.

Meanwhile, where are we to look for these royal stelas ? Were they set up in the temples, in the adjoining courts, or in the halls of the sovereign ? We know not; for no building, whether at

---

[1] WRIGHT, *The Empire*, Plate XIX. If we have not reproduced the two last-named figures, it is because they are almost Assyrian in execution. As the limits of our space do not allow of our publishing all the monuments that have been recovered in North Syria, we have confined our selection to those distinguished by quaint, peculiar aspect, so as to bring in a few specimens recently discovered. These, as a natural consequence, are not found in Mr. Wright's work.

[2] WRIGHT, *The Empire*, Plate IX.

[3] *Hist. of Art*, tom. ii. Fig. 69, p. 306, and Plate XII.

Carchemish or any other centre, has been made the subject of systematic excavations. Were these once brought to light, even though the inscribed signs continued to be a sealed book, we should find no difficulty in making out the general signification of the subjects represented.

Such are the three slabs from Saktchégheuksou, which represent a royal hunt, where we come in at the death; in which the king, recognizable by the solar disc over his head, and two more sportsmen are engaged (Fig. 279).[1] The peculiar arrangement of the animal figures, cut by the joints of the stones already referred to, leaves no doubt but that the stones were intended to decorate the base of a wall, like those still found in place at Sinjirli (Fig. 269). On the two sinister slabs are three figures that follow each other in one direction; whilst those on the dexter stones—whether the archer preparing to let go his arrow at a huge stag, which he has missed, but has hit the female in front, or the winged quadruped erect on his hind legs, or the male figure with tiara or long-handled mattock—are all turned the other way. Finally, round the corner, on the last stone, only partially uncovered by the explorers, a horse's head appears, and meets the last procession, clearly showing that here was the end of the frieze.

A certain degree of thought was bestowed upon carved stones that were meant to be applied to a wall, notably at Saktchégheuksou, which were rectangular and ornamented with a border, as against stelas than which nothing could well be ruder or more irregularly cut. Fig. 280,[2] from an excellent photograph of Dr. Gwyther, portrays two women sitting upon primitive low-backed chairs, with footstools cut out of the same wooden block, upon which the feet are placed. A table is between them, with three quaint platters and a vase. The posture, the dress, and high cap with striped or quilled border, are precisely alike in both figures. Each has a hand raised, and holds one a patera, the second a vase or cup; and each presses the remaining hand against her breast, with some object not easily determined, perhaps a vase or pome-

---

[1] This bas-relief is reproduced after a photogravure plate of MM. Heumann and Puchstein's work.

[2] A good impression sent us by Dr. Gwyther enabled us to add the inscribed characters to our drawing, scarcely visible in the photograph. Casts of all these stelas are in Berlin.

FIG. 279.—Hunting Scene. Basalt. Height, 1 m. 18 c. See p. 64.

granate. The space above and between the heads is covered with characters.[1] The thin narrow base of the next stela (Fig. 281), meant to enter the ground, is gone. But this in no way interferes with the general shape and nature of the figures, save that a child is introduced, who sits on a kind of tall stand, his feet resting on the knees of the adult female, evidently his mother. In her right hand is held a pomegranate, and in the left a four-stringed lyre, upon which a bird is perched. Chair, table, plates, vase, and so forth are precisely similar to those already seen, and are repeated on sundry other tablets of the same series, but much more worn; the only variant

FIG. 280.—Votive Stela. Height, 44 c. Basalt. Merash. Drawn by St. Elme Gautier.

is the bird, perhaps a dove, held up by the feet, forming a pendant to the patera of the opposite figure.[2]

We will terminate the enumeration of this class of monuments — which, owing to their archaic clumsy aspect may seem too long

[1] An isolated block which, from its shape and character, was designed for mural decoration, comes from Sinjirii. It consists of two figures, male and female, sitting one on either side of a table with platters, as in the above woodcut. With one hand they carry a cup to their lips, and with the other, one holds a sceptre and the second apparently a flower. Casts of all these stelas are in Berlin. See *Reisen*, etc., Heumann and Puchstein.

[2] The whole series, to the smallest fragment, will be found in MM. Heumann and Puchstein's work.

already—by one more tablet. Its size, subject, and treatment show a decided advance on those we have reviewed, and were it intact would constitute one of the most curious and interesting specimens of Hittite art (Fig. 282). Unfortunately, the whole of the left side,

Fig. 281.—Votive Stela. Height, 52 c. Basalt. Merash. After a drawing by M. Puchstein.

which was occupied by an abnormally tall figure, doubtless a deity, is broken away. But enough remains to show that he was clad in a long robe, and that in his hand was carried some kind of weapon, the end of which alone is visible; this part of the stone being most seriously damaged. The worshipper, his hair held by a fillet,

FIG. 282.—Votive Stela. Basalt. Height, 88 c. Merash. St. Elme Gautier, from
a photograph of Dr. Gwyther.

carries in his right hand a drinking cup, and in his left a palm. A table of the usual type, loaded with viands, separates the god from the hero or knight. Near the former is a plate, with what

appears to be a duck or goose; and in the second platter crescent-shaped objects, fritters, cakes, or fruit, at will. Below these figures is a groom minding the horse of his master (seen in the upper register), which he is walking up and down.[1]

There is yet the fragment of a stela, un-covered at Roum-Kalé between Birejik and Samosata, to be men-tioned among exemplars of Hittite origin. It portrays a bearded per-sonage, with a round cap, bearing a palm, the distinctive badge of a worshipper. The exe-cution, owing partly to the hardness of the material, and partly to unskilfulness, is so un-couth that it is difficult to make out the other attributes, except so far that he seems to hold a lyre in his left hand

FIG. 283.—Fragment of Stela. Basalt. Height, 50 c. *Gazette Arch.*, 1883, Plate XXII.

like that of Fig. 281, and that he wears a girdle, from which hangs a broad dagger. His tunic, heavily trimmed with fur, is cut away in front to facilitate locomotion, and discloses the legs and feet,

[1] On the base of another stela, the carving of which is obliterated, was figured a chariot

which are covered, but whether with snow or leather boots it is impossible to determine. Behind his back is slung a huge basket or leather pouch.

The general aspect and all the details about these stelas from Northern Syria indicate a votive character. Now the god is portrayed together with his worshipper and the offering; now his presence is assumed and as it were understood; the attitude of the personages, the objects offered, such as pomegranates, the emblem of fecundity, pateras, drinking cups, lyres twanged in religious ceremonies, doves sacred to Ashtoreth, leave no doubt as to their destination. The object of these stelas therefore, like many found in Phœnicia and Cyprus, including statues, was to prolong the act of adoration and sacrifice; they replaced the worshipper before the deity whose protection he had implored or imagined he had obtained.[1]

Great diversity of head-gear is observable in these sculptures; sometimes they are bare-headed, with a wealth of curly hair (Figs. 279, 282); sometimes we meet with tall conical hats (Fig. 279), with rounded caps (Fig. 269), or the type seen on Khitisar (Fig. 260); at other times the hat is furnished with a turned-up rim (Fig. 276). This shape obtained in Cappadocia, and is one of the signs that are oftener repeated in the inscriptions.[2] The most curious head-coverings are perhaps those of the two kings (Figs. 262 and 278). The presence and position of the child in Fig. 281 are sufficient indications that the round head-dress of this and Fig. 280 belonged to women. Defective drawing and general outline would otherwise leave the sex unrevealed, which the costume does not help to remedy.

The dress of the various classes seems to have been sharply defined. Thus gods, heroes, and kings are clothed in long flowing robes heavily fringed (Figs. 276, 278). Over this or the tunic was sometimes thrown a richly embroidered mantle, calling to mind those on the monuments of Assyria and Nineveh (Figs. 277, 292). Short tunics taken in at the waist by a band (Figs. 269, 282) are still of general usage among the peasantry of Cappadocia. Coats of mail covering the whole body are seen in three out of four figures in the royal chase (Fig. 279).

Bas-reliefs representing females are of but one type, and very

[1] *Hist. of Art*, tom. iii. pp. 257, 258.
[2] See Wright, *The Empire*, Pt. I., second line in first and second Hamath stone.

rare ; whilst the cloak, which completely shrouds them, yields no opportunity for observing the under-garments. Details common to almost all these figures, male and female, are the pointed cap or

tiara and the turned-up shoes, recalling those in vogue in the fourteenth and fifteenth centuries (Figs. 262, 269, 276, 280, 282). Tip-tilted boots, shoes, and slippers are worn at the present day all over the East,

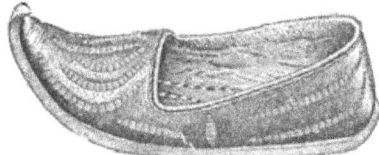

FIG. 284.—Modern Syrian Shoe.' LORTET, *La Syrie.*

be it Anatolia, Syria or Egypt (Figs. 284, 285). It is probable that in olden times, notably among the warlike Hittites, they

partook of the character of a military boot, suitable for forced marches, and not left in every quagmire, as would a Turkish slipper. The semi-high boot, open on the instep and fastened round the leg by leather thongs in true mountaineer fashion, should be noticed (Fig. 282).[1] This peculiarity of the national foot-covering was observed by the two great nations of antiquity with whom the Hittites were brought in contact.

Fig. 285.—Syrian Boot. LORTET.

As before stated, it was figured with intentional exaggeration, both at Thebes in the Ramesseum, and on the black obelisk of Shalmaneser, where tribute-bearers, in the Hittite tunic, Phrygian cap, and curled shoes, are said to have come from Cappadocia, held at that time by Hittite and cognate tribes.[2] Finally, the

[1] Some have thought to recognize this boot in the Hittite hieroglyphs (Figs. 256, 277, 280 (WRIGHT, Plate XX. Fig. 3 ; XXI. Fig. 2 ; XXV.). But that the sign in question was designed for the actual foot is abundantly proved in numbers of instances, where the ankle is distinctly drawn (Fig. 277). The engraver was so accustomed to see the foot shod, that he unconsciously gave it the characteristic curve of the boot, to make its meaning more clear. Moreover, the foot was not the only limb that had been requisitioned ; the head, arm, hand, leg, etc., had each in turn furnished signs to the Hittite alphabet (Fig. 256).

[2] This detail had escaped Rosellini, Lepsius, and subsequent scholars, who as a natural consequence did not reproduce it in their drawings. Professor Sayce, in his visit to Thebes in 1884, was the first to call the attention of his fellow-travellers to

tip-tilted shoe has been recognized on early Cypriote vases and cylinders (Fig. 286).[1]

If from the costume we pass on to weapons, we shall find that they were by no means all drawn on the same pattern. Perhaps the quaintest specimen is the mace from Sinjirli (Fig. 269). Then we have lances (Fig. 282), spears, two-headed axes (Fig. 279), long swords (Fig. 269), and daggers, both hanging from the waist (Fig. 283) and not unfrequently the bow (Figs. 269 and 279).[2]

Fig. 286.—Pointed Shoe.   Cypriote Vase.

Defensive arms were not unknown; and though the deeply indented shield has not been identified on any Hittite sculpture, we find it carefully reproduced on the Egyptian monuments (Figs. 257 and 259). In the latter, the three chief personages are protected by a long cuirass, probably contrived with bronze plates fixed upon a skin (Fig. 279).

Hittite art, far more than that of Assyria and Chaldæa, was mainly concerned in reproducing every detail of dress and equipment; and rarely attempted to represent the nude. Among the bas-reliefs, which from certain characteristics and details we are justified in ascribing to native invention, there is not a single figure which is not covered. The only exception to this rule is found in the Anath or Ishtar from Carchemish. But, as was remarked at the time, it is exceedingly hard, not to say impossible, to assign a certain date or nationality

---

this peculiarity (Wright, *The Empire*, Plates XXII., XXVI.). The accuracy of the observation was confirmed by another eye-witness, M. Maspero, in a letter to us. *Hist. of Art.* tom. ii p. 553.   Fr. Lenormant, *Gaz. Arch.*, 1883, pp. 130, 131.

[1] We reproduce one of these vases, which was published by M. Solomon Reinach, *Chroniques d'Orient*, tom. vi. p. 360, 3ᵐᵉ série de la *Revue Archéologique*, 1885. For the cylinders, see De Cesnola's *Salaminia*, Fig. 116 and Plate XII. Fig. 2.

[2] The bow is also found in a stela from Merash on which is clearly, figured a dagger with rounded hilt.

to this piece. It may with equal propriety have been due to Lower Chaldæa, Phœnicia, or a native craftsman. As the goddess was an importation, the artist would naturally figure her with the attributes by which she was universally known, albeit foreign to Hittite methods and traditions.

However mediocre—even taken at its best—this art may have been, it had none the less two distinct periods : the first decidedly original, but rude and barbarous in the extreme ; and the second when contact with neighbours in the enjoyment of a higher civilization induced greater freedom and grace in its designs.

In the first era should be classed the bas-reliefs from Sinjirli, more especially the stelas from Merash and Roum-Kalé, where the figures, hard and crude, are absolutely undiversified in dress or general outline ; and where all are seen in profile with round protruding eye. This poverty of invention is extended to symbols ; for, with the single exception of the winged lion on the Sinjirli frieze, they are conspicuous by their absence ; clearly demonstrating that when these sculptures were elaborated, the native engraver was as yet uninspired by alien sources. On the other hand, subjects and symbols conventionally treated, bearing witness to their dependence on Chaldæan and Assyrian art, are plentiful in royal stelas and in sundry fragments from Carchemish (Figs. 276, 277, 278, 279). To this category belong the winged discs figured over the heads of kings ;[1] deities standing on lions, like those at Bavian and Malthai, in the Tigris Valley ;[2] outstretched wings seen on Assyrian and Chaldæan cylinders ;[3] and sacred bronzes generally carried in the hand.[4] The influence of Assyria is most striking in the lion-hunting scene ; where we might almost fancy that it had been bodily taken from one of the palaces at Khorsabad or Kujunjik, so faithfully has the Hittite craftsman reproduced every detail about the dress of the personages, even to the discarding of the national boot for the Assyrian sandal ; whilst the harnessing of horses, the shape of the chariot, the plaiting and roundels round the border, are copied with no less exactness. Nevertheless, we have felt no hesitation in assigning this sculpture to a Hittite artist, familiar with Chaldæan models, who tried to imitate them as closely as possible. But it was easier for him

[1] *Hist of Art*, tom. ii. p. 88, Figs. 18, 19, and 343 ; tom. iii. Figs. 283 and 305.
[2] *Ibid.*, pp. 636-647, Figs. 310, 314.   [3] *Ibid.*, Figs. 314, 315.
[4] *Ibid.*, pp. 4, 8, etc.

to dress his personages in true Assyrian fashion, than modify the physical type which he saw everywhere about him, and which moreover was fixed by long usage. Hence it is that, albeit reproduced here with lighter and more practised hand, it still preserves its special physiognomy. The nose, for instance, is not hooked, like that of the Semites, but straight, long, and pointed; the treatment of the hair, too, in the central figure, is not quite what we should find on a Ninevite tablet; and the lion is at once tame and clumsy. There is an abyss between this art and the consummate skill and truthfulness with which the sculptors employed by the Sargonides expressed the impotent rage, the supreme agony, of the hunted beasts in the throes of death. And last, not least, all these sculptures are on basalt slabs, a sure test that they were carved on the spot.

The multitudinous points of touch which we have passed in review, admit of quite a natural explanation : the extension of the Assyrian empire began in the ninth century B.C. From that date the kings of Calah and Nineveh crossed the Euphrates and frequently moved their armies into Syria. They overran the twin kingdoms of Israel and Phœnicia along the shores of the Mediterranean, and, as a natural consequence, relations were entered into between the conquerors and the conquered. Such relations were doubtless of no friendly character whilst contests lasted; but these were followed by long intervals of peace, during which caravans resumed their journeys from one country to another. The clay seals with Hittite characters, discovered in the treasure chamber at Kujunjik, affixed to the bags that contained the objects paid as tribute, may have been brought by kings of Hamath and Carchemish (Figs. 287, 288, 289). At any

Figs. 287, 288, 289.—Clay Seals. Layard, *The Monuments of Nineveh*, Plate LXIX. Berlin Museum.

rate these and other petty princes of the Orontes and the Pyramus valleys, could not remain indifferent to the pomp and circumstance they beheld or had reported to them. They were stimulated by their powerful neighbours to build palaces, on whose walls their battles, hunting scenes, and religious sacrifices were portrayed. Under the influence of Chaldæa, their sculpture, hitherto rough and archaic, softened and developed apace, without reaching the level of its model or being confused with it. Sometimes, indeed, they are very near the mean of Assyrian virtuosity; notably in the flute player from Merash (Fig. 290). Notwithstanding rigidity of outline, due to the hardness of the material, the head is not wanting in dignity, and there is a certain elegance in the arrangement of the beard and hair symmetrically disposed, falling in graceful curls on either side of the face and on the shoulders.

The custom of covering animals with inscriptions, the Merash statuette and lion for instance (Fig. 275), calls to mind the cuneiform texts of the Assyrian bulls; with this difference, that the finely sunk characters of the latter never interfere or break the lines of the figure in which they occur in minute sections, destroy-

FIG. 290.—Fragment of bas-relief. Height, 32 c. Basalt. After Puchstein. Berlin Museum.

ing the general effect, as do the raised Hittite hieroglyphs, with their diversified outline. These constitute a clumsy overloading of sculpture upon sculpture, resulting in confused, blurred aspect, even where the inscription is strictly confined to the field (Fig. 277).[1]

Like the Assyrians, and all the nations whose sculptors did not work from the nude, the Hittites excelled in rendering animal forms, evidenced in the heads of bulls, wild goats, horses, asses, etc. No observer can fail being struck with the surety of hand shown in these abridged heads, which denote long practice. Nowhere, perhaps, is this merit more apparent than in the twin rabbits of the Merash lion (Figs. 254, 255). The latter animal holds a prominent place in Hittite art. At the present day, the

[1] See WRIGHT, *The Empire*, Plate IX.

sportsman has to seek him much further south ; but some four thousand years ago and more his home was still the native jungle along the banks of the rivers and in the fastnesses of the Taurus range, where the Syrian artist was within hearing of his roar, and where he had ample opportunity to observe him.   But inadequate technique stood in his way, and prevented his achieving a great success. He failed in dramatic power, in expressing the unutterable agony of life suddenly arrested in the plenitude of its strength, so graphically rendered by his Assyrian *confrère*, and which force our admiration in certain hunting pieces of Assur-nat-sirpal.   But if there is little variety of attitude, if the action of the animal is not always felicitous, none the less has the sculptor seized the leading features of the face and head of the beast, and rendered them with singular truth and vivacity. The mouth is frankly open, the deep furrows on the forehead and sides of the face, characteristic of the ferocious brute, are carefully drawn. Praise cannot be given respecting the way the body is modelled. The artist appears to have hesitated in the treatment he should adopt —finally sacrificing truth to a hankering after effect. Thus he thought to give an appearance of strength to the lion (Fig. 279) by heavy outline, making him shorter than reality, but the result was a thickset, undersized animal. This defect he avoided in Fig. 276, to fall into the opposite error by undue length of line, albeit it must be confessed with more pleasing aspect ; for it is nearer being true, and more readily expresses the marvellous agility of the great brute, the prodigious bounds which enable him to spring upon his prey from a great distance. This type seems to have obtained—at least, it is that which we shall exclusively encounter —in Cappadocia, where we propose to take the reader. The monuments of this district are grouped on a narrow space, not far from the modern town of Yuzgat, the head centre of Eastern Asia Minor.   Here the Western Hittites built their capital, here for centuries they had their principal fortress and centre of activity. Here they started on their distant expeditions across the Halys, leaving traces of their arts throughout the peninsula, on the very borders of the Ægean. Some twenty-five years ago, I spent over a month among these ruins, for the purpose of studying them and taking photographs of the remains that we are about to submit to the reader. If our harvest is more abundant in Cappadocia than it was in northern Syria, this, as was stated at the beginning of this chapter, is owing to difference of material—here soft, easily worked, but as easily destroyed; there hard and resisting. The most important and striking monuments that we shall find on our path, will not be, as heretofore, stray detached remains of buildings that have long disappeared, but rock-cut sculptures with relief and contour almost intact, against which the fury of the elements has beaten in vain, and which were accounted old when Homer wandered from city to city singing his divine poems.

CHAPTER III.

ASIA MINOR.   WESTERN HITTITES.

§ 1.—*Boundaries, Climate, and Natural Divisions.*

The climatic conditions of Cilicia are those of Syria, with which it is intimately connected by language and national development. The configuration of the country common to both does not lose its character until the narrow defiles of the Taurus range are reached, where Asia Minor may be said to begin.[1] This region was from the earliest times the cradle of many centres of ancient civilization, the theatre where more events were crowded in than in any other place of equal size.   Here Greek genius, fanned and stimulated by Oriental breezes, produced its first blossoms, its early fruits. In the fulness of its manhood and middle age it everywhere raised magnificent cities and noble buildings.

We propose, in the sequel of this study, to return here more than once and visit every corner. Hence the propriety to define its boundaries, indicate its natural divisions, and state what conditions air and earth had prepared for the nations settled on its surface.

[1] We do not hesitate to use the appellation μικρά Ἀσία, given to the western peninsula of the Asiatic continent by geographers and historians since Orosus in the fourth century of the vulgar era.   Strabo calls it "the peninsula" ἡ χερσονῆσός, or ἡ Ἀσία ἡ ἐντὸς τοῦ Ταύρου, and ἡ Ἀσία ἐντὸς τοῦ Ταύρου. Herodotus is even more vague, and calls it indifferently, ἡ Ἀσία ἡ ἐντὸς Ἅλυος, or ἡ κάτω Ἀσία, Lower Asia, in opposition to ἡ ἄνω Ἀσία, Upper Asia, extending to the rear of the Taurus and Lebanon.   From the starting-point of the Ægean, the term ἀνάβασις, "ascent," applied to the retreat of the Ten Thousand, including the march of Alexander across the central plateau to the Persian empire, is fully justified. The Greek name Anatolia, Turkish Anadolu, Natolia, for short, may from Natolia city have been extended by the Turks to the whole province.   At the present day, the old denomination of Asia Minor has been revived as best calculated to describe the country.

The area occupied by Asia Minor is as nearly as possible that of France. Three seas wash its shores—the Euxine to the north, the Ægean to the west, and the Mediterranean, with the great islands of Rhodes and Cyprus near its shores, to the south. Its only frontier is towards the east, and no matter the direction assigned thereto, it will always be somewhat arbitrary, since the peninsula is but the prolongation of the uplands, which from one end of the Asiatic continent to the other form the demarcation line between the Northern and Indian oceans. Some have proposed to find this frontier line in the mountain range and the uplands which to the north are the continuation of the Syrian heights, and constitute the dividing crest between the Pyramus and the affluents of the Euphrates, forming a natural dividing line at the base of the peninsula. But on the north-east this limit becomes undefined, so that the geographical division carried right through the plateau of Sivas, across the valley of the Ghermili or Lycus, which feeds the Ieshil-Irmak or Iris, is more or less conventional and arbitrary.[1]

Uncertainty of boundary line does not apply to the general character of the country, than which nothing can well be more easily determined. Broadly speaking, Asia Minor may be described as a rectangular plateau supported by mighty ramparts thrown out by mountain chains, which as a rule run in parallel lines pretty close to the sea coast. The rim of this plateau is surrounded by mountain ranges of considerable and various heights, here and there inaccessible. It leans against the high uplands of Armenia, of which it is but a secondary ridge, or lower terrace, covering nearly two-thirds of the peninsula. Its aspect is diversified, and the transition from the uplands to the coasts is not everywhere constant. There, where the rain which falls on the plateau is most abundant, it has created watercourses of sufficient volume to pierce through the thick barrier of the mountain side. Their bed, in clayey soil, flows between steep banks, which become deeper year by year, presenting the most violent combination of colours it is possible to imagine. As they advance, they meet with less resistance, and fluvial valleys are let in, whose charming variety of aspect serves to beguile the tedium of long ascent or descent as the case may be. Sometimes the waters stagnate at the base of the belt surrounding the plateau ere they can open out grooves for themselves, when they disappear in the

---

[1] RECLUS, *Géographie Universelle*, tom. ix. p. 462.

depths of the rock, to emerge from its clefts on the other side overlooking the lower plains.   Here the river leisurely meanders in the
alluvial soil it has formed, deltas increase with marvellous rapidity,
and many a deep bay has already been filled up.   The harbours of
Ephesus and Miletus, once the theatre of life and activity, were
within historical times choked up with mud and silt brought down
by mountain torrents.   The Hermus will do for the magnificent
bay of Smyrna what the twin Mæanders did for these brilliant
sisters, and, like them, she will become an inland city.

Asia Minor has been called "a lesser Iran, which builds itself
up out of the midst of three seas."[1]   Like the eastern waste of
Persia, some of the basins of central Asia Minor are no longer
connected with the sea, whither at some remote period they probably carried part of their flood.   Open and subterraneous canals
have been obstructed by incrustations and other causes, which
finding no outlet, were transformed into fresh-water lakes or
turned into sheets of salt water by evaporation, extending in winter
over a vast area, but almost dried up in summer.   The water that
then remains, notably that of Lake Tattæa, or Touz-Gheul, is
heavier and more saline than that of the Dead Sea.   It is collected
by the natives, who come from all parts of the country for the purpose.   In the fair season, long files of "arabas" or carts drawn by
bullocks are seen slowly moving along the roads in quest of their
yearly provision.   Many such a caravan have I met plodding back
to their hamlets, distant perhaps some twelve or twenty days'
journey.[2]   Things are not much altered from what they were
thousands of years ago, when these inexhaustible deposits were
first made, and together with the elements requisite to sustain life
to be found here, contributed to render the inland populations
stationary.   No need was there to travel to the coast for these
first commodities, and thus in the seclusion of their Alpine homes
they elaborated an independent culture and a history of their own.

Scarcity of water is felt in certain districts of Galatia, Cappadocia, notably in Lycaonia, near Konieh ; the whole region is brown
and bare and only fit for pasturage.   The spring is the sole part

[1] Curtius, *Greek History*.   The first pages of this able work, with a few broad
touches, define with rare precision and clearness the physical features of Hellas and
Asia Minor, the twofold theatre on which were enacted the chief events of Grecian
history.

[2] G. Perrot, *Souvenirs d'un Voyage en Asie Mineure*, in 8°, pp. 204, 205. M. Lévy,
1884.

of the year when, owing to abundant rains, the country is covered with coarse tall grass where graze the herds of the Turcoman and Kurdish farmers. The camels and horses seen at Smyrna and Constantinople come from these provinces, which also supply those markets with mutton and beef. But towards the end of May the grass is sere and the landscape has resumed its tawny aspect, a few green patches alone announce the presence of moisture still lingering in the hollows and which will last until the autumn. The wools of Cappadocia were much prized in ancient days, and constituted the chief revenue of the native princes.

If the plateau presented throughout the same character, there would be no need to seek on its surface monuments of the past. Hunters and woodmen build no cities, and arts are unknown to them. A fresh crop of grass, nowhere more abundant than on the spot where the nomad has pitched his tent for a season, will obliterate the trifling vestiges left by his temporal settlement. But this broad level is succeeded by well-watered, undulating country, alternating with green pastures and ploughed fields, where the monotony of the foreground is forgotten in the infinite diversity of hill and dale in the distance and all around you. These rocks are of volcanic origin, and before their fires were extinguished threw up molten trachyte and porphyry, now hardened into perpendicular or overhanging cones and needles. The highest of these cones is the Argæus, with an elevation of 4000 metres, resting upon an enormous base of lava more than thirty leagues round. The soil left on its broad slopes by the decomposition of igneous rocks is of marvellous fertility, and requires but little labour from the husbandman to produce almost everything.

If all the mountains of Asia Minor have not the gigantic proportions of this mighty cone, they are sufficiently high—averaging 1000 metres above the surrounding level—to arrest clouds on their summits which resolve themselves in snow. This, as it melts, covers their broad sides with the richest vegetation ere it is lost in swamps and lakes without outlet. Thanks to these watercourses and rivulets, many of which have but a short run, thanks to diversity of elements contained in a soil where in a small radius rocks of different formation are met side by side, the inner uplands, even if they were cut off from the subjacent valleys and the coast-land, would yet feed a population far exceeding in number that of the present day. Cities and hamlets are for the most part surrounded by orchards and gardens, where vegetables, flowers, and fruit, as fine as any seen in our European markets, testify to the productiveness of the soil, and were better methods of agriculture and less primitive implements introduced, a population five times as large would find ample accommodation.   The want of timber is severely felt in Lycaonia and sundry adjoining districts, be it for building or culinary purposes.   As in the central wastes of Asia, here also, the sole means for cooking your dinner is the dried-up dung of cows and camels.[1]   Wood, whether as rafters, doors, window-frames, and the like, is only met with in the more important houses, the huts of the peasantry being constructed with mud and uncemented stones.

Despite centuries of neglect and dilapidation, the forests on the southern slopes of the Taurus and the spurs it throws out into the twin provinces of Cilicia and Lycia, as well as the hilly ranges that run parallel with the Euxine, are not all destroyed.   These forests, besides all the trees of Europe, contain also, notably along running streams, magnificent cedar and plane trees.   Isolated cones are brown and barren, like the Argæus, but clumps of oaks fringe the ravines ; and umbrella-like pines spring out of every cleft on the hillside.   In the northern regions of Phrygia are still vast forests, in the midst of which, hidden in a valley of picturesque rocks, are the tombs and other monuments of the ancient kings of the land.   Large herds of cattle graze on the hills ; the tinkling of bells, the bleating of young lambs, break pleasantly on the ear amidst these vast solitudes.   It is a curious fact, that on this side the forest seems neither to have advanced nor retreated since the beginning of our era.   It was certainly crossed by the consul Manlius Vulso in his expedition against the Galatians, for it skirts the route from Kûtaniah to Sivri-Hissar ; and, like a good general, he wished to save his soldiers a march under an almost vertical sun. At the latter place, the Romans were obliged to forsake the covert and take the high-road, which at this point makes a great curve towards the plain.   I was able to test step by step the correctness of Livy's statement in regard to the march of Manlius, which he copied, as did Polybius, from the Antonine Itinerary.[2]   From this

[1] G. PERROT, Souvenirs, etc., p. 381.

[2] Exploration Archéologique de la Galatie, etc., exécutée en 1861, et publiée sous les auspices du ministère de l'instruction publique, par MM. G. Perrot, E. Guillaume, and J. Delbet, 2 vols, in folio, 80 planches, et 7 feuilles d'itinéraires, 1872, Firmin Didot.

it appears that Manlius, breaking up from Abbassus, reached Aleander, halting at Tyscon, Plitendus, and Alyatti in turn; after which he entered the "Axylos" district.[1] The pithy description of the great Roman writer accurately corresponds with the dreary, barren, woodless tract that rose before me as I travelled on the route followed by his countrymen nearly seventeen centuries ago. Only the day before, I had been able to enjoy the noon siesta under the grateful shade of great pines; but these were now reduced to mere sprouts, apparently of no use, save to half-starved goats.

This applies generally to the table-land, and particularly to the whole of eastern Phrygia; the lower hills which form the belt and the supporting walls of the plateau are alone densely wooded.[2]

The formation and consequent general character of these hilly ranges are not consistent throughout. We propose, therefore, to divide them into three groups, according to their special physiognomy. The northern group, with some fifteen or twenty mounts, known under the generic name of Olympus, to distinguish them from other chains of mountains, we will call the Olympian range. The best-known, or at least that venerated by the ancient Greeks, was the Mysian Olympus, near Broussa; then came the Bithynian Olympus, the Galatian Olympus, etc. It is worthy of remark that nothing can well be more confusing than the orography of this region, which consists of broad hilly masses, parallel one to the other, with progressing declivity towards the sea. The rivers that rise on the plateau, after having successfully broken through the rocky ridges which, like mighty walls, oppose their passage, discharge their waters into the Euxine.

Forests, as stated, are found on the slopes, in the intervening valleys, and wherever there is a stream. As a natural consequence, more rain falls here than in any other part of the peninsula; the air is cooler, and the growth of plants and pastures manifests greater luxuriance than on the southern slopes of the peninsula, where the sky is unclouded during the greatest part of the year.

The most important forest of Asia Minor is the Agatch-Denizi, or sea of trees, which covers the country east of the Sangarius.

---

[1] Duci inde exercitus per Axylon, quam vocant, terram cœptus. Ab re nomen habet: non ligni modo quicquam, sed ne spinam quidem, aut ullum aliud alimentum fert ignis (Lib. xxxviii. c. 18).—EDITOR.

[2] G. PERROT, *loc. cit.*

along the east of the Black Sea; the lower branches of great
planes and oaks trail in the water, and make landing impossible,
save for small boats.   In fact, the whole region watered by the
Sangarius and the Billæus, from Mysia, Paphlagonia, and the
Pontus, as a rule, presents the same features, and one who was
not pressed for time could almost go from Broussa to Trebizond
under covert.[1]

The southern group comprises the mighty Taurus range, which
we, discarding the authority of the ancients, whose definition was
vague in the extreme, will apply to the chain of mountains whose
peaks are seen from Caria, and along the coast which faces Rhodes
and Cyprus.   Sometimes the broad masses increase in bulk along the
sea shores, with lofty ridges and weird projections which support
Lycia and Lower Cilicia; at other times, they open out into valleys,
such as Pamphylia and Upper Cilicia; these again are succeeded
by precipitous walls and alluvial plains, through which sluggish
rivers meander ere they are lost in the sea; whilst to the east the
plateau of Sivas and its snowy peaks serve as intermediaries
between Anti Taurus, the Olympian range, and the high mountains of Armenia.

The development of the coast on the western side of the
peninsula amounts to quadruple its extent in a straight line from
north to south.   Here are no chains of mountains parallel one to
the other up to the very border of the sea.   The latter has
fashioned and dislocated the outward body into peninsulas, promontories, and islands, which run far out into the Ægean; such
would be Samos, Chios, Lesbos, etc.   The greatest variety of
formation is to be found here—uplands well supplied with streams
and pastures; mountains with snowy peaks; the Trojan Ida, the
Tmolus, the Cadmus, and many more.   Here, too, occurs a sudden
transition from the uplands to the coast, as will be seen by
reference to the annexed woodcut (Fig. 291).

The altitude of the table-land around Koutahia (Phrygia) is
from 800 to 900 metres; and from 1000 to 1100 near Konieh;
but Lycaonia and Cappadocia are far above this level, Kaisarieh,
(Cæsarea), the chief town of this province being 1320 metres above
sea level.   The elevation of the crest is regulated by that of the
table-land; on the west and north the average is under and about

---

[1] Respecting the northern and southern shores of Asia Minor, which we coasted,
see G. Perrot, *Souvenirs d'un Voyage en Asie Mineure*, pp. 225-255.

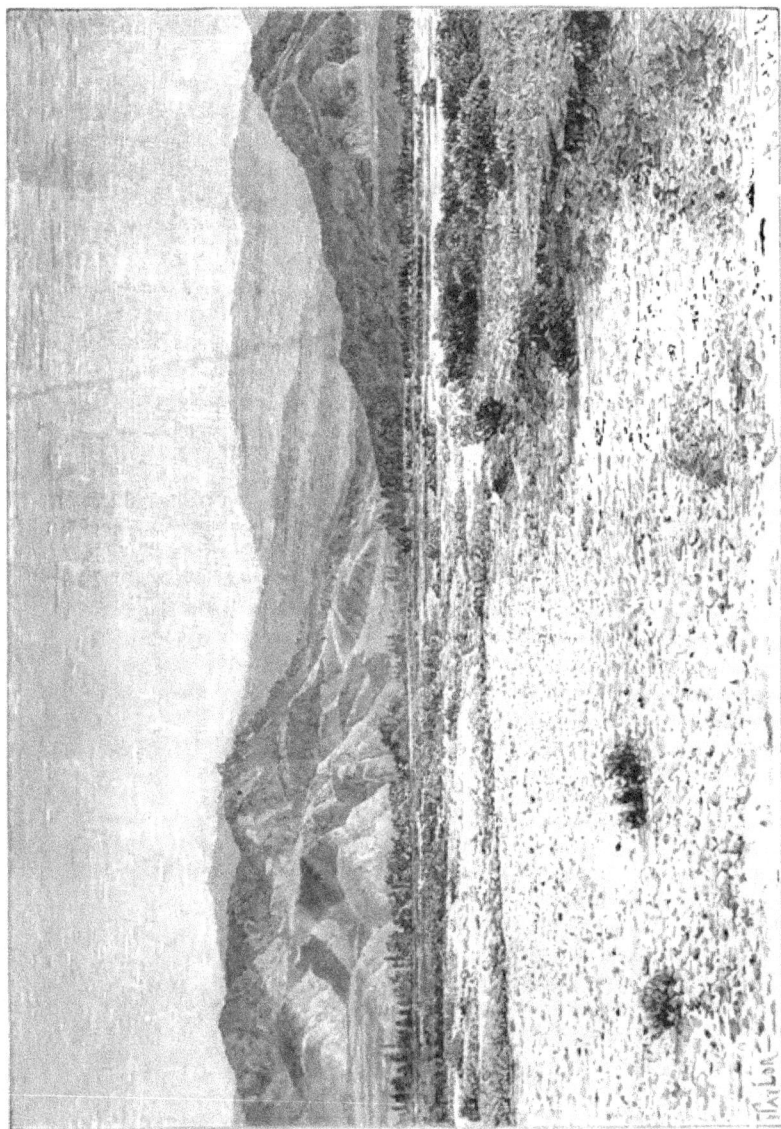

FIG. 291.—Mountain range, with Tmolus in the foreground, and Plain of Sardes. Taylor, from a photograph of M. Héron.

2000 metres ; the greatest development is manifested on the south and east, many heights being 3000 metres ; whilst the Argæus and some peaks of the Taurus range reach the limit of perpetual snow. The Olympian group, whose culminating peak (Mysian Olympus) is seen from Constantinople, is more imposing by its broad masses and its ridges, clothed with dense forests which everywhere conceal the horizon, than by any great elevation. The ascent of any particular mountain is rendered exceedingly arduous, by the interlacing of branches and a deep sea of dry leaves, through which it is almost impossible to steer your course. The difficulty of communication is as great on the south, to the rear of Pamphylia and Cilicia ; for though the rocky wall is much reduced in thickness, many summits attain the region of perpetual snow, hence the narrow passes are closed to caravans during great part of the year.

The mountain range of the Taurus can only be ascended by narrow paths winding up its rugged declivities. From its lofty edges torrents fall with rushing sound into deep ravines below. We say torrents advisedly; this region, with Caria, Lycia, Pamphylia, and Lower Cilicia, having no rivers deserving the name, except the Saros and the Pyramus, and they scarcely belong to Asia Minor. The latter, during part of its course, marks the frontier line on the south-east, and both have their sources in the mighty bulwarks which to the east build up the Anatolian plateau.

The main watershed of Asia Minor is, as a matter of course, to the west, north, and north-west. The most important basin, at least that which has the longest course, is the Halys, Kizil-Irmak.[1] It rises in the Sivas mountains, flows to the south-west, as if to carry its waters to the sea of Cyprus, but is met by the Argæus, which causes it to fall back to the north and north-east, describing a vast concentric curve which embraces the whole of Cappadocia, finally entering the Black Sea between Sinope and Samsoum castle. Although the Halys is the longest of all the rivers of the peninsula, owing to excess of evaporation the liquid mass it rolls to the sea is inferior to that of the Sakaria. It is spanned by several bridges, and fordable almost to the sea edge. Nevertheless, when swollen by rain and the melting of snow, it rises to a great height, and inundates the country to a considerable extent, doing much damage to the bridges, which are frequently destroyed, so that during

[1] HERODOTUS, i. 72.

many weeks at a time it cannot be crossed with safety. The
Halys cuts the peninsula into two unequal parts, and was
adopted in olden times as the line of demarcation between the
Median and Lydian empires. It influenced the ethnology of
the country, for it practically kept the races settled on its banks
apart. In Cappadocia lived tribes that spoke a Semitic language,
and are designated as "Syrian" by Herodotus, who ascribes a
Thracian origin to the Phrygians and the Paphlagonians, more or
less intimately connected with the Greeks on the coast.[1] A similar
division is observable in the respective art of the two races; with
rare exceptions all the monuments encountered east of the Halys
bear an Eastern stamp upon them, easily accounted for by military
expeditions and momentary conquests.

The other rivers which flow through the Olympian range,
though of less importance, are interesting from the fact that they
are specified in ancient writers. Additional interest attaches to
the Thermôdôn, on whose banks the Greek poets placed the
Amazons. Next comes the Iris (Ieshil-Irmak), which traverses
the picturesque town of Amasia (Fig. 292). The Sangarius
(Sakara), whose sinuous course through the hills which lie east to
west is necessarily slow; but as soon as it emerges into the
broad alluvial plain, it hastens to carry its flood to the Black Sea.
Caravans from Constantinople cross this broad level on their way
to Angora and Cæsarea. Though shorter, the basin of the
Ryndacus is of the same nature.

At the present day, the routes that connect Asia with Europe
have their starting-point and terminus at Constantinople. But
formerly Sardes, Smyrna, Ephesus, and Miletus, had equal claims
to be considered as intermediaries between the heart of the mainland and the Ionian coast, through the valleys of the Cayster,
Hermus, and Mæander. The river valleys on this side are less
tortuous than towards the Euxine; nor do white foamy torrents
fall over a succession of precipitous rocks, as in Caria and Lycia.
The plateau where the rivers take their sources is barely 800
metres above the sea. They, too, have to fight their way
through the rocky belt on the table-land ere they reach narrow
channels, which gradually broaden out into valleys of incomparable
fertility. This particularly applies to the Mæander and the
Lycus, its largest affluent, which rise in the very heart of the

[1] Herodotus, *loc. cit.*

FIG. 292.—Amasia, from the south-west.   Taylor, from a photograph of M. J. Delbet.

mainland, and in their lower course diffuse a loamy soil as rich as that of the Nile. Nowhere is there a closer union between the uplands and the lowlands; nowhere has nature worked so much to bring it about, and nowhere has she shed her blessings with so lavish a hand.

These contrasts from one region to the other are also found, as might be expected, in the climate. It is almost tropical in the south, but approaches that of Europe towards the Euxine, constantly refreshed by cool breezes blowing from the north. These, in winter, become icy cold, having swept over the southern provinces of Russia, then covered with deep snow. When they reach the peninsula, however, they have been somewhat softened by their passage across the Black Sea. The olive, whose growth on the Bosphorus is almost as luxuriant as in the Ionian Islands, disappears at the entrance of the Euxine, and is scarcely seen again until Trebizond. Here the Caucasus opposes its high crest against the wind; and oranges, lemons, and Mediterranean pines [1] fill the gardens and throw a wreath of verdure around the city and along the whole coast to the very border of Russia.

The western side of the peninsula is warm, and winter is scarcely known; whilst the fierce noonday heat of summer is tempered by the Etesian winds, and the nights made cool by the ἐμβάτης, the wind that passes over these coasts and penetrates inland.

Everywhere around these bays the slender foliage of the olive flutters with the breeze; the lemon and cotton plant are grown wherever there is any moisture. Palms, however, nor edible dates, will flourish of their own accord; for, lovely as is the climate of Ionia, it is less equable than that on the opposite coast or the islands washed by the Ægean.

The valleys south of the Taurus are not open to the north wind; and except Cilicia, which is almost tropical, the climate and productions are precisely the same as in Syria. The fields and roads are fenced, as in the latter country, by tall hedges of prickly pear, resplendent with scarlet blossoms; the towering slender stems of the agave yielding the needful variety of outline. Winters are absolutely unknown. On the other hand,

---

[1] As a matter of fact, the umbrella-like pine is seen inland wherever conditions are favourable for its growth. It was first observed in the south of Europe, especially along the coast, hence it came to be popularly known as " Mediterranean," or "maritime pine."—EDITOR.

during the three or four hottest months, life is a burden away from the sea breezes, when the inhabitants betake themselves to their "yaïlas," or alpine châlets on the slopes of the lower hills, amidst verdant forests and pastures.

Totally and utterly different is the natural condition of the central plateau. Though on a lower level than the uplands of Erzeroum and the snow-capped mountains of Armenia, it is of sufficient altitude to be subjected to the extreme of cold, helped, doubtless, by its utter denudation; whilst any moisture that might accrue from the seas by which it is begirt, is arrested on the lower hills, and not a drop of rain falls on the plateau for months together.

On the other hand, as soon as the sun has melted the last snow, the lacustrine region is transformed into vast morasses, over which spreads a white saline efflorescence. Rivers are reduced to mere threads of water, trickling in the middle of their wide stony beds, and the drought, which obtains from May to October, turns the table-land into a hard, barren, dusty waste, which, with the latitude of Sicily, has the climate of central Europe. The north winds in their passage over the crest of the Olympian range become icy cold, and resolve themselves into snow. This they take up, whirl and toss about, and finally cast in the depressions and clefts of the mountain side. The population of many districts of Lycaonia and Cappadocia, in order to escape the rigour of almost Siberian winters, and prevent their tenements being swept away by the violence of these northern gales, scoop out or dig caves in the hillside; the roof alone is structural, consisting of wooden rafters, over which are placed layers of earth beaten down. In process of time this is undistinguishable from the surrounding turf; hence many villages might be passed unperceived, but for the curling smoke issuing from them. It was in this way, on one occasion, whilst looking out for a night's shelter, I suddenly felt my horse giving way under me. To my utter amazement, I found myself in the middle of a village, surrounded by the startled population; and what I had taken for terraces were, in fact, the roofs of houses, one of which had subsided under my horse's weight.[1]

If we appeal to reminiscences left by our visit to the country under notice, it is better to bring out the fact that Asia Minor consisted of two distinct parts—the masses of table-land which

[1] G. Perrot, *Souvenirs d'un Voyage en Asie Mineure*, pp. 160, 176, 380.

suddenly break up into natural divisions, and wide river-beds open towards the sea, whose coast is like a piece wrenched from the European continent, and pieced on to Asia, "like a border of a different material woven on to a garment."[1] The races settled in these regions were equally distinct from each other; their development was not simultaneous, nor on the same lines. Syria and Mesopotamia were flourishing states, in the enjoyment of a cultured life, when Europe was divided into barbarous clans that used stone implements.

It was to be expected, therefore, that the uplands, as nearer to Mesopotamia, would receive the germs of civilization long before they could be transplanted on the western and southern coasts, separated by great distances and natural barriers from the radiating focus. The castellated ridges of the Taurus could be crossed through the river courses on to the table-land, where are found the numerous springs of the Halys; whilst to the southeast the "Cilician pyles," and other passes, led to the uplands.

As soon as civilized tribes were in possession of Cilicia, they held the key to Asia Minor, and were not slow in availing themselves of it. Their advance was in compact settlements, and the positions they selected on the plateau could be defended by a few against a multitude. They gradually subdued the rural populations around them, pushed yet further their conquests, penetrating to the more accessible parts of the western coast.

If the geographical position of the table-land was pre-eminently calculated to receive its first culture from anterior Asia, the seacoast had been fashioned by far-seeing nature, that the flow of ideas, the interchange of traffic between Asia and Europe should be incessant. As stated before, inland bays, some open and of great depth, others imperceptible at a little distance outside, advance between stony masses, broken up and dislocated on the coasts by the flood into secondary bays, anchorages, and sounds; where pebbly shores and safe harbours invite the mariner to sail in and out of them. Numbers of these indentations are only found in the charts of the Admiralty. But, like unwritten laws, they are impressed on the native sailor, who knows that from the Helles-

---

[1] Reclus, *Géographie Universelle*, tom. ix. p. 464. Consult also Curtius, *Die Ionier vor der Ionischen Wanderung*. "Nowhere is the contrast more marked than between the interior and the coast; this is submitted to different laws, and is like another land."

pont to Rhodes he can run in his vessel at almost every point. Moreover, this interpenetration of the sea conduces to healthiness of climate, it facilitates the foundation of cities and the opening of marts, with consequent contact of countries and peoples which seemed separated by nature, but which the sea has brought together.

A country so favoured could not fail to become the native home of a race of hardy mariners. As soon as they turned their boats towards the main they beheld before them the coasts of the Hellenic peninsula, towards which they were led by islands close at hand, yielding halting-places from coast to coast. They could thus sail from Thessaly, through the channel of Eubœa, to Attica and Argolis without losing sight of land. The European coast, too, offered everywhere safe and spacious anchorages; here land and air seemed familiar to them, and they hardly realized that they had left their native shores. Contact with the Ionian mariners awakened the spirit of enterprise, tempting the dwellers of the Hellenic coast to quit the paternal home in quest of booty or adventure.

If Ionian vessels were the first to follow on the track of the Phœnicians, this was due to the fact that the stream of civilization flowed from east to west. But whatever its origin may have been, once the wave was set in motion it never stopped, but waxed stronger, and penetrated everywhere; and the Ægean became an inland lake, common to the races settled on the opposite coasts, owning the same descent, the same language, the same alphabet, the same arts, and, with slight differentiation, the same creed. Political and religious revolutions have been powerless to break asunder the intimate connection provided by nature and confirmed by history. If the interior is ruled by the stupid, fanatical Turk, the seaboard is as much of the Greeks as it was of yore; and an Athenian finds himself as much at home at Smyrna as in his own native city.

Intercourse was not confined to this latitude. Before ever vessels were seen on the Ægean, other routes, the Bosphorus and the Dardanelles, connected Europe with Asia Minor. Here the emigrants or freebooters could cross, though ignorant of navigation, the twin straits, which are not wider than ordinary rivers. Greek etymology derived Bosphorus from *bos*, " bull ; " *phoreo*, φορέω, φέρω, " to carry." The animal was supposed to have swum across it between the points now occupied by Stamboul and Scutari, formerly Byzantium and Chalcedon.   However that may be, Greek traditions placed *here*, at a remote period, the entrance of the Brydges, Bebrydges, or Phrygians, "free men," of Thracian origin, who in their passage from' Europe to Asia, were doubtless borne on inflated skins which they used as rafts, even as the Kurds do in the present day, to go from one side of the Euphrates to the other. Here they spread on the banks of the springs of the Ryndacus and the Sangarius, not far from the sources of the Mæander, interspersed with woody tracts and verdant pastures, everywhere capable of being cultivated.   Here the invaders founded a state, which for two centuries was the most important of the peninsula.   When the traditions connected with the wealth and power of the ancient Phrygians reached the Greeks settled on the coast, they had already passed into mythical forms, and were associated with their gods or kings. But all was not fabulous or the mere creation of the fancy; such myths contained a certain documentary truth, manifested in the language and the venerable remains that have withstood the action of time and the convulsions of nature.   The names of these heroes have been discovered carved on the rocks side by side with inscriptions which, though brief, prove that they were written in characters partly derived from the Phœnician alphabet, and in a dialect closely allied to Greek.   We shall have more to say in respect to Phrygia when we describe her monuments, and show that intercourse with the other Greeks of the peninsula was incessant, be it with the northern or western coast.   Weighing all these circumstances together, we shall not greatly err in dating Phrygian civilization immediately after that of the Hittites ; *i.e.*, centuries before the Trojan War.   Trending our way towards the west, we shall encounter the Lydians, a mixed race, albeit related on one side to the Phrygians, when we shall find ourselves almost in Greece.

Their empire rose long after that of Phrygia and the Homeric epos.   The spot selected for their capital was the alluvial plain which skirts the sea, a site favourable to commerce and domestic industry.   As a quick-witted people, ever on the alert, they were sometimes allied to the Ionian Greeks, sometimes at war with them, as occasion served.   But whether they tried to subjugate them or lived in amity with them, their relations and consequent influence one upon the other were frequent and lasting.

Thus, following the main streams of the peninsula—the Halys, the Sangarius, the Hermus, and the Mæander—may be traced the history of the three nations that succeeded each other in this sphere. The Greeks took the same route, but reversed it in their conquests of the East under Thymbronus, Dercyllidas, Clearcus, Agesilas, and Alexander. But such expeditions savoured of reconnaissances, of brilliant marches, rather than permanent settlements, and therefore left scarcely any traces. It was reserved for the kings of Pergamus, Bithynia, and Pontus to spread everywhere, penetrate every corner, and bring about the complete transformation of the country.

Secluded tracts in the upper valleys of the Taurus, Pisidia, and the inhospitable fastnesses of Isauria, were in the hands of freebooters, who remained strangers to the movement and the influences that had been at work on the table land. They built their castles on rocky heights, whence they sallied forth to lay waste the neighbourhood or despoil caravans; and until the Romans put a stop to their depredations they were the terror of the rural populations of Pamphylia and Cilicia.

This applies with equal force to the wooded hilly range towards the Euxine and the higher slopes of the Olympian Mountains. No inscription, no sculpture or monument, has been discovered to enable us to judge of the civilization of the early inhabitants of this part of Asia Minor. That the country was occupied by mere savages we know on the testimony of Xenophon, who, after the death of Cyrus in the battle at Cunaxa, was obliged to march his army back across the lofty ranges of Kurdistan and Armenia; when leaving in his rear the narrow strip on the coast held by colonists from Miletus, his way led through the region occupied by the tribes in question. These, adds the historian, were the most barbarous the army had encountered; they had no cities, and lived in open hamlets built of unsquared timber and rough planks.[1] This state of affairs lasted down to the Greek and Roman occupation, when native princes—Nicomedes, Prusias, Pharnaces, Mithridates —imbued with Hellenism tried to introduce a taste for culture among their rude subjects. The Solymi or Lycians occupied the southern slopes of the Taurus. Here, amid the grandeur of mountain chains which stretch close up to the sea, they were alike cut off from the movements and the disturbances of the

---

[1] Xenophon, *Anabasis*, V. iv. 30–34. Cf. V. ii. 5, 25–27.

mainland or their immediate neighbours, whom they surpassed in all relations of civil life; whilst they were at least their equals in courage, patriotism, and knowledge of the sea. .

The origin of the Lycians is exceedingly obscure; yet it is generally allowed that, after the Hittites, they were the first to make use of writing. The antiquity of their alphabet is shown from the fact that, besides some Phœnician letters, it contains characters which closely resemble certain cursive Hittite signs, leading to the inference that it was older than the Phrygian. Monumental writing is the forerunner of the art of drawing; it leads naturally to sculpture and architecture. As might be expected, therefore, monuments encountered here, of which more anon, are in greater abundance and centuries older than those of the interior.

The reason for this is not far to seek; the southern coast (Cilicia, Caria, etc.) was among the first visited by the Phœnicians; it was early in the hands of tribes originally akin to the Greeks, and their intercourse with the coasts of the Archipelago was much more frequent than with the nations of Asia. Their vessels crossed the inland sea and reached Egypt as early as Psammeticus; yet nothing remains to attest their primitive history, save occasional inscribed characters in the face of stout walls crowning hill-tops. As a people of pirates, they swooped down to desolate the coasts; and their daring expeditions were remembered in Greek legends, which conceived them as a rude, barbarous race. Such glimmerings were older than history itself; vaguely conscious too that the impetus to a higher phase of life had not come through the "wet paths" but over inland routes, with Babylon, Nineveh, and many cities of the peninsula as starting-points, but whose names were often changed in antiquity, making their identity in sundry instances almost impossible. This wave, which never ceased, penetrated distant Sardes in the south, and Ephesus and Miletus; and the connection between the various points was fruitful and intimate. To give but an instance of the inventive genius on the one side, and of the transforming aptitude on the other, the honour of having first struck coined money is generally ascribed to the Lydians; but in the hands of the Greeks, who borrowed the craft from them, coins became beautiful as well as useful.

At the outset, by the employment of three metals instead of one, they created divisionary specie, and facilitated commercial operations in a marvellous way. Moreover, the endless variety of types and inscriptions engraved on their pieces yielded documents of inestimable historical value. Then, too, with their innate love of the beautiful, they contrived to introduce in the exiguous field, side by side with the city mark, bas-reliefs which in nobleness of style and composition may be ranked as masterpieces.

Asia Minor has been likened to an open palm, stretched out to Hellas through its mountains, its promontories, and rocky islands projected far out into the Ægean to meet the sister hand of Europe. A glance at the map will show the correlation of the twin peninsulas. How vividly this is brought home, let any one say who has performed the voyage from Piræus or Syra, to Metelin or Smyrna in a Greek barque, not much changed since the days of the travelled and experienced Odysseus. As of yore the Etesian winds fill the sail, and their regularity renders them as free from danger as they are serviceable to the mariner. Little need is there of knowledge to steer his vessel from Europe to Asia, and bring her safely back again into harbour; for he knows that before foul weather he can run her into a secure anchorage. When the cooling breeze suddenly falls, he takes up the oar for a while until the vessel is caught again by the land wind. He may be becalmed, he may have to go about to catch the slightest breath, he may be hours, nay days, before he rounds the cape. Needless to say that this is not the quickest mode of getting from one place to another; but there is no doubt as to its being the pleasantest. The only certainty is when he weighs anchor, but the end of the journey who shall declare? When he runs her ashore to procure water or victuals, he may reckon upon as comfortable a bed as man ever had on the soft warm sand of the beach, whilst lying on his back he watches the stars overhead, until refreshing sleep robs him of consciousness. In this way days grow into weeks, although it seems but yesterday that the friendly coast of Hellas disappeared in the blue distance; when he sighted other lands and other horizons, the great groups of the Cyclades, and the Sporades, the promontories of Lesbos, Chios, and Samos, those outposts of the Asianic continent; finally in the early light of an Eastern sky, the complex coast of Ionia rises before him. Yet air, sea, and land, the very trees and flowers with which he is familiar, are here to welcome him ; and but for the map he would not know that he has entered into a new world. Not once during his passage has he felt the peculiar awe which is apt to steal over the inexperienced, when the vast horizon is bounded by sky and water. I have not forgotten the impression left by a voyage so performed, every small detail of which is present with me still ; when during the long days of enforced leisure spent on deck a reflective mood will overtake even the young and thoughtless. I thought that if there was a sea calculated to bring men together, this was emphatically the Ægean ; that from the day when the nations on the opposite coasts could handle an oar and stand at the helm, the same interests, the same history were common to both. Arbitrary divisions, consequent on the accidents of war, have not been able to destroy the old tie ; made faster than ever by the power of steam, which has done so much to reduce the relative distance between them.

§ 2.—*The Pteria of Herodotus.*

Before we proceed to describe the monuments of this region— in style and some of their details precisely similar to those we have reviewed at Hamath, Carchemish, and Aleppo—a few words in respect to the district in which they occur will not be irrelevant. Our task will be all the more pleasant, that it will serve to bring to our recollection the visit we paid here in 1862, when we had the opportunity of inspecting these ruins and figured documents, whose historical value no one suspected at that time. To render our campaign as full of fruitful results as possible, we were careful to consult all that had been written about them. Unfortunately the time at our disposal was cut short by the incoming winter, which obliged us to suspend our operations. But even so we had greater leisure for noting many an interesting detail, which for that reason had escaped our predecessors—Téxier, Hamilton, and Barth— enabling us to add much to what was already known about this remarkable group. Our excavations were neither so deep nor on so vast a scale as we should have desired ; nevertheless they per- mitted us to restore an important building, and bring to light a whole series of bas-reliefs of the highest interest. Moreover, such of the sculptures as were already known have been more faith- fully reproduced by photogravure,[1] and those which, owing to lack of light and shade, would not admit of such treatment were care- fully drawn by the well-known architect, E. Guillaume.

[1] Doctor Debet was our artist.

For obvious reasons, the woodcuts that figure in this part will
not be all taken from our own work ; but where requisite for the
elucidation and better understanding of the subject, we freely
borrowed from Téxier's plates, the first traveller who visited
Boghaz-Keui, and the only one before us who made plans and
drawings of the monuments.[1] It would ill become us to ignore
or undervalue the services which he rendered to science by his
explorations in Asia Minor, Armenia, and Persia ; undertaken too
when Oriental expeditions were not the easy matter which they
are at the present time.   He had been admirably prepared, moreover, by long study of monuments in France, Italy, and northern
Africa ; and, if he could boast no superior acquirements, this was
amply compensated by natural intelligence, quickness, energy,
great perceptive powers, and indefatigable industry, evidenced in
his sketches, which betray a ready pencil and a light, crisp touch.
In an evil hour he conceived the idea of having improved drawings made from them, that they might look better in the splendid
work he was about to publish, forgetful that truth and accuracy
are of far greater worth than mere prettiness.

Comparison of certain copies of Téxier's plates with his original
sketches revealed the truth to us.   This, the testimony or breach
of confidence of the draughtsman whom he had employed for the
purpose served to corroborate.   Consequently, much as we should
have wished, we have refrained giving his general plan of Boghaz-
Keui, which, had it been accurate, would have enabled the reader
to form a clear idea of the locality and the relative position of the
monuments which we are about to describe.   His architectural
and sculptural drawings are decidedly better ; but even they show
that the engraver softened the rude modelling, and repaired the
ravages of time.   Hence our reason for admitting only those which
we were able to test on the spot as being less removed from
reality will be appreciated.

The part of Cappadocia upon which attention was directed
some fifty years ago by the discoveries of Téxier is unimportant,
thinly populated, and not specified by modern geographers.   It
lies between the town of Tchouroum on the north, and Iusgat on

[1] *Description of Asia Minor*, 1833–1837. Publiée par le Ministère de l'Instruction
Publique.   Beaux-arts, monuments historiques, plans et topographie des cités an-
tiques.   Ch. Téxier, gravure, Lemaitre.   Paris, Firmin Didot, 1839–1849, 3 vols.
in folio.

the south ; the latter a city of some importance, with a "resident,"
or waly, whose power extends over the pashaliks of Angora and
Cæsarea. A lofty hill, 1700 metres in height, called Hapak-Tepe
(north of Iusgat), forms the southern spur of the Keuch-Dagh
range.[1] It is connected with the Olympian heights towards the
north, while to the south it runs out, like an inland promontory,
amidst the vast table-lands which it overtops. The base of these
hilly ridges is washed by the Halys and the Iris, and the table-
land is interspersed with woods and fields ; whilst numerous small
streams swell the two rivers as they descend from the plateau.
This is broken up into narrow defiles, edged on either side by
precipitous rocks which it is exceedingly difficult to scale ; indeed,
the whole district may be considered as a gigantic natural fortress.

The physical configuration of the country has led us to identify
it with that alluded to by Herodotus, under the name of Pterium,
whose town, Pteria, was taken by Crœsus, after he had crossed
the Halys and marched into that part of Cappadocia which is
opposite Sinope. Or, to give the words of the historian, "Crœsus
having crossed the Halys, marched into that part of Cappadocia
which is called Pteria, the most inaccessible territory of that land,
and almost on a line with Sinope, a place on the Euxine. He took
the city, reduced the inhabitants to the condition of slaves, and
ravaged the country of the Syrians, although they had given him
no cause for complaint."[2] Here he was encountered by Cyrus,
and a great battle was fought without any decisive result, but
which obliged Crœsus to effect a retreat.

The description given by Herodotus agrees in every particular
with the actual position and nature of this district, where alone

---

[1] Hamilton visited Asia Minor in the same year (1835–1836) as Téxier. He
was observant and accurate, and his book (*Researches in Asia Minor*. London,
J. Murray, 1842) may be consulted with advantage. He brought away 455 careful
copies of inscriptions, but he could not hold a pencil.

[2] *Herodotus*, i. 75. Of the misleading character of Larcher's translation of this
passage, which has been repeated in subsequent versions, we have spoken in another
place. Thus ἡ δὲ Πτερίη ἐστὶ τῆς χώρης ταύτης τὸ ἰσχυρότατον, κατὰ Σινώπην πόλιν
τὴν ἐν Εὐξείνῳ Πόντῳ μάλιστά κη κειμένη, is rendered, "Pteria, the strongest district
of that country, is near Sinope, a city situated near the Euxine." But κατά in this
instance does not indicate proximity, but direction, alignment ; for if Pteria had
been near Sinope, it would have belonged to Paphlagonia, and not Cappadocia.
Moreover, μάλιστά κη κειμένη refers to Pteria, and not to Sinope. The error is
probably due to Larcher having read κείμενην. But anybody could have told him
that Sinope is "super mare," and not any distance from it.

monuments of remote antiquity are found. Had ancient Mazaca (Cæsarea), to the south of Cappadocia, been intended, it is hardly credible that the historian would have omitted to name so important a place ; nor would so remarkable a feature as Mount Argæus, close by, have escaped his observation ; and last, not least, at this height, *i.e.* before the Halys is joined by the numerous streams that escape from the Keuch-Dagh, its crossing would not have endangered the safety of the army, as stated by Herodotus.[1] There is internal evidence that the campaign took place in summer.[2]

We have no particulars with regard to the march of Crœsus, but it is not probable that when he broke up at Sardes he would take his army through the unwatered plains of Phrygia Paroreia, and Lycaonia, but he would naturally follow the well-known line across the lower Olympian hills, sure to find good quarters almost everywhere, and an unfailing supply of water. Finally, if Herodotus brings Pterium in juxtaposition with Sinope, it is clear that the former must be sought near the Black Sea, and not so far inland as Cilicia. Sinope was given as a known starting-point, a station visited by every Greek sailor, and likely to convey some idea of the whereabouts of Pteria to his countrymen. It is at least worthy of remark that Boghaz-Keui is nearly under the same meridian as Sinope.

Stephanus Byzantinus specifies two Pterias : " Pterion (Pteria), a town of the Medes ; and Pteria, the principal place of a district near Sinope, called Pterinos, from which Pterium, Pterienos, Pterieni, to denote the inhabitants." It is evident that the twin Pterias were meant for one and the same place. The mistake may have arisen with Stephanus himself, or his copyist, who, finding the name in notes wide apart, too hastily assumed that they referred to two distinct towns. Had such a station or dependency existed in the environs of Sinope, we should find it in other historians and later geographers ; nor would it have been left out by Xenophon. Finally, it is believed by some that in the early language of Babylonia *ptera* (*n.p.*) signified fortress, castellum, and was applied to the acropolis of that city ; whilst we need not travel far to find examples of a dual ethnical form to denote the same people.

[1] *Loc. cit.*

[2] *Ibid.* The words attributed to Crœsus when he dismisses his soldiers are to the effect that they must be ready to follow him in another five months, in winter, when he may count upon the concourse of his allies.

The character of the monuments unearthed in this region is in perfect accord with our theory. From Nefez-Keui to Tchouroum we lighted upon no monuments save scattered vestiges of Greek hamlets, one single tomb, with an incipient attempt at decoration, and some rude stelas. But at Boghaz-Keui and Eyuk are venerable remains, both architectural and sculptural, with symbols of a markedly archaic Oriental nature.

If our hypothesis that Pteria was an important political and religious centre be admitted—and monuments are there to prove it—then nothing is more natural than that Crœsus should have marched against it, perhaps to punish a rebellious vassal and occupy the fortress situated at the head of an important pass, which commanded the approach to the principal plains of western Asia Minor, and was the meeting-point of two routes : one running from Ephesus to Phocæa, and the other from Smyrna to Sardes. The old name of Pteria, so often associated in ancient times with the struggles between Cyaxares or the Medes on one side, and Alyattes or Lydians on the other, is forgotten ; and the appellation of the modern town is simply *boghaz,* " pass," *keui,* "village."

The fact that this district was thinly populated during the Greek and Roman period may have been due to the invasion of Crœsus, who transported the population beyond the Halys ; an example not without parallel in ancient history. To name but an instance : Etruria was covered with flourishing cities, which were destroyed by the Romans, and have never been rebuilt. Everything concurs, therefore, in viewing the ruins about Boghaz-Keui as those of old Pteria ; to which may be added the remains of less important places in the district specified by Herodotus ; whose relative position is indicated in the adjoining map (Fig. 293). These ruins we will divide into three groups, according to the site in which they are found : Boghaz-Keui, Eyub, and Alajah ; which we will take up in their order of succession.

§ 3.—*The City of the Pterians. Civil and Military Buildings.*

Boghaz-Keui is a town of about 150 houses, five hours northwest of Iusgat, on the banks of a stream whose course is towards Songourlou, whence it joins the Halys. At the outset, the road leads through barren grey hills, clothed here and there with stunted oaks; then it follows the bottom of the narrow ravine, and high up along the broken cliffs, while pointed rocks rise out of the broad igneous masses, when the valley widens out, presenting well-wooded patches, until the plain of Boghaz-Keui is reached.

The mountains continue to follow the right bank of the stream;

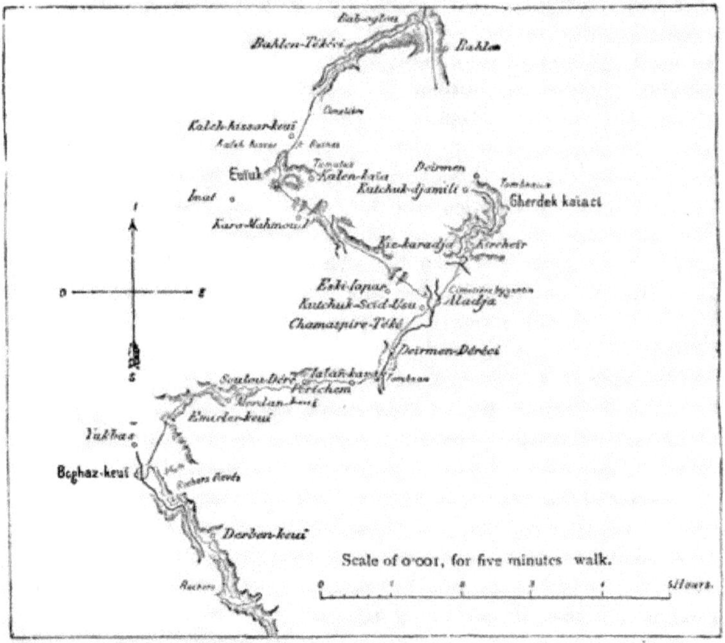

Fig. 293.—Map of Pteria. Perrot and Guillaume, *Exploration Arch.*, Sheet C.

but on the left they leave it at right angles, with progressing declivity, to form the plain, with direction from south to north. On the lower slopes rises the modern town of Boghaz-Keui; but the former city occupied the hill from base to crest.

We propose to divide the monuments into two groups: the city, with its fortress, on the left bank of the stream, and the open chamber, called Iasili-Kaïa or "written stone," on the opposite side. We will begin with the former, and try to prove, what has been questioned, that an important place once stood here.

The city wall is from five to six kilometres, and covers too great an area to have been designed, as proposed by the German traveller Barth, for a mere entrenched camp, where in troublous times the rural population found shelter under tents or temporary shanties.[1] A similar supposition from a sagacious observer is only to be explained from the fact that his visit to Boghaz-Keui was of but one day. Totally different would have been his opinion, had time permitted him to inspect the monumental remains of the building on the banks of the stream, which must have been a palace. And a palace presupposes a man in authority, with a numerous retinue, and a settled population. Nomadic tribes would have left no vestiges. When stone edifices are encountered, built, like this, of massive blocks well prepared, we may safely assume that the people who erected them were accustomed to live under structural roofs. Moreover, we are here in the heart of Asia Minor, at an elevation of 960 metres above sea level, where the thermometer falls to zero at the beginning of November, followed by snow in December, which, said the natives, will remain on the ground.[2] The notion, therefore, that these villagers would consent to forsake their dwellings partly excavated in the rock, to spend months, perhaps, of winter under the poor shelter yielded by canvas or unsquared timber, must be abandoned. But even without these massive ruins, the numerous fragments of tiles or painted pottery strewing the ground about the base of the walls, cisterns, silos, rock-cut stairways, subterraneous passages, apartments, portals, terraces, and so forth, sufficiently indicate that structural houses formerly existed here.

Examination of the surface above ground proves that the rock was untouched in many places; for at such points no traces of structures have been found, leading to the conclusion that similar sites were reserved for gardens, a custom still prevalent all over the East.

Our guide took us straight to the ruins described by Texier as a temple to Anaitis,[3] which Barth—with whom we agree—recog-

[1] H. BARTH, "Reise von Trapezunt durch die nördliche Hälfte Klein-Asiens nach Scutari, 1858, mit einer Karte von Dr. A. Petermann" (*Ergänzungsheft zu Petermann's geographischen Mittheilungen*, in 4°, 1860, p. 57).

[2] From observations taken by Dr. Delbet.

[3] The natives call the ruin *Bazarlik*, "small bazaar."

nized as a palace. The superstructures have entirely disappeared, leaving nothing but the foundations, which are perfect throughout, and still preserve, in places, the second course, with a salience of about 60 centimetres (Fig. 294), quite enough to enable the explorer to make out the main dispositions of the building. The plans of Téxier and Barth betray signs of hurry; that of the former is invested with an appearance of regularity and a state of preservation which are apt to mislead. To look at his walls, we should never suspect that the blocks of the lower course were anything but consistent in size. Again, he does not seem to have observed that the sinister passage of the central hall was closed at the back, a detail which calls to mind Assyrian palaces (11 in plan);[1] whilst he left out the north-west angle of the building, perhaps on account of its worn condition. Nevertheless, even on this side, a patient observer is able to trace the walls. On the other hand, subsidiary buildings, a little in front of the main entrance, which are omitted in Barth's plan, are carefully indicated in Téxier's albeit somewhat too near the palace. They were built of small stones, and in Barth's estimation would scarcely have been noticed, when juxtaposed with the huge blocks of the larger edifice.[2]

Further diggings would doubtless bring to light the foundation-stones hidden underground, as well as all the inner dispositions, perhaps remains of pavement, decoration, etc., and enable the architect to make a perfect plan. Our time was too short to attempt doing more than compare on the spot the drawings of our predecessors. On the eve of our departure, we were still at work at 9 p.m., by a clear moonlight, trying to finish our verification. Barth made a complete plan of the building under notice, which we reproduce as being on the whole the more accurate of the two (Fig. 295).

To adopt his measurement, the edifice, properly so called, was about 57 m. long by 42 in width; it formed a rectangle, except at the north-west angle, now disappeared. Some of the foundation-stones are 5, 6, and even 7 m. long, and 2 m. high. The supporting walls are sometimes as thick as the outer wall, sometimes thinner.

These walls were obtained by bevelled masonry, i.e. the stones fitted one into the other like carpentry, recalling a similar arrangement at Passargæ. The vertical faces are rough and rudely cut,

---

[1] Téxier, loc. cit., tom. i. Plate LXXX.
[2] This is the reason he adduces for not having drawn them.

FIG. 294.—View of Boghaz-Keui, showing Remains of Palace. TÉXIER, *Description de la Chersonèse d'Asie*, in 8°, Plate VI.

but the top is carefully dressed throughout. In many of the
stones are circular holes or sockets, averaging from 40 to 45 c.
in diameter, 3 to 4 in depth, and 25 to 33 apart. At first sight,
these holes might be supposed to have been intended to receive
metal pins or poles, for fixing drapery, except that they are too
small and unevenly distributed to have been put to such uses.

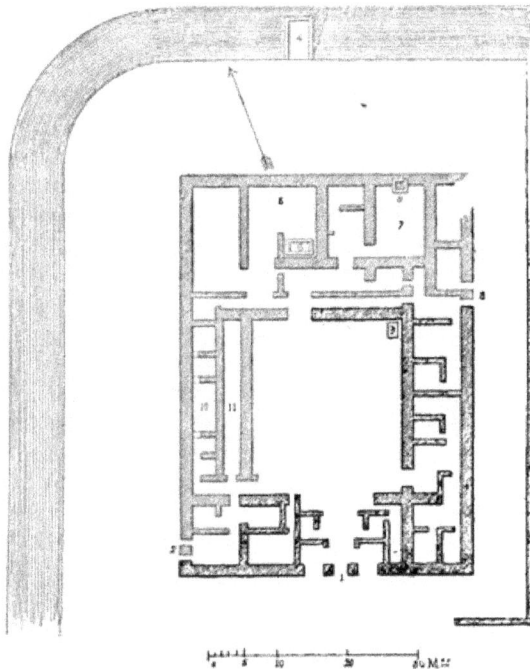

FIG. 295.—Plan of Palace. BARTH, *Reise*, p. 48.

Curtains, beside their inadequacy against the rude climate of that
alpine district, would have been superfluous, since there is no
doubt that proper doors existed, as hinges about doorways everywhere attest. Had these holes been designed as cramp-irons for
joining stones one to the other, as in Greece, the accumulated
rubbish left by the falling in of the superstructures would be found
around the building, but nothing of the kind occurs. The only
reasonable supposition is that, as at Nineveh, here also the

foundation was alone stone built, but that the superincumbent layers consisted of unbaked bricks, which have been reduced to powder or mud. Did the holes serve to unite the first layer of bricks, by having small pointed pieces of wood stuck into them, which in their turn entered the under-part of the brick, and which, being filled with soft clay, through induration became incorporated with the superincumbent bricks? Both contrivances are possible; but the same result could have been obtained at less expenditure of labour, by mere indentation in the upper face of the stone.

That the bricks in crumbling away should not have formed a mound, under which the foundations of the edifice would have been buried, is explained by the fact that it stood on the slope of the hill, hence torrential rains and the melting of the snow have cleared and washed away all that was not stone or adhering to the rock (Fig. 294).

The other explanation that has been proposed is that the building of the palace was interrupted by the Lydian invasion. But against this hypothesis are the following facts: that both esplanades are blocked up with rubbish; that the cyclopæan blocks are not everywhere above ground; that there are traces of hinges, and that a few paces from the entrance was a throne, now overturned, decorated with twin lions, that have sunk in the ground, from which we had no time to rescue them. This is our reason for having reproduced the annexed woodcuts (Figs. 296, 297, 298) from Téxier's drawings.[1]

As will be observed, the manipulation recalls Assyrian and those Hittite examples which we have passed in review in a former chapter. Here, too, the body of the lion is unduly elongated, and the impression of high relief is obtained by the same means. The throne stood formerly in the court of the building, but was dragged out by the inhabitants in the hope of finding a treasure which they thought might be concealed beneath it.

The main division is a vast rectangle 25 m. long by 21, covering nearly half the surface built over. Three doorways (1 in plan), with a double vestibule, gave access to it from the outside. That this was a court where, as in Assyria, stood the throne (found outside) on which the monarch sat on stated days to transact

[1] The dimensions given by Téxier do not seem to us to be quite correct; nor is the throne of marble, as stated by him, but of white calcareous stone, like the foundation wall.

public business, the absence of any traces of pillars or other means for supporting a roof, place beyond the shadow of a doubt.

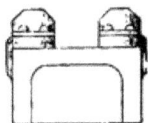

FIG. 296. — Plan of Throne. TÉXIER, *Description,* Plate LXXXII.

FIG. 297.—Front View of Throne. TÉXIER, Plate LXXXII.

The only covering it could have had would have been an awning, and this, considering the size of the court, would not have been an easy matter.

FIG. 298.—Side View of Throne. TÉXIER, Plate LXXXII.

Chambers were distributed on three sides of this open area, to the south, west, and east, with free access outside, either through the wide bays right and left of the main portal, or a servants' door at the side (2 in plan). These apartments are all of different sizes; but to the west a large chamber interposes between a set of small cells, probably occupied by the household. This part of the building was doubtless the male quarter, or selamlik, whilst the harem must be sought in the after-part of the edifice, beyond the door at the end of the court. The narrow opening in the east wall (3 in plan) may have belonged to it, as well as a chamber close by, with no outlet save towards the court, which we must consider the room reserved to eunuchs.

However this may be, there is no doubt as to five or six apartments, three of which are rather large, forming a block by itself at the end and side of the court. Two of these chambers (5 and 7 in plan) have rock excavations of unequal size, probably intended as bath-rooms (6 and 8 in plan); a depression or tank in the main court (9 in plan) should also be noticed. It may have served to collect rain water, brought about by a slight incline in the pavement. Diggings would probably reveal the channel excavated through the rock for draining purposes.

The decoration about the throne, and a cavetto moulding on either side of the foundation wall, show that the chisel of the sculptor had been freely employed to beautify a building whose proportions, with its thirty apartments, great and small, make it clear that it was the most important in the place. The general disposition of the edifice is akin to that of the palaces in Chaldæa, Assyria, and Jerusalem. On the supposition of its having been a temple, it is not easy to account for, nor what use could be assigned to the series of small apartments ranged around the central court, whilst there is no chamber sufficiently distinct from the others to have been the habitation of the deity. A similar temple would have had none of the characteristics of those we have described, or shall describe in a future work.

On the other hand, all its features—the terraces, for instance— seem to have been calculated for a domestic and not a religious dwelling.

Fronting the palace, at a height of five metres from each other, were two esplanades, carefully laid out, each measuring 140 m. in length by 110 m. in width.[1] Leading to them, on either side of the hill, were two magnificent flights of steps, indicated on the

[1] The measurement is taken from Téxier's plan, and within a few yards coincides with reality.

north-west of the hill by the slope of the ground, and on the
opposite side by three beautiful steps still extant. To diminish
the steepness of the ascent, which on the north-east is almost
perpendicular, the stairway, between the lower and upper terraces,
described a long westward curve. About half-way up the flight
of steps is a stone block, believed to be an altar by Téxier, but in
which Barth recognizes a lobby, of frequent occurrence in Assyrian
architecture, to break uniformity of outline ; but from its narrow
dimensions and circular holes on its upper face, as if to let in
some superincumbent object, we are inclined to think was a
pedestal of some kind. It is possible that it may have supported
a symbolical figure, perhaps a colossal lion, supposed to guard the
city. Some little way beyond, but on a line with this block, is
a huge rock excavation, about 3 m. 25 c. broad at the base,
2 m. 90 c. high, and 1 m. 60 c. deep. Its use is not apparent ;
it may have been designed for a monumental statue, or a secluded
place whence the beautiful view of the valley might be enjoyed.

The lower terrace is supported by a foundation wall, 6 m. 50 c.
high, consisting of stones of regular and irregular courses.
A series of small chambers or cells, almost obliterated, ran for
about 58 m. along the east side. Connected with this building
were two subterraneous passages, mentioned by Téxier. The one
(to the east ?) which led from the bed of the stream to the upper
terrace, he could still follow for about 100 m ; and the other, to the
west of the hill, with perpendicular walls well smoothed over, he
ascertained was cut right through the cliff, and might still be used.

Of the character of the superstructures, now disappeared, we
can form no idea. But the well-chosen position of the palace, on
the brow of a hill commanding an extensive prospect, its imposing
portal towards the city, the size and beauty of the stones of which
it was built, testify that the people which erected it had reached
an advanced stage of civilization, and were familiar with the
methods and types of the great nations of anterior Asia, whom
long experience had trained to use the means at their disposal,
not only to satisfy their needs, but to produce the greatest possible
effect. Though inferior in point of size to the buildings of Calach
and Nineveh, we venture to say that, were this structure better
preserved, it would merit to take rank among them.

The favourable impression left by this building is increased as
we ascend the slopes which led to the wall of enclosure, with

towers to strengthen it, so as to render the city capable of sus-
taining a siege, and close up the pass if necessary. A complete
drawing of the system of defence would be highly interesting ;
but, for obvious reasons, all we were able to do was to check
those of our predecessors and note some details which had
escaped them.

On the city side, the palace was protected by two forts of
about equal size, midway between it and the wall. The cliffs
which supported them are defended by steep precipices towards
the north of the hill, and at the other sides by a double wall,
which encompassed the area on which rose the towers, thus forming a citadel of considerable strength. They are called *Sari-
Kalé* "Yellow Fortress," and *Ienije-Kalé*, "New Fortress," by
the natives (Fig. 299). In the construction of these forts they
adhered as a rule to what is technically called "ashlar" work ;
but here and there specimens of frankly polygonal masonry are
encountered ; and besides chambers, each had a cistern excavated
on the top, so that the garrison, if victualled, could hold out even
when the town was in the hands of the enemy, until relieved by
reinforcements from without. Beyond the wall, along the bed of
the stream, were advanced posts or redoubts. The place on this
side was strongly guarded by precipitous rocks, which extended
to the bottom of the ravine ; but if the enemy approached the
town across the mountain ridges, they would be on a line with
these commanding positions ; and against this eventuality walls
with polygonal arrangement had been provided.

The city wall, from four to five metres in thickness, ran between
these outposts and the inner towers. Its construction was more
or less irregular ; the larger blocks were reserved for the exterior,
and the space between the facings was filled in with rubbish and
small stones. A more careful system of masonry is observable
about the gateways. A ditch with retaining wall, which in places
(where it was rock-cut) is still in good preservation, surrounded
the town on three sides, at the distance of 20 m. from the
rampart, sloping at an angle of 39 or 40 degrees, and constituted
a glacis partly rock-cut, or flagged over to prevent the earth
slipping down. A walk over it must at all times have been a very
arduous undertaking, and even now would be impossible, but for
the grass and shrubs which have grown between the stones. It
is only by placing the foot against them at each slab, and holding

FIG. 299.—Suri-Kalé. PERROT, *Exploration Archéologique*, Plate XXXIV.

on to the branches, that an upright position can be maintained.
In former days, when it was kept clean and in good order, a few

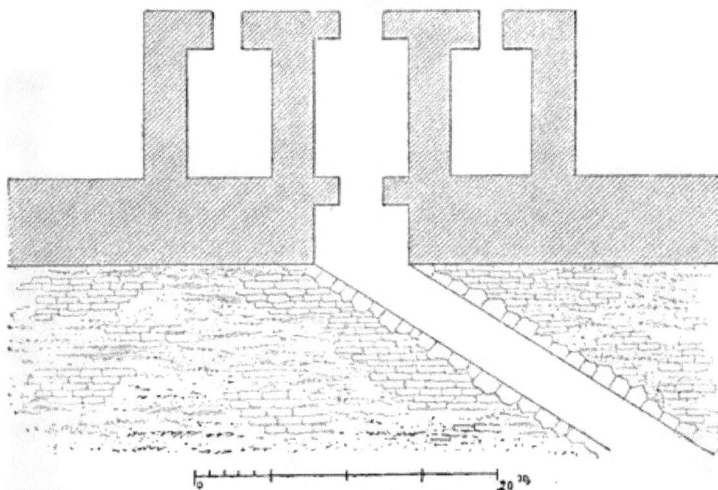

FIG. 300.—Main Doorway of Area. Plan. TÉXIER, Plate LXXXI.

stones let loose—always to be procured from the surrounding
rocks—would send rolling down whoever attempted to scale the
wall on this side. The position of the assailants was scarcely

FIG. 301.— Principal Gate. Perspective View. TÉXIER, Plate XXXI.

improved by taking the circuitous path over the glacis; for
though the ascent was easy, they would be longer exposed

to the missiles of the garrison. The annexed woodcuts (Figs. 300, 301, and 302) will enable the reader to judge of the nature of this piece of military engineering. This winding path abuts to a deep sinking in the wall of nearly three metres, with a guard-room on each side, and an opening at the end which looked into a chamber with folding door. As in Assyria, here also, the city gate was an independent structure, almost 18 m. deep. The

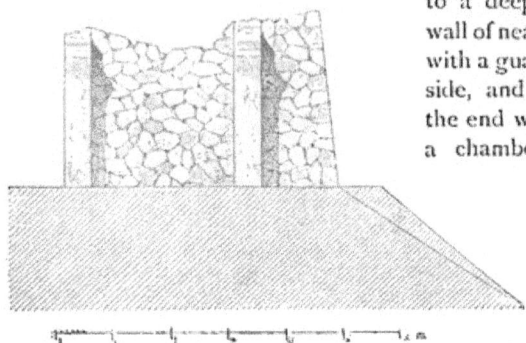

FIG. 302.—Principal Gate. Longitudinal Section. Texier, Plate LXXXI.

posts were formed of monoliths; on the outside of each were sculptured lion's heads (Fig. 303). The symbolism represented by these animals placed over the side openings does not require explanation at our hands, nor is it necessary to insist that the central doorway, now disappeared, terminated in a horizontal or false arch, and that the scroll moulding which began towards the top of the posts was extended to the massive lintel they supported. This is an arrangement which we have frequently encountered before.

FIG. 303.—Lion's Head on Doorway. Texier, Plate LXXXI.

The gateway was not the only means of communication the garrison had with the exterior. In many places are remains of narrow passages under the rampart, with outlet to the moat below the retaining wall. The most remarkable is to the west of the gate, superficially occupied by a plantation of oaks. It was obtained by a double set of five rude stones, projecting one beyond the other, till one smaller stone closed the top and made the vault complete (Figs. 304, 305). It is the nearest approach to an arch, and holds a middle course between the false vault and the radiating scheme or true archway. The door belonging to this passage opened into the moat, and is still in good preservation ; whilst the hinge sockets are as good as if cut but yesterday (well seen in Figs. 306, 307). But the arch at the back of the huge lintel has given way, and the stones are strewing the ground.

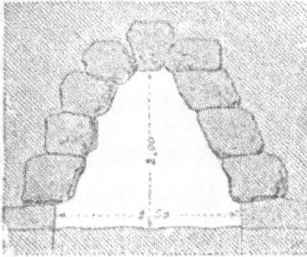

FIG. 304.—Subterraneous Passage. Transverse Section. PERROT, *Exploration*, tom. i. p. 329.

FIG. 305.—Subterraneous Passage. PERROT, *Exploration*, p. 329.

The restoration of the entrance was achieved by measuring the actual blocks of which it formerly consisted (Fig. 308). This passage may be entered through the hole left by the falling stones, and which can be followed for about 45 m., on a deep incline, with direction from south to north, until it is met by the

FIG. 306.—Entrance to Subterraneous Passage. PERROT, *Exploration*, p. 329.

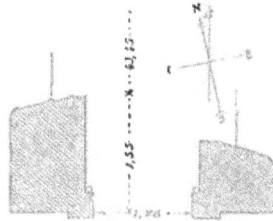

FIG. 307.—Subterraneous Passage. Plan of Entrance. PERROT, p. 329.

wall. In our second visit to this curious gallery, which calls to mind similar structures at Tiryns (save that here it is 15 m. longer and built of smaller stones), we discovered its inner outlet hidden behind the rampart ; a shrubbery may have concealed the exterior one. At the other end of the passage, we noticed remains of foundation walls, consisting of cyclopæan blocks, which doubtless supported a public structure, either civil or military. Scattered on the surface of that portion of the rampart which is over the subterraneous passage, are massive stones, with a cyma moulding rudely carved upon them, which formerly belonged to a doorway, now fallen in.   In troublous times, when the enemy tried to force this gate, a sortie through the unsuspected inner passage might be effective from its very suddenness.

These few indications suffice to give an idea of the defences of a city, which we hope will be completed by some future explorer, when the elements upon the art of fortification used by the nations of Asia Minor, before their point of touch with Hellas, will be brought to light, enabling us to compare the resemblances and divergencies which are observable in the methods of Oriental as against Greek engineers.   Nor is this all; it is quite possible that the traditions relating to the foundation of Greek cities, which told of heroes who had come from Asia, would find their fulfilment here; and that strong analogy would be discovered between the fortress under notice, and those of Mycenæ and Tiryns.

Fig. 308.—Subterraneous Passage.   Restored Section of Entrance.   Perrot, p. 329.

It should be noticed that the wall curtain, so far as we examined it, is nowhere flanked by towers, not even about doorways.   The omission is the more striking that a similar mode of defence was resorted to in Egypt, Mesopotamia, and Syria, from the remotest antiquity, to prevent the enemy approaching the wall.[1]   In the present state of the structure, the question of whether the lacune was supplemented by embattlements cannot be decided with absolute certainty, but all tends to prove their non-existence.   The Cappadocian architect, therefore, with his smooth wall top, without salience, shows less skill and knowledge of his art than his Assyrian colleague.   Moreover, he does not appear to have foreseen or calculated that the length of line of the city wall was out of all proportion with the smallness of the place and consequent garrison entrusted with its defence; so that when surrounded by a superior

[1] *Hist. of Art*, tom. ii. p. 350.

FIG. 309.—Iasili-Kaia. Perspective View of Main Court.

force, the besieged would be reduced to guard the points attacked, and prevent surprise, but could never hope to take the offensive. Whilst noting this error, and the evil results which might ensue, justice should be rendered to the ingenious contrivances of the builder ; the skill and patient industry of the masons in his employ, shown in the subterraneous passages, notably the glacis, conceived and executed with thought and care.

To sum up, the qualities and the defects of this military architecture bear witness to an independent and original art, whose aspirations to a high standard of excellence were partly realized. It is an art which had progressed, beyond merely using the means at its disposal, to a useful end ; its aims were already loftier ; directed to producing an agreeable effect, evidenced in the sculptured lions, the mouldings about jambs and lintels, etc. If the skill of the ornamentist and the sculptor, therefore, were required upon structures which, after all, might have dispensed with it, it proves the existence of artists accustomed to go to nature for their inspirations, who used their knowledge in translating the creed, the religious ideas of the community at large, into symbolical forms, be it of men or animals. An assertion which we shall have occasion to prove in the sequel of this study.

§ 4.—*The Sanctuary. Iasili-Kaïa.*

Ascending the hill on the right bank of the stream, about two miles east of the palace, near the base of the escarpment of a ridge of limestone rocks, are the remarkable bas-reliefs known in the locality as Iasili-Kaïa.

They may be ranged under three heads : the more important, numbering forty-five figures (A K in plan), cover the walls of a large excavation, almost rectangular in shape, measuring 11 m. 40 c. in width, and about 25 m. from end to end (Fig. 310),[1] which opens to the south-west towards the town, the rocks at the sides being from 8 m. to 10 m. high (Fig. 309).[2] The second group, east

---

[1] The woodcut was obtained by M. St. Elme Gautier, partly from Téxier's Plate LXXII., and partly from Plate XXXVI. of our *Exploration Archéologique*, etc.

[2] The plan shows a horizontal section of the rocks, at the height of the bas-relief, with the main and smaller chamber or passage and outlets. Each bas-relief is marked with a corresponding letter, so that its position can be easily found in Plate VIII. The sculpture is nearly double its real size ; the scale in plan indicates 2 m. 40 c., whereas it only measures 1 m. 40 c.

of the preceding, consists of twenty-two figures carved upon the
same solid rock (N P in plan), and the third is represented by two
figures inside a small hollow, interposing between the principal
chamber and the passage (L M in plan). The wall, to the height
of a few feet, was cut perfectly smooth, followed by the figures,
which formed a raised band, but above them the rock was left
rough, constituting a rude natural frame, not devoid of a quaint
charm of its own.

A layer of yellowish glaze was added to these sculptures, perhaps to heighten their effect, certainly to protect them at the same
time against the injurious action of the elements. Notwithstanding these precautionary measures, owing also to the nature of the
limestone on which the figures are carved, which is coarser and
less resisting than marble, many of them are much worn and nearly
obliterated, notably those furthest removed from the centre, where
the sun never penetrates, but where wind and rain are free to
carry on their work of destruction. No wonder that large patches
of mould and lichen should have spread over these rocks, making
the figures hard to distinguish from the surrounding surface.
Hence it often happened that M. Guillaume, before he proceeded
to photograph them, was obliged to scrape off with the knife the
green vegetation, guided thereto by his fingers, which felt for the
general contour, and the details of the pictures, throughout in
very flat relief.

The pavement of the main chamber is now covered with grass
and brushwood ; that this was not so in olden times we proved
by clearing a small space of the earth and rubbish which have
accumulated, when the rock-floor perfectly levelled out, and traces
of a side canal (Plate VIII., A B C) came to light.

Fronting the bas-relief on the right (Plate VIII., G), is a ledge
with a projection of 10 to 12 c. from the rock. It may have been
an altar or a pedestal, more likely the former, as a statue placed
on it would have been right in front of an important figure carved
on the rock behind it, and so have concealed it from public gaze.
The base of this altar, which we disengaged, is indicated by dots.
We also took soundings at the entrance of the main chamber and
the rock above it, for the purpose of ascertaining the existence of
some kind of door or roof, but without result. Consequently, it was
from the beginning an irregular excavation open to the sky. A
certain amount of thought was bestowed towards securing diversity

of aspect, by opposing smooth to raised or rough surfaces, resulting

FIG. 310.—Iasili-Kaïa. Plan. PERROT, *Exploration*, Plate XXXVII.

in a happy combination of nature and man's skill. Relief was
obtained by sinking a shallow groove around the figures, sixty-

seven in number, further heightened by colour, and in vivid contrast with the fantastically broken, sombre background, which is
not without a certain rude quaintness *sui generis*.

Superficially viewed, the composition may be defined as the
meeting of two processions, extending along the two sides of the
chamber (Plate VIII.). The longer, which is on the left, as a
natural consequence, yields greater variety in accessories and
postures, whilst that to the right, except the second figure, which
falls a little out of the line, and walks second in the procession,

Fig. 311.—Iasili-Kaia. Bas-relief in Main Chamber, letter F in Plan. Height of second
figure, 81 c. *Exploration*, Plate XLVIII.

consists, seemingly, of women, all cut on the same pattern, robed
in long flowing garments, with plaited hair, which falls behind their
backs, and high square caps, akin to those on the Merash stela
(Figs. 280, 281). It is the same head-gear, but the shape has
undergone a change, and is more elegant ; the fluting, too, and
the top edge show a decided advance on the plain surface of its
predecessors (Fig. 311).

The close-fitting tunics, over which is sometimes thrown a
mantle (as in northern Syria), ending in a long point behind, which
covers one leg but leaves the other exposed, and high conical
caps of the figures of the left row, some of whom wear beards,

FIG. 312.—Iasili-Kaia. Bas-relief in Main Chamber, Letter A in Plan. Height, 86 c. *Exploration*, Plate XXXIX.

leave no doubt as to their belonging to the stronger sex [1] (Fig. 312) (Plate VIII. D). Doubts may be entertained with regard to the two central figures of this group, who, but for the hair, which is cut short, and smoking caps (see Figs. 262, 269), might well pass as women, with their trailing robes and redundant outlines. We are of opinion that these, and the two larger effigies in Figs. 314 and 321, were eunuch priests.

The two principal figures on each side are nearly 2 m. high; those immediately attendant upon them are 1 m. 70 c., and the others from 80 c. to 75 c. Such a difference of scale is common to all primitive people, and was born of the desire to indicate the relative importance of personages, which in their simple conception could only be reached by marked difference of stature. Hence the rank and file were never apportioned the height of kings and priests, these in their turn yielded the palm to deities.

Agreeably to these notions, which it is not necessary further to develop, it is clear that the two figures heading the procession (which we take to be gods) are the most important in the group.

Opinions are divided as to the subject these figures were intended to represent. At first Téxier considered them as the meeting of the Amazons and Paphlagonians; later "Ashtoreth calling to immortality an impeccant prince;"[2] with the gods Amanus and Andates, who, on the statement of Strabo, were worshipped on the same altars with her.[3] Raoul-Rochette and Lajard, on the other hand, believe that they were intended for the two great Assyrian deities—the god Sandan and Mylitta, Ashtoreth, Aphrodite. Others again, among whom Hamilton,[4] are inclined to recognize in them the meeting of two conterminous kings, to commemorate a treaty of peace concluded between them, under the auspices of their respective deities.

But which nations, we may ask, were they? We know abso-

---

[1] M. Ramsay recognizes a certain number of women in this group. His reasons, which he published in an interesting account ("On the Early Historical Relation between Phrygia and Cappadocia," *Journal of the Royal Asiatic Society*, vol. xv. Pt. I. pp. 14–21) of these bas-reliefs, which he carefully examined, failed to carry conviction to our minds.

[2] The citation is from E. Vinet, whose article, "Les Missions de Phenicie et d'Asie Mineure," published by Didier in a miscellaneous volume, entitled *L'Art et l'Archéologie*, 1874, was suggestive of many an instructive comparison.

[3] *Memoire sur l'Hercule phénicien et assyrien* (*Académie des Inscriptions*, tom. xvii. 1848, p. 180). LAJARD, *Recherches sur le culte de Venus*, p. 119.

[4] *Researches*, tom. i. pp. 394, 395.

lutely nothing of Eastern Asia Minor previous to the Median invasion, and our inability to decipher the inscriptions renders darkness more complete.

Again, these bas-reliefs were meant as a reminiscence of a victory obtained over the Saces, which was celebrated throughout the Median empire in a national festival under the name of "Sacæ" (Saces);[1] whilst M. Kiepert sees in the figures with tall conical caps the warlike Scythians (Saces) who invaded Media,[2] and whose power was felt in Anterior Asia, down to Alyattes and Cyaxares I.[3] Finally, Barth, moved by more peaceful sentiments, recognizes a pageant of a domestic character : the marriage of Aryenis, daughter of Alyattes, with Astyages, son of Cyaxares, which put an end to the war between Media and Lydia.   More than this, he fancied he saw the solar and lunar discs, in the hands of the twin monstrous figures carved in the small hollow ; which he argued were symbolic of the total eclipse reported by Herodotus as having so frightened the soldiers that they could not be induced to fight, and thus led to the conclusion of peace.[4]   We found nothing of the kind on the stone in question (L M in plan, Figs. 315, 316).

According to us, not an historical composition, but rather a concrete expression of the religious ideas and the images of the deities worshipped by the nation who carved them should be sought here.   This, our assumption, is borne out by the winged figures, which do not belong to the material world (letter D in plan, Plate VIII.).   If in Assyrian bas-reliefs of a marked historical colouring, winged genii, more or less fantastic deities, are encountered, they are almost always associated with the solemn act of prayer and sacrifice ; analogous to the subject which we think we can divine here.   But they never mix with the human crowd ; and when introduced in hunting or war episodes, their exalted position, the sacred ring around their middle, and outstretched wings, leave undoubtful their divine origin.   We unconsciously feel that, though in it, they are not of it ; hence, notwithstand-

---

[1] *Asie Mineure (Univers pittoresque)*, p. 615.

[2] Their invasion lasted twenty-eight years.—EDITOR.

[3] KIEPERT. *Archæologische Zeitung*, Berlin, 1843, p. 44.   *Herodotus* vii. 64. BARTH.   *Reise von Trapezunt nach Scutari*, p. 45.

[4] The sculptor forgot to remove the thickness around the finger-tips, in figure M, left by the blocking out, and stars or spheres were made out of this amorphous, insignificant mass.

ing their presence, the picture always retains its realistic character.

Of all the explanations proposed, that which is dependent for its existence upon the conical caps, seems to us the most futile : Herodotus writes nowhere that the Cimmerii were the only tribe that wore them ; and neither in the marshalling of the groups, nor the attitude of the different actors, is there aught that faintly calls to mind the so-called victory under discussion ; not to mention the absurdity of recognizing the sturdy warriors of Media in these effeminate, long-robed figures on the right side. Barth's theory of a royal marriage, and consequent large retinue of officials, personal attendants, and so forth, alone coincides with certain features of this bas-relief ; but, though fascinating, it melts away into nothingness when subjected to the searching light of criticism. For we do not read in Herodotus that Pterium was the theatre of the final meeting and of the negotiations which ended the war between the contending parties. But, granted even this, it does not follow that the matrimonial alliance was concluded here rather than at some other place. On the other hand, we contend that there is no foundation for the belief which would attribute to this domestic alliance the importance implied by the magnitude of these sculptures. If Herodotus alludes to a battle interrupted by an eclipse, this was done for the sake of extolling the wisdom of Thales, who had predicted it, and of whom his countrymen were justly proud. An incident so gratifying to their national pride was not likely to be forgotten ; thus it came to pass that whilst the details of the struggle between the Medes and the Lydians were unrecorded, its final episode lived in men's memory. Does this prove that the event has the importance which we are tempted to ascribe to it at the present day ?

Moreover, is it credible that the Lydians would have had a great work like this placed beyond their territory, where there would have been few opportunities of viewing it ? And if due to the Medes, should we not find here at least some lines of their writing akin to the trilingual inscriptions of Iran, associated with Persian and Assyrian epigraphy ? Whereas the signs on these bas-reliefs belong to no variety of the written system, indifferently called arrow-headed, or cuneiform ; but we meet with its prototype among the hieroglyphs of Northern Syria. One of the characters which we find oftener repeated in Hittite monuments is the following : ⊙ ⊚, considered by Professor Sayce as a determinative prefix to denote the names of different deities.[1] Now this sign, albeit obliterated in many places, is seen in front of sundry figures in these groups (Plate VIII.).   Sometimes it is a simple oval ring crossed by a vertical bar at the extremity of a slender stem ; sometimes the stem is furnished with a leaf on each side, or a flower forms a pleasing device ; at other times it crowns a puppet god or a small figure a span high (Fig. 313).[2]

If Professor Sayce's conjecture is correct, each group of characters which begins with this peculiar sign must be the determinative prefix of a deity; and, as a matter of fact, it occurs in most inscriptions of Hittite origin. Nor is this the only indication which should warn the observer to be on his guard against ascribing these sculptures to the Medes. Laying aside the nature of their connection with Cappadocia, which we know was transitory, there is not a single detail in these figures, be it of dress or arms, which recalls in the remotest degree the Median costume, as described by Greek writers or seen in the monuments of Persia and Media. But we find here many an adjustment, many an accessory, which are encountered nowhere else, except at Eyuk, some little distance from here, and which, though different in manipulation from those at Iasili-Kaïa, betray community of school and traditions. In presence of instances such as these, will anybody be found bold enough to urge that the remarkable bas-reliefs at Eyuk were the creation of the Medes, and that stone and brick palaces, subterraneous tombs, sculptures cut in the solid rock, and the like, were not due to the race called by Herodotus Leuco-Scythians, whose capital was Pteria (Boghaz-Keui) ? It is not to be supposed that because they acknowledged the supremacy of the Medes, by paying a tribute until the sixth century, and occasionally also to Assyria in preceding ages, that they would have gone out of

---

[1] Variants of this hieroglyph will be found in the Carchemish inscription (Fig. 256) ; as well as in Plates V. and VIII. of Wright's *Empire*, where it occurs without the stem.

[2] We have said in another place (see Vol. i) that we were formerly inclined to view the two corresponding leaflets as the capsules of the mandragora ; a fruit connected by Eastern natives with aphrodisiac and fecundating qualities. As symbol of life and its various phases, the mandragora seems to have played an important part at Iasili-Kaïa. Those interested in the subject may read our conjectures—for they do not amount to more—duly set forth in our *Galatia*, pp. 332-334.

their way to celebrate the deeds of their foreign masters, whose

FIG. 313.—Iasili-Kaia. Principal Carving in Main Chamber, E in Plan. Plate XLV.

sudden attacks meant ruin and starvation, and whom, when their backs were turned, they were not likely to wish to remember.

Far more natural is the theory that several generations of

Pterians were engaged in carving upon the indestructible rocky

Fig. 314.—Iasili-Kaia.   Bas-relief in Main Chamber.   Height, 2 m. 24 c.   Plate XLV.

surface the images of their deities and public acts of worship, in order to win their favour.

For obvious reasons, the gods in the two side groups meeting

each other are not only taller than the figures after them, but
they are made to stand on plinths, to add to their height.   The

FIG. 315.—Iasili-Kaïa.   Carving at Entrance
of Passage.   Height, 1 m.   Plate XLVIII.

FIG.   316.— Iasili - Kaïa.   Carving   at
Entrance of Passage.   Plate XLVIII.

FIG. 317.—Iasili-Kaïa.   Face N in Passage.   Plate L.

secondary genii, introduced by the artist in the left row, were supposed to belong to the sublunary world, their life being intimately

interwoven with that of man. To the same category belong the
three winged figures (C D in plan) already alluded to. Nor
should the twin quaint central figures (in bas-relief C) be left
unnoticed. Unlike the others, they are short and thick-set, and
drawn full-face. The features, however, are obliterated, though
a protuberance, a long ear or horn, at the side of the face, as
well as a goat's cloven foot, is still distinct in the figure to the

Fig. 318.—Iasili-Kaia.   Face P in Passage.   Plate I.

right, leading to the inference that something like a Greek satyr
was intended. These fabulous beings stand upon pedestals, cut
cartouche-fashion in the plinth; in their outstretched arms they
hold an object which may be a boat or a crescent, emblem of
the moon-goddess.

   To describe all the accessories of these figures, such as sceptres,
terminating in knobs or balls, two-headed axes, upright or crooked
staffs, scythes, horns, pateras, flowers, etc., would far outstretch
our limits. We will only say that every detail, sacred utensils,
each of which had a special use and was handled by a special
official, to the grave attitude and gestures of the personages—all

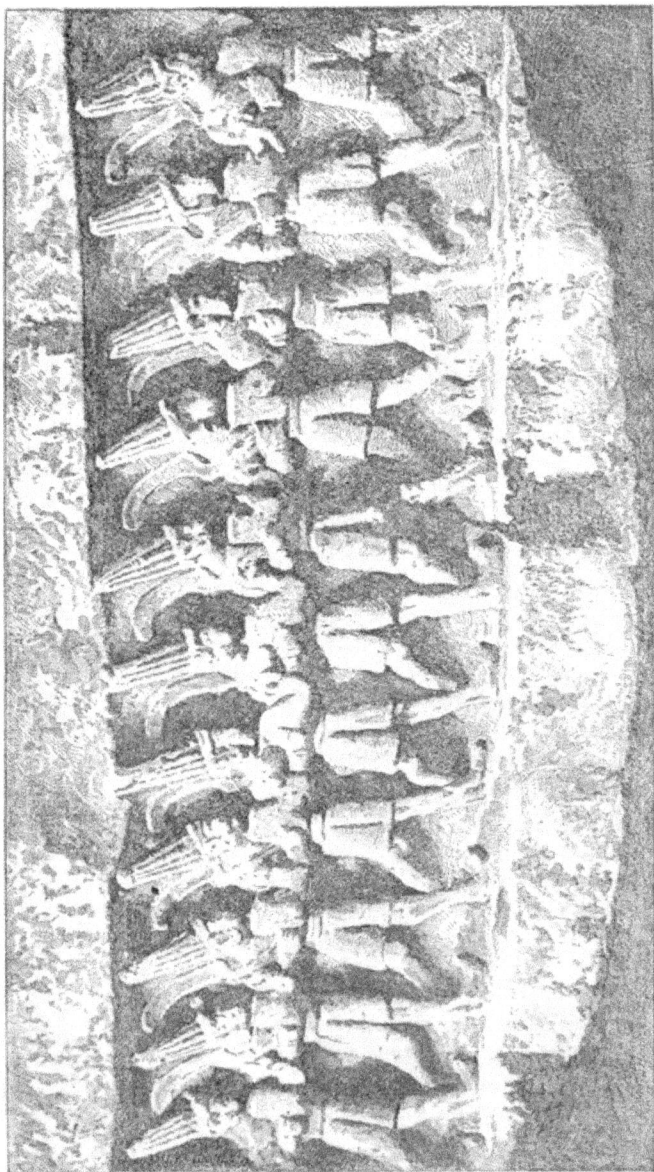

FIG. 319.—Iasili-Kaia. Sculptures in Passage. Height of bas-relief, 82 c.; length, 2 m. 60 c. Plate LII.

was calculated to stamp the composition with a markedly hieratic character. Such are the mitred bulls projecting beyond the two principal figures; the hills and men's shoulders supporting deities on the left; the panther and double-headed eagle bearing those on the right (E in plan). But this religious and symbolic character is particularly noticeable in the figures away from the twin main groups.

Facing the centre of the principal chamber rises the tallest figure of the whole group (over three metres high), standing upon twin hill-tops, one of which is broken away. He holds an œdiculum in his right hand, and in the sinister a "lituus" or crooked augural rod. His tight-fitting cap is like the Turkish "tarbush," minus the tassel, and his robe reaches to the ankles; whilst the beginning of a hilt is seen about the waist. The œdiculum is supported by Ionian columns; a mitred genie occupies the centre, with robe ornamented by a tooth-edged device; and divine bulls, one on each side, fill up the space.

At the entrance of the narrow passage are two winged monsters, already referred to (L M in plan), which we were the first to reproduce—the one with a dog's head, the second apparently a lion's. Judging from their gesture, they seem to have been placed there to guard against witchcraft or to keep off the profane (Figs. 315 and 316). At the southern extremity of the next rather wider passage, which runs through the broad rocky mass, are the groups seen in the annexed woodcuts (Figs. 317 and 318), of which the heads were alone visible (as drawn by Téxier and Barth), but which we completely disengaged.[1] On the walls behind the bas-reliefs are three rude niches, circular in plan, which could be closed; for traces of slabs about their apertures can still be detected. Two out of the three are in the west face, upon which are carved a dozen figures, armed with scythes, filing past as though on the march (Fig. 319, N in plan).

Of the three tall figures on the east wall, the tallest is un-doubtedly a god (Fig. 320, O in plan); his splendid head is placed upon a bust formed by two lions back to back, their muzzles coming out at the sides over the armpits. Suspended to stumpy arms below are two other lions, whose heads rest upon a huge sword-blade, which supports the whole mass. The remaining

---

[1] They made drawings of what they saw, without attempting to clear them of the accumulated rubbish.

two figures are on the right of this, in the centre of a small hollow (Fig. 321); the taller recalls the second figure of the main group (Fig. 313), whilst the other is akin to Fig. 314; and we find it again, this time with a winged disc (in bas-relief D, Plate VIII., first figure). Both sets are distinguished by similarity of costume, arms, and long, curved staffs. The god (Fig. 321) holds under his arm the smaller figure, in an attitude of solicitous regard; in his right hand, stretched towards the man-bodied lion, is a symbolic puppet-god, intended to recall the name of the deity. On the wall behind this tall mitred god is an œdiculum, surmounted by a winged sphere or solar disc, exhibiting the same arrangement of Ionian columns and probable divine bulls (nearly obliterated), as in the preceding temple, save that the central genie is replaced by a phallus. Nor should the cap of the deity, with ring device, be left unnoticed.

The conclusion to be reached from this succint analysis is that we are brought here face to face with the principal sanctuary of Pterium, perhaps of Pteria. Its disposition—the passages, for example, which connect the two chambers, the smaller being hidden away in the depth of the rock—is suggestive of an oracle. The main recess is spacious enough to have admitted of a double procession, as figured on its walls, albeit reduced and simplified. The local deities were supposed to dwell amidst this convulsed, wild alpine scenery, in the gloomy shade of sacred woods. Here, twice or three times a year, festivals, corresponding with the changes of nature, were celebrated by the whole population. Clothed in gay apparel, the Pterians issued from the city portals in long files, headed by their princes, priests, and priestesses. With them they slowly ascended the winding path which led to the high place. Whilst the chiefs of the nation performed the sacred rites within the precincts, externally the multitude lounged about on the verdant slopes overlooking the stream, spending the day eating and drinking, with due accompaniment of dancing and music.

It was a panegyria of the kind I have often witnessed in the East, the scene of action being always some secluded, picturesque spot on the bank of a stream, amidst cascades and a wealth of greenery. Such festivities partook of a national character, so that people would repair from great distances to join in them. Besides plying their own different trades, it gave them an opportunity to

FIG. 320.—Iasili-Kaia. Bas-relief in Passage. Height, 3 m. 23 c. Plate XLIX.

D

K

Plate 86

view some works freshly executed, of greater intrinsic value than
all that had gone before.   These public rejoicings were doubtless
wound up, as they still are in the East, with a fair.   Some days'

FIG. 321.—Iasili-Kaïa.   Bas-relief in Passage.   Height, 1 m. 70 c.   Plate L.

journey from here is the modern town of Zela or Zileh, where,
towards the end of November, an annual fair is held, attended by
traders from the whole peninsula, and even from distant Persia.

It was a place of great importance in antiquity, when a celebrated temple to Anaitis stood here, which attracted people to worship at the shrine from all parts of Asia. The traditions attaching to the spot, though long forgotten, have still the power to make it the one great meeting-place for Anterior Asia.[1]

Pterium, the capital of the district, the head of an important pass, situated midway between Sinope and Tarsus, was on one of the high roads followed by the trade of the interior; and as such could not but have a sanctuary of its own. The leading idea which pervaded the rites celebrated here was doubtless connected with one of the many divine dual forms variously called Báal and Ashtoreth, Tammuz and Báaltis, Sandan and Mylitta, Reshep and Anaït, Adonis and Aphrodite, Atys and Cybele—according to the localities in which they were worshipped—albeit all were originally mere epithets of one supreme, formless God. In Him was embodied the twofold principle of all terrestrial generation, the male and female, without which life could not be produced. But for the general worship, this pure and abstract monotheism was obliged to borrow symbols and images, in order to convey to the imagination the duality expressed by two persons.[2]

What was the appellation borne by the twin deities of Cappadocia? . It is impossible to say; but we shall not greatly err in assuming that the female manifestation was closely allied to the Cybele of the Greek Pantheon; conceived by the Hellenes, in their ignorance of her true origin, as having been born at Pessinus, where she had a famous temple. Cappadocian civilization is certainly older than the Phrygian—the latter borrowed largely from the former, even, it may be, this divine type and appellation. Classic art represents the Phrygian goddess in a chariot drawn by lions, with a turreted cap, the prototype of the mural crown seen in all the figures of the group to the right;[3] the first figure standing on a panther or lioness.

Numerous are the examples of a similar disposition in the

---

[1] With regard to Zileh and its ancient sanctuary, see *Exploration Archéologique de la Galatie*, pp. 459–466; G. Perrot, *Souvenirs d'un Voyage en Asie Mineure*, p. 378. If there ever was a fair near Boghaz-Keui, it probably fell into desuetude after Crœsus's expedition, when the country became little better than a wilderness.

[2] De Vogüé, *Mélanges d'Archéologie Orientale. Inscriptions Phéniciennes de Cypre*, pp. 41–85.

[3] In the first figure of the dexter row, considerably larger than the rest, this detail is perceptible (*Exploration Archéologique*, p. 356).

plastic art of Asia; the Greeks however, with unerring taste, discarded an arrangement that savoured of barbarism, and the griffins, vultures, eagles, and wild beasts generally that served as supports to Asiatic deities, were put to draw the chariots of Aphrodite, Dionysius, Cybele, etc. Like all the foreign elements introduced into Hellas, the costume, attitude, and physiognomy of Ma, or Cybele, were modified to suit her new surroundings. But, for all that, she retained enough of her former features to render her recognizable wherever she wandered.

These are very apparent in the first figure of the female procession—conceived here in her oldest and primitive simplicity; but in whom we are fain to see the great mother Ma, that which for the Phrygians, and subsequently for all the Greeks, at home and abroad, personified the earth and its everlasting fecundity.

According to this hypothesis, the god heading the male procession is Atys, of whom Phrygian myths told that he was the son and then the husband of Cybele, whose priest he became after his voluntary mutilation.[1] It is certainly a curious fact, that in the main chamber he should be represented bearded and of virile aspect, whilst in the passage, where he is repeated twice, his face is smooth and effeminate. In the same category may be classed the unbearded priests in long garments of the left row (letters D and K in plan). They are the forerunners of those Græci-Galli, or eunuch-priests of the great Phrygian goddess, whose mysteries they celebrated to the last day of paganism.

At first sight, the presence of the second figure in the female row is somewhat bewildering. Although beardless and differently arrayed, this personage has the air of being a repetition of the corresponding one in the opposite group. The anomaly is more apparent than real; for if we come to look at it more narrowly, the idea that the dual principle, male and female, in its concrete expression should have been juxtaposed, will approve itself to our judgment. Such reduplication was calculated more vividly to impress upon the mind of the worshippers the eternal idea of the intimate and inseparable unity of the divine couple; wherein the abstract concept of life and supreme force, one and manifold at the same time were incorporated.[2]

[1] The official title of the high priest of Cybele at Pessinus was Atys. See Mordtmann's paper, entitled, "Gordium, Pessinus, and Sivri-Hissar" (*Sitzungsberichte der Akademie*, etc., July 7, 1860, p. 184).

[2] De Vogüé, in his exhaustive survey of Syrian cultus, states that the Eastern

Notwithstanding obscurity in detail, and perhaps also the
unfathomable enigmas that here exist, the general economy of this
barbarous Panathenean composition is easily grasped.   The
epithet may startle some ; but the relative proportions being preserved, we venture to say that, within certain limits, the Cappadocian sculptor was the predecessor of the Parthenon frieze.
There is, as a matter of course, in the execution the wide distance
which separates the archaic from the inspired perfect creation of
a people in the zenith of their artistic power ; but the theme is
almost identical, and though rudely treated, no less than eighty-
five figures, many of colossal size, were sculptured here.   In both
localities, on the main sides of the parallelogram formed by the
sanctuary, a double procession is portrayed slowly ascending
towards the poliote deities.   These, at Iasili-Kaïa, are represented
by the group which occupies one of the smaller sides in the main
chamber ; the same arrangement, the same combinations of reality
and idealism are common to both.   The deities are supposed to
have descended upon earth in their tangible visible forms, in
order to be present at the solemn public acts of worship performed
in their honour.   As might be expected, the distinction between
the divine, as against the human world, is less distinctly marked
in the Asiatic bas-relief than in the Greek one.   In the former,
supernatural beings, secondary gods and genii, are jumbled along
with priests and Pterian chiefs.   But in other respects the subject
exhibits singular analogies: the procession of the Asiatic priestesses
coincides with that of the Attic Canephoræ ; the horsemen gallop-
ing through the Ceramicus correspond with the rhythmic march
of the twelve personages that close the pageant.

In the Parthenon, the first chapter of the grandiose work
written upon the frieze of the main face was protracted and completed in the entablature and frontels.   But on the façade, that it
might be read by all, was represented the traditional, solemn, and
most brilliant festival connected with the city ; whilst metopes and
spandrels received, carved in high relief, the myths dearest to the
fancy of the Athenians.   The same idea is apparent in the Asiatic
sculptor ; but the rude surface he had to decorate did not lend
itself to felicitous and varied combinations as the Greek temple.

goddess, Anaitis, is almost in every instance figured standing or seated upon a lion.
This he explains from the fact that here the lion, as the sign of male force, is not
to be taken as a symbol of the goddess, but of the god with whom she is associated.

To complete the translation of the main instances of his creed by means of tangible forms, the Pterian artist had no other resource than filling in every available part of the pronaos and utilizing the walls of the adytum. And so far he was not unsuccessful. At the entrance of the main chamber, the eunuch priest erect upon the summit of a hill, grasps in one hand the crooked staff, emblem of his priestly office, and holds up with the other the œdiculum, upon which is carved the image of his god. The conspicuous position he holds, coupled with his abnormal size, testifies to the importance and veneration attached to his person. In the adytum, this priest and his god are placed side by side; they form a group which is not wanting in nobleness and expressive value. The relative proportion of the two figures was well thought out; the gesture of the god, instinct with tenderness, is as that of a father pressing his son or daughter to his heart; whilst the phallus in the centre of the œdiculum behind the group is sufficient indication of the naturalistic character of the local religion. In the colossal figure which follows are we to seek for a mere abstract image of the deity just referred to, or do not rather the fantastic complex members of which this strange type is composed, reveal the effort of the artist to lend a shape to the supreme deity, in whom no longer dwells sexual difference, but that indetermined mysterious force of which the god and goddess leading the twin processions are but emanations and reflexes? In the absence of written documents to enlighten us on the subject, this must remain a mere hypothesis—an hypothesis, however, not devoid of a certain degree of probability; in accord, too, with what we know of Syrian religions, and of their characteristic tendencies. From certain indications, a critical authority believes he discovers here ternary series, triads vaguely outlined; the twin visible manifestations of which always remain more or less in shadow; i.e. fall in the background.[1]

These considerations lead us naturally to inquire as to the probable destination of the various members of this monument. The large hall is the pronaos, or public section; the lateral chamber is the inner sanctuary, or adytum, where the priests and the images of the worshippers were alone admitted. The latter are represented by the twelve warriors, who file past the god and his chief priests. Externally the only means of communication

[1] DE VOGUÉ, loc. cit.

with the adytum are two exceedingly narrow passages, which
could be easily closed or blocked up (see plan, Fig. 310). The
stones strewing the ground in front of this small recess may very
likely have formed part of walls which formerly barred these
avenues.   Reference has been made to the part assigned to the
twin monsters at the entrance of one of the passages, and to the
nature of the two great bas-reliefs, as coinciding with their destination.   One represents the close union between god and priest;
and in the second, this same god, seen hitherto with a human form,
has assumed a totally different aspect : his image is entirely made
up of symbolic members which could not blend and become fused
in a living organism.   We recognize here a mystic creation dear
to the sacerdotal fancy, which looks abroad for emblems by means
of which it may give utterance to its inner consciousness, in vain
endeavour to express the inexpressible.   The outcome is the
strange composite figure which we find in the holy of holies, but
which would have been out of place in the more frequented part,
where the forms should be simple and easily read.

   This brings us to the circular recesses right and left of the
passage (Figs. 310, 317, and 318), which it is clear were used as
cupboards for sacred utensils, amongst which may have been chests
akin to the ark of the Israelites.   What gives colouring to this
supposition are the twin œdicula front and back of the great bas-
relief (Figs. 314, 321); for they have all the appearance of being
intended as richly ornate reliquaries, or coffers, wherein were kept
sacred objects handled by the priest alone, which on stated days
he held up to the gaze of the assembled multitude.   If in composition and excellence of detail these movable chapels are far
superior to the surrounding sculptures, we may be sure that models
on wood or metal, with ivory inlay, perhaps of foreign manufacture,
had long been known to the Pterians.   If the artist assigned them
so conspicuous a position, if he reproduced on hard stone so elaborate an arrangement, it was because he was conscious that mere
sight of them would call to the remembrance of his countrymen
a special public act of worship in which they all had taken part.

   The first impression produced by the loneliness of the place is
apt to bring up the query as to whether a stone or bronze door
sufficiently guarded the precious objects placed in these recesses;
or if they were brought from the city when required.   But then, is
it credible that they would have laboriously excavated them, if

Fig. 322.—General View of Mound at Eyuk, from the south-west side. Plate LIII.

there was no use for them ? On the other hand, if the importance of these sculptures be allowed, the inference becomes irresistible that we are face to face with the principal temple of the Pterians, where daily worship was performed to the deities whose images are still carved on its walls, and that priests and Levites had their dwellings in the immediate neighbourhood ; so that the sanctuary was not left to take care of itself, but was at all times jealously watched over. Excavations made around Iasili-Kaïa might possibly reveal the group of houses under notice.

A complete exploration is much needed, and could not fail to uncover many an interesting detail ; albeit we venture to say that, despite discrepancies in our documents, they would not materially alter our conclusions in regard to the monuments just described. It is possible that other valuable remains of this civilization may yet be unearthed at other points of ancient Pterium, to add to that already known ; though not highly probable, from the fact of this locality having been so often visited. However that may be, our inquiries during our stay were far too searching not to make it pretty certain that the ruins at Boghaz-Keui are far away the greatest and most important encountered in the district. Here rose its capital, the main centre of Cappadocia, whose existence implies a flourishing country, thickly interspersed with hamlets surrounded by gardens, orchards, and fields, which could be irrigated even in summer. Hence it is to be supposed that in other localities will be found examples bearing upon them the unmistakable stamp peculiar to the race, though different in some particulars from those at Boghaz-Keui ; remarkable instances of which will be dealt with in the next chapter.

§ 5.—*The Palace. Eyuk.*

The ruins of the building which we have called "palace," were first discovered by Hamilton. But he reached Eyuk one day and left next afternoon, having made but a hasty drawing of them.[1] Barth, long afterwards, followed in his track ; his visit, however, occurred in the heart of winter, so that his stay was not protracted beyond a few hours. He expressed the earnest wish that these important remains might receive greater attention than had devolved upon him, remarking at the same time upon Hamilton's

[1] *Loc. cit.*, p. 282-284.

inadequate sketch. This stricture particularly applies to the sphinx, which he mistook for some huge impossible bird.[1] On the other hand, our visit extended over five days (Nov. 18–23), during which we were able carefully to examine the tumulus and its approaches, as well as the surrounding village. We excavated wherever ancient remains appeared above ground, made plans of each structure as it was uncovered, and used every available hour of the short days to obtain photographs. As until the publication of our volume these sculptures were practically unknown, we shall not attempt to draw from the meagre sources alluded to, but will confine ourselves to condensing our former account, reproducing our own sketches and plans.[2]

Eyuk is a hamlet of about 30 houses, built upon the small plateau of a hill, 12 or 13 m. high, with a gentle slope towards the surrounding plain (Fig. 322). On the south-eastern limits of the village is an ancient gateway, facing the south. Trachytic monoliths form the door-posts. On the outer face of each is carved a sphinx, whose claws are still wholly uncovered—a proof that the ground has not shifted its level since antiquity. The wall which advances on either side of the entrance is ruined; but on the lower course, which is left, may be seen a line of sculptures cut in low relief in the same trachytic rock to be met with everywhere about here.[3] These rows of bas-reliefs are interrupted on the south by a modern fountain, and on the opposite side they are lost to view at the beginning of the tumulus or hillock. Within the gateway an avenue of large sculptured blocks extends some distance into the village (Fig. 323). The summit of the mound which covers the ruins of the ancient building, the principal entrance of which we have just described, measured crosswise, is about 250 m. It was doubtless quadrangular, but

[1] Barth, *loc. cit.*, pp. 42, 43. Consult also his article entitled, "Ueber die Ruinen bei Uejük im alten Kappadocien" (*Archæ. Zeitung*, 1859), with accompanying Plate CXXVI., the drawings of which are not much better than Hamilton's.

[2] The Eyuk sculptures have been adequately described in a recent work; and although its author is not a professed archæologist, will repay perusal. It is entitled, *Travels in Little-known Parts of Asia Minor*, etc., by the Rev Henry J. van Lennep, 2 vols. in 8°. New York, 1870. The chapters (xix. and xx.) devoted to Boghaz-Keui and Eyuk contain several sketches, which, though on a small scale, give a pretty good idea of the monuments.

[3] Van Lennep (*Travels*, vol. ii. p. 119) calls the rock "a black granite of fine grain and great hardness;" and he remarks that it accounts for the remarkable preservation of the sculptures.

FIG. 323.—General View of Ruins, south side. Plate LIV.

the action of time, of man, notably of the cattle grazing on the slopes, has broken the edge at several places. Large stones strew the ground on the western face, and may possibly have belonged to a second gateway. In one of them were holes, such as we had noticed on blocks about the palace at Boghaz-Keui. Our time was too short to attempt exploring on this side'; nor was it necessary for our purpose, which was to make a plan of the structure and find out its probable destination.

The regular outline of the tumulus, and its smooth level top, made us suspect that it was not due to nature. To make sure of this, we had shafts sunk to a certain depth, but nothing except loose soil was encountered, and nowhere did we light upon the rock; whilst its slopes, cut by the winding footpath which leads to the village, revealed the same fact, and confirmed our first impression that, as at Khorsabad, Kojunjik, and Nimroud, we had here an artificial mound formed by the crumbling of unbaked bricks. Its sides, like those of the tells of Mesopotamia, face the cardinal points.[1]

We may assume, therefore, that these are the remains of a palace, built for a native prince, on a plan that closely resembles that of the Ninevite builder. The southern gateway, if not the only one that was let into the walls of the structure, was undoubtedly the main or royal entrance; and as such, more elaborately enriched—perhaps the only one upon which the chisel of the sculptor had been required. What tends to confirm this supposition is that here, but nowhere else, do we find stones projecting beyond the heaps of dust which have accumulated about them. Had dressed or sculptured blocks existed at any other point, like the monoliths of the gate-posts, and the huge stones or lion avenue ranged in front of the entrance, after the fashion of Egyptian "dromos," all traces of them would not have disappeared. Nor would entire blocks, such as one we found near the fountain, eight metres from the foundation wall, and a second on the same line, but 82 metres beyond, besides worked fragments which had evidently belonged to the same series, and which strew the ground on this side, have escaped our search for them.

Lack of time obliged us to confine our efforts to the gate as the portion which even in its present ruinous state testifies to the

thoughtful care bestowed upon it by the builder. To this end
we engaged all the available hands the place could furnish to clear
the entrance and its approaches of the earth under which the
stones were buried, all except the top;[1] setting up such as had
fallen on their faces so as to judge of the carving upon them.
Our plan (Fig. 324) shows the disposition of the structures; and
its relief is indicated in the general elevation (Fig. 325) and
longitudinal section (Fig. 326), even as they appeared when we

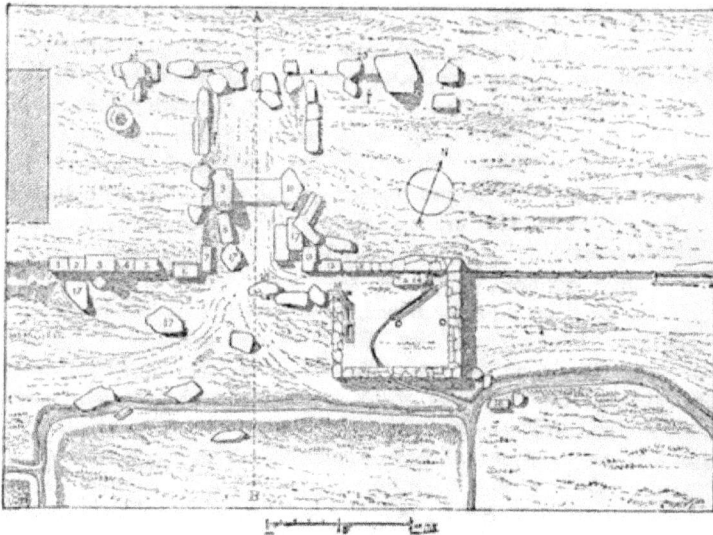

Fig. 324.—Plan of the Ruins of Eyuk.   Plate LV.

had uncovered them. A stage or landing, 5 m. 20 c. broad, stood
outside the front wall, and formed a kind of vestibule, to which
a gentle incline or paved ramp may have led from the plain, as at
Boghaz-Keui (Fig. 301), for we could find no vestiges of steps
having been there. But the monolith forming the threshold is
still in place; the lintel, however, has given way, and a fragment, trapezoidal in shape, lies some paces in front, with the neck
and claws of a lion carved upon it, which may have belonged
thereto (Fig. 324, 18). Lions, it will be remembered, were also

---

[1] Barth did not attempt to disengage them, and his drawing only shows the upper
part.

introduced as a means of enrichment about the main gate at Boghaz-Keui (Fig. 301). The top of the right hand gate-post is ruined; it was occupied, moreover, at the time of our visit by a stork's nest, which we did not like to disturb; but the left is still entire, and exhibits an inclined plane, as if intended to support the end of the lintel formed of one single block (9 in plan, and Fig. 327). The palace gate, 3 m. 41 c. wide, seems to

FIG. 325.—Elevation of Ruins. Plate LV.

have had but one single opening, for the threshold towards the right-hand post, though much worn, has still the hinge socket intact, albeit no trace of it exists at the opposite side.

Within the gateway the avenue lets in a vestibule, 6 m. 50 c. by 5 m. 20 c., which probably gave access to a court. Here the wall (20 in plan) advances on each side, and may have consisted, between the outer casings, of crude bricks, or formed a massive

FIG. 326.—Longitudinal Section through A B. Plate LV.

block, 13 m. thick, in the depth of which were side chambers. Had the outer stones been carried to any height, we should find them in greater number about the place; whereas they are comparatively few, even about the entrance. They all belonged to the second course, with the exception of one single block still *in situ* (No. 3), and their irregular shape and "bossed" face,[1]

---

[1] Owing to the small scale of our drawing (Fig. 325) this detail is not seen.

including a certain proportion of those in the first tier (block 1),

Fig. 327.—Left-hand Sphinx.   Plate LXV.

show that the scheme of masonry was, on the whole, polygonal,
as at Boghaz-Keui, and that the same method obtained in both

localities. This applies with equal force to the foundation wall; and we have no reason to suppose that it differed in essentials from that of the mother city.

The fountain prevented our ascertaining the whole extent of the sculptured stones to the right hand of the entrance (see plan). No such impediment exists on the left, where our diggings uncovered the whole plane and enabled us satisfactorily to establish that they continued on each side of the gateway some three

FIG. 328.—Eyuk. Bas-relief. Plate LVI.

English feet above ground. A disposition, it will be remembered, invariably selected by the Assyrian architect, in order to invest the façade of his palace with the utmost possible air of grandeur. It was calculated to strike the imagination of the beholder and impress him with the awful majesty of the sovereign, whose image formed the central figure about the gateway, amidst his protecting deities, the grandees, and chief officials that composed his court.

The figured decoration at Eyuk, though different, occupies the same position, and forms part of the same constructive mode of enrichment—the man-headed bulls and divine lions that guard the palace in Mesopotamia, Assyria, and northern Syria, have been replaced by Egyptian sphinxes. The mother idea is indeed borrowed from the Nile valley, but treatment and details are modified, and closely resemble Assyrian style. Thus, for example, throughout the range of Egyptian art, the sphinx is figured in low relief, in a recumbent posture about the doorway. Here, however, he is sculptured in the round, and set up on his hind-quarters on either gate-post, facing the palace avenue. Then, too, in the former country, the headdress has two side lappets which encircle the face, but the Cappadocian artist, discarding his national "klaft," has taken the ringlets or volutes which characterize Hathor's head-gear.[1] With him again the ear occupies its proper position, whilst in figures of Egyptian origin it is invariably carried too high, above the line of the eyebrow, sometimes even above the fillet surrounding the brow. This applies to the necklace, which is made to touch the chin, but in the rare instances where it occurs in Egyptian sculpture it falls low over the breast. The result is a composite work, which holds a middle course between Assyrian and Egyptian style. On the other hand, the influence of the Nile valley is not apparent on the sculptured stones extending along the wall. In details they call to the memory the monuments at Boghaz-Keui; in a general way, those of Assyria and Persia, albeit neither suggest historical scenes such as are current on the walls and stairways of Ninevite, Susian, and Persepolitan palaces. As at Boghaz-Keui, here also we see a double religious procession meeting near the entrance, on the block next to the corner-stone (6 in plan), with an altar and two figures, male and female, carved upon it (Fig. 328). The personage with a crooked staff is almost identical with the priest at Iasili-Kaia

Fig. 329.—Bull Idol. Eyuk. Plate LVI.

---

[1] *Hist. of Art*, tom. i. Fig. 244. See also Merriam, " Arrangement of the Hair on the Sphinxes at Eyuk " (*American Journal of Archæology*, vol. i. pp. 150–160).

(Fig. 314). On a tall pedestal, right of the altar, stands a bull, evidently an idol, finely sculptured, with mouldings about him, doubtless of hieratic import (Fig. 329). All the figures on this side of the wall, whether on the right or left of the altar, are turned towards it.[1]

Fig. 330.—Eyuk. Bas-relief. Plate LVIII.

The left-hand procession is headed by a bull of far more archaic make than the preceding. An object, apparently an altar, is carried on its back, and two discs are sculptured about its forelegs (Fig. 330). Next come two personages, the one playing upon an

[1] Block 8 in plan forms no exception to the rule, for it has been displaced from its proper position.

instrument not unlike a mandoline in shape, with ribbons fastened about the top (Fig. 331); his companion, as far as can be judged from the worn state of the stone, holds a small animal —hare or kid, for the sacrifice. The next stone has three figures in pretty good preservation, which allows the details about their heads to be seen. The tallest seems to blow a trumpet; he wears a low, rounded helmet, with raised border, which forms a rosette on the forehead. Large rings depend from his ears, and a long pigtail falls behind his back. The other two seem to have been buffoons, whose part was to amuse the crowd and keep it in good humour. A huge block from the second course has fallen right in front of the figure standing at the foot of the ladder in a posture of expectancy, so that his feet cannot be seen. The next is half-way up the ladder, or rather the uprights, a clumsy con-

Fig. 331.— Carving at Eyuk.   Plate LXI.

trivance resorted to by the artist to show the steps rendering doubt in respect to the object portrayed impossible. The arrangement about the head of this figure should be compared with that of Fig. 336, which it closely resembles. The head is shaved, all but a top piece, twisted into a pigtail, which falls behind. The next stone is occupied by priests, whose costume and attitude are precisely alike, so far as may be judged from their worn condition, the heads having suffered most. The dexter hand of the first and last figures are raised, as though in the act of blessing. The latter is

the only one whose sinister, holding a lituus, is preserved. The
interposing figure is even more mutilated; the hand is gone, but
the curved bit which extends to the following block apparently
belonged to some kind of instrument carried in the hand. We
now come to the most distinct group of the series, that upon which
the skill of the carver is seen to greater advantage. It represents
a priest clothed in the usual long robes, whose head is much
injured and one arm almost obliterated. He is followed by two

FIG. 332.—Carving at Eyuk. Plate LXII.

sets of rams driven to the sacrifice, the one on the same plane with
the priest, and the other immediately above it (Fig. 334). By
this conventional arrangement the artist wished to convey the idea
of a large number, a whole flock.[1] Here a stone, 93 c. long, which
must also have been worked, is wanting (see plan, Fig. 324).

If, as seems likely, the altar (Fig. 328) and the bull (Fig. 329)
were the counterparts of personages that at Iasili-Kaïa stand upon

[1] In respect of the ignorance of perspective betrayed by a similar contrivance,
see LAYARD, *Monuments of Nineveh*, vol. i. Plates LIX. and LX., and early part of
this work.

animals, they would constitute the centre of the scene, and the
beginning of the second part of the first procession would be found
in the four figures occupying the corner stone on the left-hand side
of the gateway (7 in plan).   One angle is chipped off, and has
taken with it nearly half the figure to the left.   The curious jagged
outline of the head and misshapen leg in the next figure (Fig. 335)
should be noticed.   At first we thought that it was some nonde-
script animal, and not until the ear and the huge earring were un-

Fig. 333.—Carving at Eyuk.   Plate LIV.

covered did we become aware of the real nature of the picture.   A
staff interposes between these two figures, each grasping it with
one hand and holding it to the ground, evidently intended to show
the intimate connection which existed between them.   Both wear
short tunics.   That the third figure belongs to an inferior class is
indicated by his lack of clothes, diminutive size, and his position
in the background, at a respectable distance from the exalted
personages whom he dares not approach.   The priest, easily
recognized by his dress, holds out to him a sceptre, furnished with
a moon-crescent, to be kissed or worshipped.

The next block (Fig. 336, 8 in plan) consists of six personages,

who advance with measured step. In their bearing and the place
they occupy in the procession, they closely resemble the Iasili-
Kaïa figures (Plate VIII. A, and Fig. 319), with this difference,
that here they are unarmed. Their costume is a short tunic, with
or without belt or sash. The conspicuous pigtail of the second
figure has been referred to. The difficulty of setting up this stone
(which was overturned) in its proper position explains the fact of

Fig. 334.—Carving at Eyuk. Plate LX.

the figures moving away from the altar, and not towards it, as they
should.

Sculptures of the same description seem to have existed on the
opposite side of the gateway, where they were not cut into halves
by the principal decoration. They extended as far as a bas-relief
which covered a depression in the wall, in touch with the inner
face of the sphinx. But this block was of the number that, for
lack of time, we were unable to move, hence it is impossible to say
what was carved upon it. From Mr. Ramsay's drawing, we think
that it is that which stands left of No. 17 in our plan.[1] On this

---

[1] *On the Early Historical Relations*, etc., p. 17, with drawing and plan.

side the sculptured plane has been pulled about to build the fountain, in the erecting of which the smaller stones were freely used,
so that to examine the whole series of pictures would necessitate
the demolition of the fountain, and the moving of the larger stones
which strew the ground.

In June, 1881, Sir C. Wilson and Mr. Ramsay, on their way
to Sivas, stopped at Eyuk, to see its ruins. They made no excavations, but had some of the blocks turned about, in order to examine

Fig. 335.—Carving at Eyuk.   Plate LVI.

the carving upon them ; when on a stone, facing the unnumbered
one left of No. 17, they lighted upon a picture of the highest
interest, of which, unfortunately, no sketch was made ; so that
we are reduced to Mr. Ramsay's verbal description, from which
we quote : "On the right of the picture, carved upon one of the
faces of the slab, is a seated goddess ; her feet rest upon a footstool, the right being stretched out a little in front.   The figure is
much worn, but what is left agrees in every particular with that
published by Perrot (in his *Exploration Archéologique*, Plate
LXVI.).   Towards this goddess moves a procession led by a
figure, in which, with Perrot, I incline to recognize the eunuch high

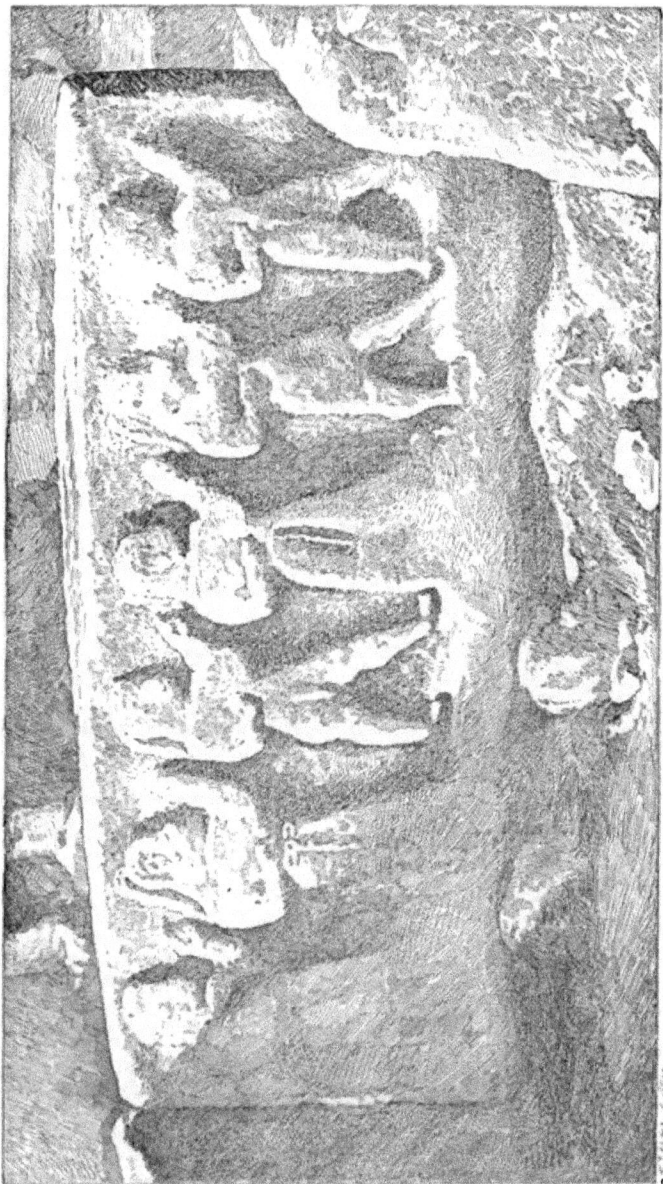

FIG. 335.—Carving at Eyuk.   Plate LXIII.

priest of Cybele, as at Boghaz-Keui. His costume is exactly the same as in all the other bas-reliefs of Pterium where his image has been met with. As usual, a lituus is carried in his right hand ; but with his left he pours out of an œnechoe a liquid over the feet of the seated goddess. Behind the priest walks the priestess, whose hands make the gesture which seems to characterize women in the plastic art of Cappadocia. Her right hand holds to her face a round object ; the left carries to her lips some other indistinct symbol. It is impossible now to say if she wore earrings. This priestess is dressed in the same flowing robe which distinguishes her in the group represented in Plate LXVI. *Exploration Archéologique,* Fig. 1 (our Fig. 328). Behind them are two other figures, almost obliterated, whose costume seems to have consisted of a short tunic and a mantle so as to cover one leg, leaving the other exposed. By a lucky chance, the central figures have least suffered ; so that we can distinctly see the priest and priestess, who also figure in the other part of the decoration, on the left side of the gateway." [1]

The Cappadocian artist, as stated, did not dispose of a great variety of forms ; thus it comes to pass that the types here described are found in other places. If we except the libation detail, which is novel, the priest and priestess are almost identical with the central group imaged in Fig. 328, and the seated goddess to whom these public rites were offered is repeated on the eastern side of the portal (11 in plan), together with the bull (7 in plan, and Fig. 329). From some unexplained cause, the side face of block 11 in plan was unworked, whilst its opposite neighbour (7 in plan) had half a dozen figures carved upon it (Fig. 336). The only image on the former occurs on its exterior section. Like Mr. Ramsay's goddess, it portrays a woman seated and habited in a long garment. Her hair falls in long ringlets about her neck and shoulders ; her boots are more than " tip-tilted," they actually form a ring in front. With the dexter hand she carries a cup to her lips, a detail which seems to suggest the libation just referred to ; with the sinister she holds an indistinct object, perhaps a huge water-lily (Fig. 337).

On the right of this picture (12 in plan, and Fig. 338) the decoration looked to the left ; but all the figures are much worn, and the upper part is almost gone. We should not have reproduced

[1] *Loc. cit.*

them but for the thick raised line in front of them, which to our knowledge, has not been found anywhere else, with the single exception of Iasili-Kaïa.   M. Guillaume and I puzzled our heads in vain to make out what it stood for : whether it was a cord trimming to the woollen cape slung over the shoulder or the border of an oblong shield.   The bar in "cameo" across the

figures, which may be taken for a leather strap to carry the shield, seems to favour the latter conjecture.   The next block (13 in plan) had three similar figures, of which the lower part alone remains.[1] The three or four stones needed to complete this part of the decoration are in all likelihood among those that were used to build the fountain ; the damaged state in which we should find them, however, would scarcely repay the trouble or cost of looking for them.   We have asked the question, without being able to decide, whether block 14 in plan (Fig. 339) belonged to this series.   Our

Fig. 337.—Seated Goddess.   Eyuk.   Plate LXVI.

reason for hesitating is not because it was out of the alignment, as this might be purely accidental, but because it wants 40 or 50 centimetres to reach the height of the other slabs still in place. On the other hand, the subject would form a fitting pendant to the rams (5 in plan) on the opposite side. It represents an infuriated bull, his head down, preparing to butt.   There is little doubt but that it was intended for the sacrifice.   But the artist, in order to impart life and movement to his picture, has figured it as though it had just broken loose from its captors.   The next block (15 in plan) is in fairly good preservation ; and shows a lion that has just sprung upon a ram, holding him down with his fore-feet.   The treatment and general form of the

[1] *Exploration Archéologique*, Plate LVI. Fig. 4.

animal at once call to memory those of Northern Syria and
Boghaz-Keui. Like these, the body was carved in low relief
on one side of the stone, the other being left flat, whilst
the head was in the round on its anterior section, as reference
to the annexed woodcuts will show. Some of these pictures were
left unfinished; so that the mode of elaboration is distinctly seen.
It consisted in tracing out the figures and cutting them down along

FIG. 338.—Carving at Eyuk.   Plate LXIV.

the edges, which were suffered to remain straight and angular (Figs.
340 and 341). It is probable, therefore, that this slab was built
with one side against the wall, to decorate the doorway of the
outer vestibule. The lion figures carved upon the blocks in the
monumental avenue in front of the palace were similarly treated;
but, owing to their having been exposed for thousands of years
to the deteriorating influence of the elements, they are in a deplorable condition—well seen in Fig. 342, which gives a front and
side view of one of them.

Our description of these sculptures would be incomplete should mention not be made of a most curious detail, first noticed by Hamilton and Barth, our precursors in this field of inquiry.   On the inner face of the dexter-hand door-post is a carving of a

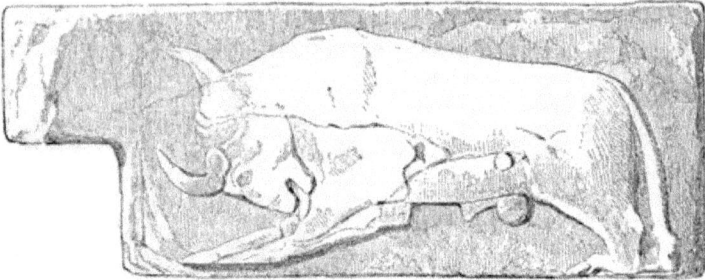

FIG. 339.—Sacrificial Bull.   Eyuk.   Plate LVII.

double-headed eagle, which is precisely similar in shape to that at Boghaz-Keui.   In each claw is clutched an animal, which from its size and long ears we take to be a hare (Plate VIII. E, Fig. 343).[1] Of the figure which stood upon it nothing remains but the end of

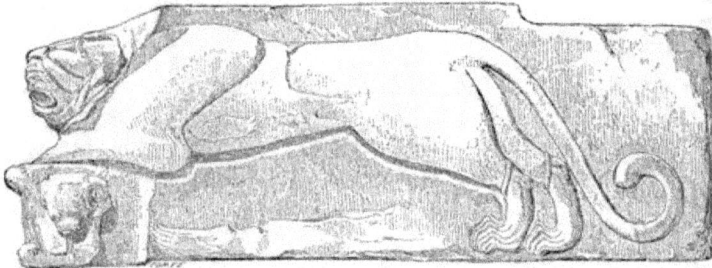

FIG. 340.—Lion devouring a Ram.   Side view.   Eyuk.   Plate LVII.

his long mantle, and a "tip-curved" shoe—the latter a significant detail unnoticed by Hamilton, both here and at Boghaz-Keui;[2]

[1] Barth thought it might be a mouse.   The modelling is so rude and indistinct that it is difficult to give a decided opinion.   We may however remark that the hare is of frequent occurrence in Hittite engravings ; that the eagle swooping down upon a timid hare was a favourite theme in Oriental art ; and that a wee mouse would have been poor game for the king of birds.

[2] But Hamilton wrote before the Hittite theory had been started.—EDITOR.

hence his supposition that "the eagle may have been a later addition." Similarity of style, however, between this and the surrounding sculpture, coupled with the part assigned to the eagle in the Iasili-Kaïa bas-relief, where it supports personages insepar-

able from the rest of the composition, have induced us to reach a totally different conclusion. Old Mahommedan traditions give the name of "Hamca" to a fabulous creature which coincides with the bicephalous eagle carved on the rocks of Pterium. Bronze coins with this emblem were struck by Turcoman princes early in the thirteenth century; the symbol was also emblazoned on the walls of their castles, and carried in their battles, figured on their flags. It was brought to Europe by the crusaders, and

FIG. 341.—Front View of Lion. Eyuk. Plate LVII.

adopted by the German Emperor in preference to the single-headed Roman eagle, from whom it has passed to Russia.

Thus a symbol that originally belonged to an Asiatic cultus of remote antiquity[1] was imported to Europe; and through a whimsical trick of fortune, the same eagle that had witnessed the

triumphal march of the Turks to the banks of the Euphrates and the Bosphorus saw them waved back at Belgrade and Lepanto.

There are details about these sculptures upon which we could not lay stress whilst endeavouring to convey

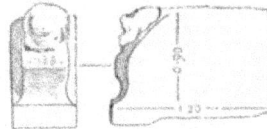

FIG. 342.—Lion in Dromos. *Exploration*, p. 342.

a general idea of them; but which point to similarity of creed with Boghaz-Keui: the lituus, for example, carried by priests (Fig. 328). and carved about animals (Fig. 341), accompanied by one or two

[1] Our information is derived from an interpenetrating suggestive article in the *Ancienne Revue Archéologique*, 1845, tom. i. pp. 91-102, by Longpérier, upon the then recent discoveries of Téxier and Hamilton. It also contains a copy of a coin struck by Malek el Salah Mahmud (1217), as well as two seals by Adalbert Beaumont, Plate CLIX., with the double-headed eagle upon them, described as : Sassanid ; one being a facsimile of the Eyuk example. This charming writer, unfortunately, is more of an artist than archæologist, and does not tell us where he met with the originals ; hence the impossibility of checking their date. We regret the omission, as it would be of some interest, in tracing the history of this symbol, to find an intermediary point between the remote antiquity of Eyuk and 1217 A.D.

small roundels, which we incline to think are but reduced copies of the discs in Fig. 330; whilst the importance of the crescent as a religious symbol throughout Asia-Minor, and seen here about sceptres, is too universally acknowledged to need further comment (Fig. 335).

The nature of the creed embodied in these images is far more difficult to unravel than at Baghaz-Keui. This partly arises from their being on a much smaller scale, and consequent soft indistinct

Fig. 343.—Two-headed Eagle.   Eyuk.   Plate LXVIII.

outline, and partly from the state in which they are found, as well as the discrepancies that here and there occur. The conjecture, however, which we think must present itself to the mind of every observer is the following: The procession, which extends on the façade and the walls of the outer vestibule, is divided into two distinct parts, which counterbalance each other, albeit each forms a perfect unit. The priests in two rows, the civilians in single file, move towards the seated goddess, seen twice on the eastern wall; whilst the bull on the left, or west, is evidently the symbol to which homage is paid. Nor should it cause surprise to find this animal in juxtaposition with the goddess, Ishtar, Anait, Cybele; for we suspect that in the ordering of this double series of pictures, the artist wished to represent the adoration of a divine couple, akin to that at Boghaz-Keui. It is even possible that, with small variants in attitude and outward semblance, they were the same deities. It should be borne in mind that in Asia divine types never acquired the fixity of forms which they assumed in Greece. Deities, in the plastic art and poetry of the Hellenes, were transformed into living creatures, each with a distinct physiognomy and special expression, like beings kneaded and fashioned by nature. Oriental art lacked this peculiar quality of the Grecian mind, and to the end its concepts floated indistinct in mid-air. Hence it happens that at a few hours from Eyuk, a warrior resting upon his club represented the male principle, whilst here the animal pre-eminently typical of virile force was selected to fill the same part. Whatever the truth may be, the principal portion in the building, which we hold to be a royal mansion, was reserved for the beardless priest or eunuch, as at Boghaz-Keui (Figs. 314 and 321). The king, however, so conspicuous a figure in Assyria, and easily singled out by his tiara and the formidable bow he wields, from amidst officiating priests,[1] is not found in the temple of either place, where we might expect to see him moving side by side with the high priest; but what is more extraordinary still, there is naught to remind us of a royal personage in the palace. To explain the absence throughout Pterium of the personage who is wont to wield supreme authority, we must suppose one of two things—either that the priest took precedence of the sovereign, or that the twofold dignity was vested in the same individual. This is mere presumption—albeit it seems to receive some weight from the words of Strabo; to the effect that the high priest of the god Mên, and the priestess of the goddess Mâ, be it in Pontus, the two Comanas, Cappadocia, Cabira, Zela or Zileh, were temporal princes as well. Like mediæval abbots and bishops, they were mostly recruited from the royal stock, and yielded to the king alone.[2] They ruled with absolute power over the temple or cathedral town, as well as the adjacent country. The peasantry cultivated their lands, and numbers of the citizens, male and female, were told off for the various services of the temple. Customs such

[1] *Hist. of Art*, tom. ii. Fig. 330.
[2] STRABO, XII. ii. 3; iii. 31, 33, 36, 37.

as these are the work of time; found only in communities that
have enjoyed a settled state of existence for long ages.

It may be that here, even before the advent of Cyrus, the priest
was almost on a par with the prince; that close to Boghaz-Keui,
the stronghold of the warrior-king, was Eyuk, an open city, the
residence of the high priest, with a palace and probably a temple.

These are hypotheses which future explorations will confirm
or invalidate. Meanwhile, we will direct our steps to another
group of ruins, indifferently described as Royal Tombs and Priests'
Sepulchres.

§ 6.—*The Necropolis.*

The large hamlet of Alajah is situated five hours' distance from
Boghaz-Keui in a northern, and three hours from Eyuk in a
southern direction (Fig. 293). It rises in the centre of a plain
watered by the Alajah Chai, which flows to the north towards the
mountains to join the Iris, where the broad level narrows into one
of those gorges of common occurrence in a hilly district. Here,
about four miles from the village, are the tombs discovered by
Hamilton as far back as 1835.[1] As we neared the mountain
ridges, we noticed that in sundry places the rocks were perforated
by caves, apparently enlarged by artificial means to serve as
domestic dwellings. Presently we hove in sight of the tomb
known to the inhabitants as Gherdek-Kaïasi (Fig. 344).[2] It consists of twin chambers of unequal size, and of different adjustment,
faced by a long porch some 2 m. by 90 c., and over 1 m. in height,
built on the side of an insulated rocky mass, detached from the
mountain range, with direction to east. It is supported by three
Doric columns of rude proportions, narrowing towards the top,
like the very early examples of this order, except that in this
instance they are accompanied by an archaic base. The portico
is approached by a flight of steps, and opens at each end into a
mortuary chamber, lighted by a small doorway and square apertures or windows cut through the outer wall. Opposite the door
of the main chamber on the left hand was an excavation several
feet deep, doubtless intended for the body of some distinguished

---

[1] *Loc. cit.*, tom. i. pp. 401, 402. Through the stupidity of his guide, Barth passed
within a few miles of these tombs, which he was looking for, without seeing them.

[2] In respect to the meaning of this word, see our *Exploration*, p. 339.

personage. Like the tombs of Phrygia and Etruria, the ceiling
of both chambers sloped at the sides. Our plan (Fig. 345)
and longitudinal section (Fig. 346) show the relative dimensions

FIG. 344.—Gherdek-Kaïasi. Ch. Chipiez, from elevation by Guillaume. Plate XXXIII.

and appearance of these apartments. The antæ to the left are
still extant, and traces of their capitals have not wholly disappeared. The ancones of the window-frame were probably
carved, but their injured condition makes this mere conjecture,
beyond which we cannot travel. The window to the right is a

simple aperture. Beneath the floor, a double chamber, now entered by a side hole, a late addition that did not belong to the original scheme, had also been scooped out. The section (Fig. 347) shows the commencement of another sepulchral memorial, which was left unfinished, as well as the talus of the hill, on the face of which the column was cut. It will be seen that the rule laid down by

FIG. 345.—Plan of Gherdek-Kaïasi.   Plate XXXII.

FIG. 346.—Gherdek-Kaïasi.   Longitudinal Section under the Porch.   Plate XXXIII.

Vitruvius [1] was strictly adhered to, the weight being thrown on the exterior line.

It is not easy to date this monument, for it may with equal propriety have been due to Hellenic influence, as it may be a primitive type borrowed by Asiatic Greeks. Pillars belonging to

FIG. 347.—Transverse Section, Gherdek - Kaïasi. Plate XXXIII.

early Grecian art, and closely resembling these, adorn the rock-cut tombs at Cyrenæ; [2] in them, however, nor in the monuments of Assyria, Egypt, and Phœnicia, so far as we know, were antæ introduced—at least, not in the way they are in this instance. On the other hand, the absence of frontel, frieze, or cornice about this portico, recalls Oriental arrangement and methods. Thus an insignificant capital alone interposes between the pillar and the entablature, which is formed of a double fascia extending along the whole porch. The lower band is a mere outline; whether this was in the original plan, as in the Persepolitan tombs, or brought about by exfoliation of the rock cannot be determined. The capital has none of the features proper

[1] Tom. iii. chap. v. Doric columns are not bounded by "vertical" lines, as was at first assumed, and as stated in the text.   It is now found that they have a convex profile.—EDITOR.

[2] Consult PACHO, *Voyage dans la Cyrénaique.*

to the Doric order, and is a plain ogee moulding, of frequent occurrence in Phœnician cornices;[1] whilst the double band of the window-frame on the left is akin to that of doorways in the tombs at Amathontis,[2] and more particularly the windows of small terra-cotta models in honour of Ashtoreth.[3] Could the carving which decorated the windows be examined, it would no doubt help us to solve the question of date and origin in regard to this structure, which in our opinion should be placed between the invasion of Cyrus and the Roman conquest. For, as stated, it was the time of the greatest mental activity of these populations, which, as a lotus flower, unfolded under the fostering care of the Italian consuls—evidenced in the countless imposing remains which everywhere occupy the sites of ancient important centres. This policy was continued by their successors; and almost all the inscriptions that have been found are written in the inferior Greek which characterizes the Lower Empire. It is self-evident that the tomb known in the place as Kapoulou-Kaïa, "pierced," "holed stone," belongs to the time of the Cæsars; be it from the architectonic disposition of its façade or the central medallion of an Apollo in true Græco-Roman style.[4] This in no way applies to the sepulchral memorial of Gherdek-Kaïasi, which is wholly devoid of elements, decorative and otherwise, such as would furnish a clue to the student upon its possible date and origin. Had it been encountered on the Euxine or the Mediterranean, rather than in the heart of Cappadocia, there would be little difficulty in viewing it as one of those composite structures which hold a middle course between two styles, and are distinctive of all early Grecian art, ere it laid aside imitation and invented forms of its own of unsurpassing beauty.

Careful and close analysis of the data which are before us will oblige us to choose between two alternatives: either we must place the monument we are considering somewhere about the Macedonian period—but against this are elements about the porch that are absolutely insurmountable—so that we are driven by the force of circumstances not to separate this from cognate monu-

---

[1] *Hist. of Art*, tom. iii. pp. 124, 125, and Fig. 63.
[2] *Ibid.*, Figs. 153, 154.   [3] *Ibid.*, Figs. 208 and 641.
[4] *Explor. Arch.*, p. 351; Plate XII., fig. 293. In it Kapoulou-Kaïa is described as a tomb on the south-west of Alajah, midway between Iatan-Kavak and Deirmen-Deresi.

ments in Pteria, and class it among those that were erected before the campaign of Crœsus, *i.e.* coeval with the princes who resided at Boghaz-Keui and Eyuk.[1]   At any rate, there can be no two opinions with regard to this monumental sepulchre being as perfect a specimen and as picturesque as any to be met with in Asia Minor or Greece herself.   Its position at the head of the ravine, with its grand background of rocks streaked with crimson red, set aglow by the sun, that seems always to be shining on the porch, impart to it an air of magnificence that it would not have in a different light.

On the left hand is another tomb, almost destitute of ornament. It is entered by a plain rectangular doorway, or, rather, it may be approached by a ladder; for, owing to the smooth surface of the perpendicular rock, nothing else will meet the case, as we had occasion to learn.   Needless to say that in this secluded spot it was an object not to be procured.   As at Kapoulou-Kaïa, here also is a subterraneous passage which connected the terrace, 8 or 10 m. high, with the bottom of the ravine occupied by the torrent. Other stairways, open to the sky, conducted from the platform to the summit of the pinnacle, yielding no room for fortifications; indeed, we found no traces of structures anywhere.   The only possible explanation for their presence in this and other instances— from Alajah to Kutchuk-Yamili, for example—is that they led to natural caves, inhabited by the natives, seated side by side with the tombs of the dead; the friable schistose stone could be easily pierced and the grotto enlarged for either purpose.   In fact, there was here, as in many other parts of Asia Minor, a troglodyte group, that used these winding paths, now obliterated, for ascending to lofty caves, which have become inaccessible.   They were the lanes of these peculiar hamlets.

[1] Compare Gherdek-Kaïasi with Dikili-Tach, "raised stones," so called because of a tall column, formed by a number of superimposed drums, the sole fragment of a Byzantine building, perhaps a church, to judge from the style and inscription preserved on the pillar.   The antæ, and stout columns tapering towards the top, one on each side of twin sturdy pillars composing the portico in front of the sepulchral chamber, seem to be of more ancient date, save the frontel, which belongs to an earlier Greek style.   Whether the massiveness of these supports was due to the forethought or ignorance of the builder, there is no doubt that it admirably harmonizes with the rugged surface of the cliff out of which they are carved.   This monument was published and described by Téxier in *Description de l'Asie Mineure*, in folio, tom. ii. pp. 84, 85; Plates XCII. and XCIII.

§ 7.—*Industrial Arts in Pteria.*

The nature of the stone documents recovered in Pteria bears on too narrow a plane to do more than to aid us to form some small idea of its military, civil, and religious architecture. For although its statuary is represented by upwards of a hundred figures, these —except here and there, in attitude and costume—were conceived and executed on precisely the same pattern. Metal, wood, and terra-cotta objects, found in such abundance in the old graves and sites of ancient buildings of Egypt, Mesopotamia, and Syria, which were so helpful in gauging the industrial arts of those countries, and which enabled us to pick out imported from among native productions, are hard to find in this instance. Besides, these pictures, as we observed, lacked from the outset the sharp, fine outline, the precision of detail which the Ninevite artist was able to impart to the more delicate material he had to work upon. Such as they are, however, they and they alone can tell us what was the dress, the weapons, furniture, and personal ornaments in vogue with the old Pterians.

The costume undoubtedly belongs to a people whose civilization had reached the stage when classes are sharply defined—evidenced in difference of apparel—albeit these natives lagged far behind the Assyrians in taste, luxury, and habits of daily life. The popularity which the short tunic seems to have enjoyed (Figs. 313 and 315) was no doubt due to its being found convenient in a mountainous district; but how inferior to the elegant magnificence of the Assyrian mantle, with its deeply fringed embroidered border! The only ornament about the priestly robe is a plain band; sometimes, indeed, as also in the female dress—scarcely less simple—the skirt of the high priest and winged genii was plaited (Plate VIII. D). Nor was the headdress less plain; it consisted of a tight-fitting cap, or a pointed tiara, the latter with variants already referred to (Plate VIII. B, and Figs. 313, 314); whilst a tall circular cap, without a single exception, seems to have been the female head-gear. As at the present day, one and all were in all likelihood of felt, the manufacture of which is still in favour in this goat-rearing district; the hair or wool is used in their fabrication, as well as in the making of abbas, carpets, and the like, in hand looms set up anywhere—a shed, courtyard, or

in fine weather, along the roadside near the village. The export
is in the hand of the Greeks, whose commercial instinct is, as of
yore, very remarkable indeed.

The character of their defensive arms was in harmony with their
other industrial productions; these were broadswords with crescent-
shaped hilts, double-headed axes (Fig. 313), clubs ending in a
huge knob (Plate VIII. E), or scimitars (Fig. 319). It is possible,
though not certain, that a shield was intended in Fig. 338. Bronze
coats of mail, and helmets, of frequent occurrence in late Assyrian
monuments, were unknown to the Pterians, nor were they familiar
with leggings. If we have no shield in Fig. 319, this may have
arisen from the ignorance of the artist, whose resources were not
equal to placing it among the serrated figures. On the other
hand, to judge from the rest of the equipment, if a shield was used,
it was no more than a wooden board covered with a bull's hide.
The presence of crooked staffs (Figs. 314 and 328), necklaces,
earrings, wind and string instruments (Figs. 331, 332), no less
than the art of putting together pieces of wood for making ladders,
chairs, tables, of quaint but agreeable aspect (Figs. 332 and 337),
elaborate œdicula (Figs. 311 and 314), testify that the old native
artificer had learnt the chief secrets of his handicraft; that he no
longer confined himself to hammered work and simple forms, but
knew how to cut, pierce, chisel, rivet, and solder metals together
into complicated designs, etc.

Certain elements about these œdicula—the pointed cap, and
peculiar ornament on the dress (Fig. 314), but in a special degree
the phallic emblem (Fig. 331)—seem to indicate indigenous invention, for it is quite certain that they did not originate in Mesopotamia or Phœnicia. Granted our premiss in respect to these
details, the conclusion cannot be doubtful or its importance contested. As often observed before, the metal-worker draws his
inspiration from architecture, and his forms are frequently reproduced or suggested by the monumental buildings he sees around
him. The peculiar column, too, may be called composite; some
of its features, the absence of base and its convex outline, for
example, recall early Doric, whilst the double spiral or volute about
the capital is decidedly primitive Ionic in character. But it lacks
the refinement, the beauty of detail, the taste and feeling evidenced
in the Erechtheium, on the Acropolis at Athens, where the elegance of the volute, the Assyrian honeysuckle below it, the egg-

and-tongue moulding, form as exquisite architectural details as are anywhere to be found, in striking contrast with the ill-proportioned, elliptic capital of our pillar, which seems crushed out of all shape by the superimposed weight. Nevertheless, if the Ionic column and its capital were introductions from Asia, and all tends to prove it, we must recognize here the primitive form adopted by the Ionian Greeks, purified by them into a far more beautiful order than ever existed in its native home. Persia is out of the running, for when her monuments were erected, the great epoch of Hellenic art had begun. Besides, the volute in the capital at Persepolis and Corinth, is only introduced as a secondary member, subordinated to the bulls' heads and foliated ornament which distinguish them. By reference to Assyrian pillars,[1] it will be found that in many essentials they are nearer to the Pterian than the Ionic column. Of the first, some have bases; an abacus interposes between the volute and the architrave, and the astragal is sometimes replaced by a triple torus which recalls the deep collar about the Erechtheium.[2] On the other hand, the shaft of the Khorsabad column is smooth, but though rudely carved, there are unmistakable traces of flutings about the Pterian style. They yield, in fact, two variants of what may be called Proto-Ionic or Primitive Ionic. Both have volutes as chief members of the capital, astragals below the capital and bases, whilst in both all the parts found in the Ionic style are likewise found, and, except in beauty of execution and detail, the same forms and feelings pervade them. Henceforth, properly to comprehend the origin of Grecian art, we shall have to give the same attention to the columns in the Iasili-Kaïa bas-reliefs, as to those of the Tigris valley.

Bearing in mind the principle laid down by us, it will be readily admitted that the œdiculum figured on the cliff was a reminiscence of a monumental façade; the hollow of the bay being replaced here by an idol, there by a symbol. The sphinxes at Eyuk were taken from Egypt, and the function of guarding the doorway was entrusted at Boghaz-Keui to Assyrian bulls, set up beside strong supports, the forms of which were derived from metal, but could be imitated in stone. A frontispiece for a temple or palace, not devoid of dignity, might be restored from the data furnished by these œdicula, which seem to have been preserved for the purpose

---

[1] *Hist. of Art*, tom. iii. pp. 218-222, Figs. 71, 75, 76-80.
[2] *Ibid.*, tom. ii. Figs. 41, 42.

of showing that the Pterian architect disposed of greater resources than these ruins seem to imply.

Thanks to the care taken by the sculptor to imitate art objects, justly admired for their execution and the material employed, we can form some idea of the skill of the native silversmith ; but we have no such instance to guide us in our appreciation of their earthenware.   For although the art of the potter is the oldest and most prolific of all handicrafts, its very popularity causes it to be viewed with disfavour, as of small account, and its shapes are not likely to be reproduced in more precious materials.   Nevertheless, clay, when it is properly burnt, will resist destruction better than natural stones or metals ; and long burial in the ground will not injure it—abundantly proved by the prodigious number of vessels that have been found all over the world, in tombs and in the ruined cities of prehistoric peoples, wherever excavations have been made.   That Cappadocia forms no exception to the rule is shown by the quantity of broken pieces of vases and pottery that strew the ground within the area of the palace at Boghaz-Keui. We collected enough to fill a case, but unfortunately it was among the items that miscarried in our home journey.   If my memory serves me right, these fragments were all of unlustred yellowish clay, ornamented in simple geometric patterns, in dull colours of red and brown, quite distinct from Greek ceramics of any period. We had, however, forgotten their very existence, when going over the Jerusalem examples (Figs. 244, 245, 246, 247, 248) suddenly revived our recollections of them.

It should be stated in this place that the only vessel figured in the Pterian sculptures is evidently a bronze bowl, and closely resembles the multitudinous specimens that have been unearthed in Assyria (Fig. 337).   To him who can penetrate beyond the surface, the humble fragments of pottery heaped about the base of the ruins of ancient Pterium go a long way to confirm the testimony of Herodotus, in regard to the destruction of the town by Crœsus, an event which virtually arrested the onward progress of civilization for centuries.

§ 8.—*General Characteristics of Pterian Monuments.*

The conventional forms and symbols carved upon the rocks of Cappadocia, in so far as they are cognate with those familiar to us

in the great Eastern countries of the world, including Egypt, may
be read at once as in an open book ; just as we deciphered the
Hittite sculptures of Kadesh and Carchemish.   The tall figure
of the god (Fig. 320) recalls Dagon or Oannes, worshipped
throughout Mesopotamia ;[1] and although the actual type (Fig. 316)
has not been met up to the present hour in Assyria, examples of
analogous combinations are not rare, notably in the presentment
of Nergal, the man-headed lion, mighty hunter, war-god, etc.[2]
Winged figures, too, are abundant, and eagle-headed deities ;
Nishroch, for example, or the lion-headed, as Figs. 315, 316, are
plentiful.   Again, bulls, antelopes, lions, and many more, which
here serve as supports to gods and goddesses, are often introduced
in Assyrian sculptures and engraved gems ; indeed, every part
found in the Tigris valley, be it mitred bulls, female types, down
to the proto-Ionic pillars, finds its counterpart in Cappadocia
(Figs. 313, 314, 321), with this difference, that the Nineveh
column is somewhat less archaic in character.[3]   To these may be
added the custom of placing flowers in the hands of royal personages (Plate VIII. E) ;[4] stout clubs, double-headed axes, winged
spheres (Figs. 314, 321), the latter being encountered throughout
the East, fully exemplified in our former volumes.[5]   Nor is the
impression left by the Boghaz-Keui sculptures effaced when we
come to Eyuk :[6] the bull engaged in deadly conflict with the lion,
which forms so conspicuous a feature in the art of Anterior Asia,
where, from Chaldæa to Persepolis it had a symbolic significance,
is replaced in Fig. 340 by a ram ;[7] and the rabbit figured at
Nineveh as devoured by eagles and vultures is despatched by a
lion at Eyuk (Fig. 343) ;[8] whilst Ninevite ivories exhibit women
who in some respects recall our seated goddesses (Figs. 280, 281,
337).[9]   The Eyuk example, above all others, resembles the queen
at Kûjûnjik,[10] carved side by side with Asur-nat-sirpal ; the

[1] *Hist. of Art*, tom. ii. Fig. 224.   [2] *Ibid.*, Figs. 114, 278 ; 8, 343.

[3] *Ibid.*, tom. ii. Figs. 6, 7, and Figs. 310, 313.

[4] LAYARD, *Nineveh*, vol. ii. p. 463, Plate LI.

[5] *Hist. of Art*, tom. ii. pp. 310, 313, 223, 224, 280, 281.

[6] *Ibid.*, Figs. 75, 76, 78, 79 ; 29, 235, Plate X.   RAWLINSON, *The Five
Monarchies*, vol. ii. pp. 64, 65.

[7] *Hist. of Art*, tom. ii. Figs. 246, 273, 338, 407, 443 ; tom. iii. p. 652, Figs. 475,
476, 544, 624.

[8] *Ibid.*, tom. ii. Fig. 409.

[9] *Ibid.*, Fig. 247.

[10] *Ibid.*, Fig. 273 ; see also Fig. 14, representing goddesses carried in a procession.

attitude and movement of the hands, the one holding a bowl and
the other a flower, are precisely alike. Then, too, on one of the
bas-reliefs at Nineveh, figures are seen scaling the wall of a
besieged city by means of ladders on which they figure in exactly
the same clumsy posture as at Eyuk (Fig. 332), showing that the
skill, or rather want of it, was pretty evenly balanced in both
artists.[1]

Perhaps no set of rock-cut monuments come nearer the Pterian
examples than those at Bavian and Malthai, north of Mosul, both
in details and general character, be it in the mixture of human and
animal forms (the former standing on real or fantastic feræ), the
large rings about sceptres to facilitate their carriage or suspension ;
with this variant, that in the Bavian group the object furnished
with a hoop was a fan.[2] As might be expected, Assyrian altars
are more elegantly shaped than at Eyuk (Fig. 328), but both are
top-heavy.[3]

If the art of Boghaz-Keui and Eyuk is so often in touch, to
a certain extent this was due to the same models having been
used ; nevertheless it should not be overlooked that it possesses
features unlike any observed by us in this and former works,
In the dearth of our knowledge with regard to the architectural
buildings of Cappadocia, it would be futile to try and form an
opinion on the subject. But, as stated earlier, the mode of defence
that prevailed was essentially different from that of Anterior Asia ;
nor did the Pterian builder go to Assyria for the rock-cut tombs
which distinguish the Alajah Chai valley.

The old Assyrians excavated canals and cisterns in connection
with their rivers and streams, they carved inscriptions and pictures
on the rocky hill-side, but I am not aware of their ever having
scooped funereal chambers out of the solid rock. The hypogees
of Egypt, on the other hand, were too far removed to induce the
belief that they could have been borrowed from thence. This
does not apply to sphinxes, whose type, impressed upon clay or
metal art-objects, and small pieces of furniture, was scattered
broadcast by the Egyptian and Phœnician artificer at enormous
distances from its native country.

These instances, meagre though they be, are all we can offer in
regard to the Cappadocian style of architecture ; but no matter how

[1] Botta, *Monuments de Ninive*, Plate XCVII.
[2] *Loc. cit.*, Fig. 310.   [3] *Ibid.*, Figs. 108, 109.

scanty, they enable us to gauge its real nature, and to perceive that if quick in availing itself of foreign elements, it did not, on that account, abdicate its modicum of originality and inventive genius.

Sculpture, whereby the peculiarities which permit Pterian monuments to be classed in one distinct group, yields richer material to the student.   Many are the characteristic details which distinguished it; but of these none, we venture to say, can vie with the double-headed eagle at Iasili-Kaïa (Plate VIII. E, and Fig. 343), a type which we feel justified in ranging among those proper to Cappadocia, since it was unknown to Assyria, Egypt, or Phœnicia.   Its position is always a conspicuous one—about a great sanctuary, the principal doorway to a palace, a castle wall, and so forth; rendering the suggestion that the Pterians used the symbol as a coat of arms plausible, if not certain.   It has been further urged that the city was symbolized by it, that the place called by the Greeks, Pteris, Pteria, Pteron, "wing," was the literal translation of the name it bore with the aborigines, that in a comprehensive sense it came to signify the whole district, the country of wings, *i.e.* of numerous eagles, "double-headed and wings outstretched."[1]

Another feature, only seen at Boghaz-Keui and Eyuk, is the augural rod (Figs. 314, 321, 328), and the bar outlined in front of the figures at Iasili-Kaïa and Eyuk, which is not unlike a staff in shape, and serves to support the arm (Plate VIII. and Fig. 328). The long, pointed cloak, trailing behind like a bird's wing, is likewise peculiar to Cappadocia (Figs. 314, 321, 328).   As referred to, the posture of the personages is appreciably the same.   With the short tunic it was almost impossible to conceal the arms; but the peculiar movement imparted to them, the one outstretched, the other bent back beyond the line of the body, under the cloak or chasuble, could be distinctly seen (Fig. 328).   Having attained this much, the artist seems to have been quite satisfied, and never to have looked further afield for a more artistic arrangement.   The hair of the female figures at Boghaz-Keui and Eyuk is invariably worn loose (Figs. 313, 328); but the pointed tiara, the broadsword with a moon-crescent hilt, are found at Boghaz-Keui only (Plate VIII. and Figs. 312, 321).   This, however, is no conclusive proof of their not having obtained in

[1] BARTH, *loc. cit.* p. 45.

the former place, and may have been due to the discrepancies alluded to in the last section.

The general style and make which distinguish Pterian monuments are no less characteristic and distinct. They betray summary, rapid handling, rather than bold elaborate manipulation ; the articulations lack the precision, the surety of hand, which form so remarkable a feature in Assyrian sculpture. The modelling is of the simplest description ; but this we feel was due to want of technique, and not to subtle arrangement and refinement. As with the art of Assyria, here also the body was always covered, so that a general outline and apportioning of broad masses were alone aimed at ; but these are not wanting in truthfulness and fidelity. The absence of the stirring scenes of the chase or hot affrays may have been due to the destination of these bas-reliefs ; more particularly, however, to the unskilfulness of the sculptor, whose experience and training were utterly inadequate to the ordering of such complex compositions as these imply. Here and there, the limbs of his figures are massive, and almost always dumpy ; in this respect also his work resembles that of the Chaldæo-Assyrian artist. But, unlike him, he never attempted to portray violent, contorted postures ; although he is not devoid of ingenuity and rhythmic sequence in the grouping of his multitudinous figures.

The difference in detail and fabrication which distinguishes the Boghaz-Keui as against the Eyuk sculptures cannot wholly be attributed to the material employed having been a friable schistose in the one instance, and a hard trachyte in the other. The sculptured basaltic stones of Northern Syria prove that the native artificer could cope with the difficulty and was provided with suitable tools for the purpose. The deduction to be drawn from the works at Eyuk, which reveal widely different qualities of workmanship, is that the craftsmen who executed them were possessed of less technique than their neighbours. The rams driven to the sacrifice, the bull preparing to butt, are designed with spirit and vigour ; the latter would favourably compare with Assyrian work (Figs. 334, 339). On the other hand, if the priest and priestess in the procession are just passable, it is difficult to imagine aught more barbarous than the musicians and tumblers ; the drawing is below criticism, and would disgrace a mere stripling (Figs. 331 and 332). The bas-reliefs at Boghaz-Keui are a decided improvement upon these, and evince greater freedom and accuracy in their elaboration. If the animals introduced as accessories in the central bas-relief are conventionalized into mere heraldic emblems (Plate VIII. E), and carelessly sketched in, the lions that decorate the throne, the heads about the city gate, are modelled with a vigorous hand, albeit in somewhat bulky proportions (Figs. 297, 298, 303), and decidedly superior to the Eyuk exemplar (Fig. 341). This difference is even more marked in the treatment of the human form; which is almost arbitrary at Iasili-Kaïa, where the figures ring no change in their attitudes. But whilst we feel that the art is still in swaddling clothes, we are conscious that it has out-stepped the rude Eyuk stage, the contemplation of which is apt to call up a smile; whereas, in the former locality, some personages (Figs. 320 and 321) are already invested with elements of beauty.

Such instances lead to the inference that Eyuk is older in date: whether this should be counted by years or centuries it is hard to say; but the presumption is that a wide space divides the two monuments. This our conjecture is based upon the superiority of the Boghaz-Keui sculptures; but more particularly upon the fact that Egyptian interference, still in full swing at Eyuk, had yielded the palm to Assyria at Boghaz-Keui.

Not to weary the reader with vain repetitions in regard to the fortunes which attended the existence of the Hittites as a nation, we refer him to a former chapter on the subject, and will confine ourselves to the statement that their acquaintance with Egypt, whether as invaders, friends, or vanquished, was of a nature to arouse in their breasts the utmost admiration of which their mind was capable; i.e. when brought face to face with the architectural splendour which everywhere met their gaze. Some reflex of the impressions they thus received were embodied—so far as the resources at their command would allow—in the monuments of Cappadocia and Syria. Agreeably with this theory, the Eyuk palace, with its sphinxes and lion avenue, would be coeval with the Ramessides. On the other hand, the terraces at Boghaz-Keui, in front of the palace (Fig. 294), the mitred bulls and the like (Figs. 314, 321), recall Nimroud and Khorsabad. The ascendency of Assyria began to be felt beyond the two great streams about the ninth century A.C., i.e. on the formation of the second empire. In this lapse of time, extending over 340 years, to the advent of Cyrus (560), should be placed the Iasili-Kaïa sculptures. It is

possible that they are later than the palace and the wall of the
neighbouring city; perhaps they were just finished when Crœsus
turned the country into a wilderness.

The closer we examine them, the clearer is the conviction forced
upon us that they are not of remote date; but that they represent
the most felicitous effort of the primitive civilized tribes that
inhabited Asia Minor, the development of which was arrested by
the rapid growth, the prestige and all-invading art of Hellas,
whose types and methods finally bore down adverse opinion and
opposition.

We have now gone over Pterian or Cappadocian art, if preferred, in its bearings with the civilization of Anterior Asia, and
such claims as it may have to be considered original. One side
still remains to be sifted, namely: are there beyond Asia Minor
monuments that bear a closer affinity to those of Cappadocia
than these do to the stone documents of Assyria? Do we know
of a group connected with the Pterian by analogies at once so
intimate and special as to suggest the idea that they were the
work of one people? And is the comparison likely to throw light
on the origin of the creators of these palaces and bas-reliefs?
Will it aid us to identify the Pterians of Herodotus, with one of
the nations accounted great in the old world long before the
Greeks entered upon the scene? A first gleam of light is found
in community of written signs. We called attention to a character, ⊕⊕, of frequent occurrence in the Hamath inscriptions;

FIG. 348. — Hit-
tite Hieroglyphs.
Iasili-Kaia.

and which, slightly modified, reappears at Iasili-Kaia.[1]
It should be noted here, that when our photographs
and drawings of the sculptures under discussion were
taken, their importance and the issues involved in
the hieroglyphs accompanying them were not even
suspected. Hence we were not as solicitous as we
should be, and as everybody is at the present hour,
to seek and tabulate with the utmost care any vestige,
however minute, of such emblems left on the wall of
enclosure. In order to supplement our deficiency in
this instance, we have reproduced the more accurate sketches
kindly forwarded to us by Mr. Ramsay (Figs. 348, 311). The first
shows three signs in front of a figure on the right hand side
(Plate VIII. F), and the second, besides the prefix of divinity

[1] *Hist. of Art*, tom. iv. p. 636.

reproduced by us, has a mule or ass's head; a character often repeated in the Hamath and Carchemish inscribed stones (Fig. 256).[1]

If this mode of writing is only represented by insulated characters in the sanctuary of Boghaz-Keui, it is not so in the town itself, where to the south of the palace, and close to it, I lighted upon an inscription of ten or eleven lines carved on a rock sloping upwards. The field on which the bas-relief occurs is 6 m. 50 c. by 1 m. 70 c. in height; it has been chiselled and prepared for the work, but the rest of the rock surface remains in its natural state. The inscribed characters are sharply defined by dividing lines, and both are in cameo; the height of the symbols is about 15 c. Owing to the damaged, confused state in which they are found, which is quite as bad as that of the cognate monuments (Figs. 254, 255, 256), we at first were uncertain whether we had before us a series of narrow friezes—a supposition induced by the human, animal, and other forms therein contained—or letters of an unknown alphabet. If, on the one hand, the inscription is so obliterated that not a single sign can be identified with those of the Syrian monuments, its arrangement, manipulation, and general aspect at a short distance render it undeniable that we are confronted by a Hittite document of the nature of the Hamath, Kadesh, and Aleppo inscribed stones. As stated, the fact that a number of signs met with in Syria have not been encountered in Asia Minor may arise from the dearth of monuments in the latter country, and the mutilated state in which they are discovered; but nothing forbids the supposition that, as in the alphabets derived from the Phœnician, here also, local forms prevailed. Notwithstanding minor and altogether secondary distinctions, affinities are sufficiently striking to justify the hypothesis we uphold, *i.e.* that as the same style of epigraphy is observable from the Orontes to the Halys, this implies a common origin and culture in the tribes to which it belongs.

[1] Those interested in the subject will find all the names of the deities in the inscriptions at present known, in a pamphlet by Professor Sayce, entitled, *The Monuments of the Hittites*, pp. 8–11, after the plates of various authorities, including our own. In it the learned professor expresses the opinion that the characters denoting a deity (Fig. 311), the prefix and the hand of the female figure, are alone distinctly shown in the cut.

Excellent casts of these bas-reliefs exist in the Berlin Museum, and it is to be hoped that with their aid the whole question will be reconsidered and finally settled.

Nor is this our only means of testing the near kinship which connected the Pterians with the Hittites of the Naharain; we can likewise prove our thesis by comparing the costume, accessories, methods, arrangement, and peculiarities which stamp the two styles of art. We need not insist upon the "turned up" Hittite boots at this time of the day;[1] but we may remark that nowhere is this national feature more emphasized than in this region (Fig. 337). Variants in costume, which may be called local, exist from one monument to another; but if we take the whole of Syria and Cappadocia respectively, we shall always find that such diversities occur in both. Each is distinguished by the short tunic (Figs. 269, 279, 282, Plate VIII. *passim;* Figs. 331, 332, 335); the Assyrian mantle (Figs. 262, 277, 279, Plate VIII. D E); the long flowing robe (Figs. 269, 276, 278, 282, 314, 321, 328, 333); the straight pointed tiara (Figs. 269, 276, Plate VIII. *passim;* Figs. 319, 320); or round cap (Figs. 262, 269, 282, 314, 321, 328). Whether we picture to ourselves the Kheta, as figured in Egyptian sculptures, or in the rare national works still extant, they are never represented except as soldiers lightly armed. With them, defensive armour, which formed so important an item in the equipment of the Assyrian soldier, was and remained of the most elementary character. They are figured as having fought bareheaded (Figs. 259, 349), or with no better protection than a felt hat; and without shield, cuirass, or leggings (Fig. 352).

We pointed out that some figures at Eyuk were closely shaven, all but a piece on the top of the head twisted into a pigtail that falls behind (Fig. 336). Now, among the barbarians fighting in the ranks of the Kheta, against Ramses at Kadesh, some are portrayed with this identical appendage by the Egyptian carver; others have the front part of the head shaved, but the hair is suffered to grow at the back and sides (Fig. 349). The female dress on the Merash stela (Figs. 280, 281) and at Iasili-Kaïa (Plate VIII.) is pretty well on the same pattern, and consists of a loose robe which reaches to the ankles. These points of touch hold good in regard to the furniture; in Syria and Cappadocia, goddesses are seated on high chairs fitted with footstools (Figs. 280, 337), in the one hand is held the usual bowl, in the other a flower (Figs. 280, 281, 337). Again, the lion is an equally favourite subject in the valley of the Pyramus, the Iris, and the Halys,

[1] *Hist. of Art*, tom. iv. pp. 562–564.

where he is set up, with mouth wide open, in front of palaces (Figs. 275, 340, 341, 342), carved on the city gates (Figs. 301, 303), and in the interior, or the chief ornament about the throne (Fig. 298), whilst in pictures dealing with the spiritual world, the abode of deities, he serves as pedestals to these (Fig. 313), finally at Saktchegheuksou, kings show their prowess by shooting lions (Fig. 279). In fact, wherever we turn, we are confronted by the

FIG. 349.—Hittite Warriors. ROSELLINI, *Monumenti*, Plate CIII.

king of the forest, in as many different aspects as the Hittite artist could command.

Correspondence in workmanship is no less striking and suggestive to the student. If we omit a certain class of monuments, in which Assyrian influence is specially noticeable, no two sets of monuments could be more alike than the Merash stela and the Eyuk slabs, the Iasili-Kaïa sculptures and those at Sinjerli and Carchemish (Fig. 269). What we said with regard to the mode of art production in Pteria is fully applicable to the monuments we are considering. Here, too, hasty execution, flat relief, a proneness to attenuate the contour, and suppress the inner model, invest the pictures in question, even when subjects and forms are borrowed from Assyria, with an impress foreign to the Tigris valley.

The points of touch we have indicated, the resemblances we have verified, lead to a conclusion which will long ere this have been anticipated, *i.e.* of an intimate link of parentage having existed between the Syrian Hittites (whose history we have almost entirely restored from Oriental documents) and the early inhabitants of Cappadocia, whom we only know from some passing words of Herodotus, and the meagre remains of their plastic art. These Western Hittites were a branch of the Syro-Cappadocian stock, a race of emigrants that we recognized on the northern and southern slopes of the Taurus and Amanus, as far as the edge of the Mediterranean, and the vast regions which stretch away to the Euphrates, including the eastern portion of the central plateau, on to the right bank of the Halys, whence they gradually spread over the whole peninsula, leaving everywhere traces of their passage and settlements. The influence they exercised on the religion, writing, and arts of tribes weaker and inferior in culture will be dealt with in a subsequent chapter, when we shall inquire as to the share they contributed to the general stock of knowledge and progress in that remote antiquity, be it as mediums or inventors, and which Hellas transmitted to the modern world with the stamp of her own genius.

CHAPTER IV.

ART MONUMENTS OF WESTERN HITTITES.

§ 1.—*Plan of Study.*

THE art productions which mark the presence of the Hittites north of the Taurus, and on the left bank of the Halys, may be divided into structural and sculptured. These may be subdivided into mutilated statues, inscribed stones, rock-cut pictures or chiselled slabs; including small objects, such as clay seals, cylindrical and conical in shape, which still preserve the impress left by the stamp, to which may be added bronze figures and jewellery. With regard to the first class, they could not be removed, and therefore still cover the site on which they were raised. But great difficulty is experienced in trying to localize the others, for as they were intended for exportation, their size, material, and make were such as could be conveniently carried to enormous distances from their native country, hence the exact spot where they were first discovered cannot with certainty by traced.

We propose to take up the principal monuments of the first category, whose presence on any given point proves that the race which built them was settled for a longer or shorter period in the district where their ruins are found. Respecting the smaller portable documents, wood, clay, or metal, the origin of which is more or less open to criticism, it will be readily admitted that regions in which they occur in great abundance are more likely to have given them birth than localities where their presence is almost unknown. It should also be noted that we were careful to select such specimens, out of the thousands we possess, as had claims to be considered as types on account of the hieroglyphs and the forms which distinguish them, and which bring them in touch with those of Pterium and Northern Syria.

§ 2.—*Hittite Monuments in Phrygia.*

Some of the monuments we are about to describe were found in
the province which, about a century before our era, began to be
called Galatia, from the bands which settled in it after their discomfiture at the hands of the kings of Pergamus. It is a name
that we shall not adopt, but will adhere to the old appellation,
inasmuch as we are concerned with an age when these tribes
were not.

Phrygia consists of that tract of land which extends from the

FIG. 350.—The Kalaba Lion. *Exploration*, Plate XXXII.

left bank of the Halys to the lower course of the Sangarius, the
Hermus, and Mæander, on to the western edge of the Anatolian
plateau. "The Halys," wrote Herodotus, "is the line of demarcation between Cappadocia and Phrygia."[1] The early Greeks
connected likewise the Phrygian empire and the myths pertaining
thereto with the Sangarius valley.[2] Now the monuments which
will occupy our attention for a while, are thickly distributed about
the springs which feed the Sangarius.

The large town of Angora, ancient Ancyra, became the capital

[1] Herodotus, i. 72.   [2] Homer, *Iliad.*, iii. 187 ; xvi. 719.

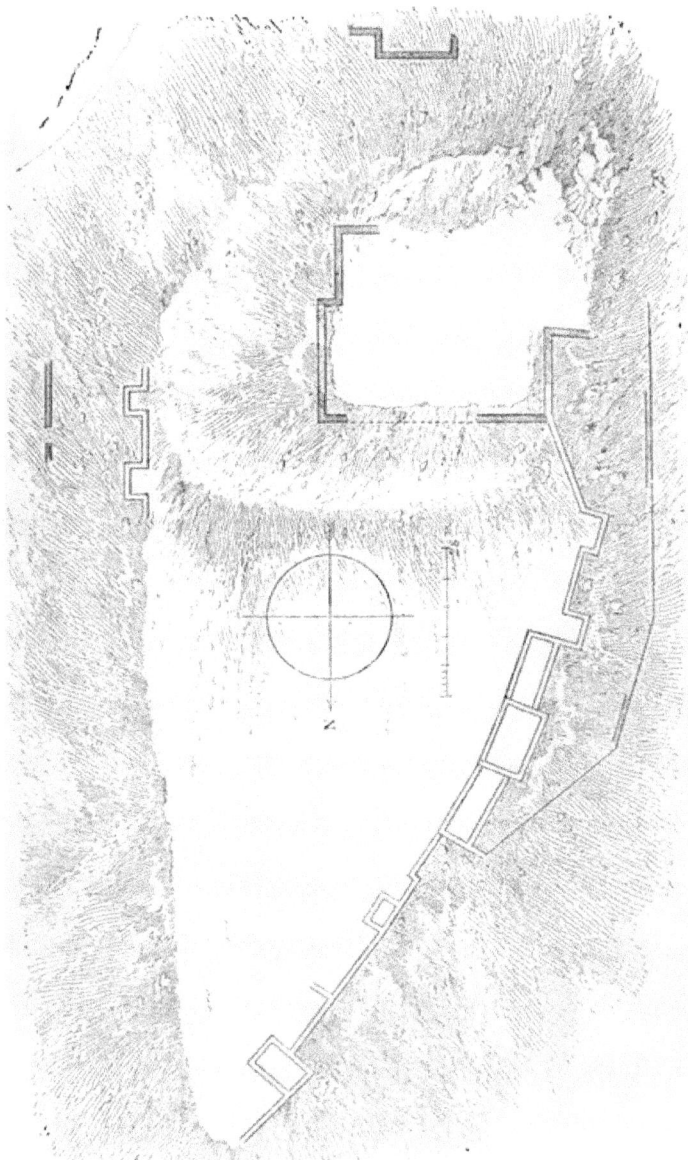

FIG. 351.—Plan of Ghiaour-Kalessi.   Plate IX.

of Galatia at the time of the Macedonian conquest ; and was said
to owe its foundation to the Phrygian Midas. It is possible,
nevertheless, that when the Phrygians arrived here the insulated
hillock on which stands the present citadel had long been occupied
and strengthened by the aborigines.[1] It was an important centre
under the Romans ; its population is even now considerable, and
stated to equal that of the largest cities of Asia Minor.   Ancyra
has often been destroyed, and rebuilt as many times from its
ancient materials ; hence its antiquities cannot be carried beyond
the Roman age.   The only monument of remote date is the lion
shown in the annexed woodcut (Fig. 350), which we had the
good luck to discover. The slab on which it stands has been used,
along with other old blocks, to build a fountain by the roadside,
at the edge of the site occupied by the Alpine hamlet called
Kalaba, about two kilometres east of Ancyra.[2] Following the
knoll, some yards above the fountain, is a sepulchral chamber
excavated in the centre of the rocky wall. We were at first
inclined to believe that the stone on which the lion is carved had
been used to close the tomb ; but careful measurement of opening
and slab caused us to change our view ; for the latter exceeds the
height, and is 17 c. wider than the actual aperture, so that it could
never have been a proper fit. Moreover, the chamber shows no
trace of outer decoration. It is probable that the stone under
notice formed part of the exterior casing in some important
edifice, as at Sinjirli (Fig. 269), Saktchegheuksou (Fig. 279), and
Eyuk (Figs. 328–338). This is one reason for believing that the
lion stood where we found him ere the Thracian tribes reached
the country.   As far as our knowledge extends, there are no data
to warrant the assumption that the chiefs of these tribes built the
palaces, the exterior and interior walls of which were ornamented
at the base by sculptured plinths ; but we have positive proof that
the Hittite builders of Cappadocia and the districts bordering on
Assyria borrowed this disposition from the older culture of the
Tigris valley.

In our estimation, the work of the Kalaba lion tells this tale even
more explicitly. As in Assyria, the body is elongated, the drawing good and characterized by knowledge of the animal form. It
is vastly superior to the Kumbet lions on the tombs of the

[1] G. PERROT, *Exploration Archéologique*, Plate LXIX.
[2] See photograph, Plate XXXII., *Exploration Archéologique*.

Phrygian kings,[1] which rank as the most successful efforts of
Phrygo-Hellenic art, and so distinct that nobody could think for
a moment that the two sets of monuments had emanated from the
same people. We feel that in the Kalaba lion the artist was very
near his Assyrian models; notably the modelling of the head and
limbs. The work is at once original and striking, albeit it lacks
the elaborate finish which long practice had taught the Ninevite
sculptor to bestow on the minutest detail. If opinion may be
divided in respect to this specimen of old art, it will not apply to
a monument which we discovered in the district of Haimaneh,
some nine hours on the south-west of Angora, hard by a village
called Hoïajah, which rises on the site of the ruins known to the
natives as Ghiaour-Kalessi, "the fortress of the infidels."[2]

Ghiaour-Kalessi occupies the summit of a truncated hill, which
overhangs a narrow gorge with a copious stream, along which
runs a path, probably the old road which in former days connected
Ancyra with Pessinus, calling at Gordium. The highest portion
of the hillock forms a fort or dungeon, rectangular in shape, 16 m.
by 34 m. It is partly surrounded by a wall of rude masonry. The
stones are laid together without cement and in irregular courses;
but where the escarp of the rock is almost perpendicular, this
mode of defence was not resorted to. The thickness of this and
other walls about the hill averages one metre. The rest of the
area describes an isosceles triangle about 125 m. long. The wall
seems to have been constructed with regular rather than polygonal
masonry; for its upper surface, now level with the ground, is
perfectly horizontal. On the west side are remains of structures
with no greater salience than the surrounding wall, which may
have been towers. Similar in character was another outer wall,
traces of which are visible in places. It extended in front of the
fortress, but its relief was greater than that of the upper rampart,
and distant from it 10 m. to 30 m. The stones, though massive,
one measuring 1 m. 98 c., and another 1 m. 20 c., are smaller than
those of many city walls in Greece, Tiryns, and even Mycenæ and
Samicon for example. The blocks had been thoroughly prepared,
but joints as well as courses are irregular (Fig. 352).

Taken by themselves, these ramparts have no better claim to
our consideration than scores of like description. The interest
which attaches to them is due to the twin figures carved upon the

---

[1] Perrot, *loc. cit.*, Plate VIII.   [2] *Ibid.*, *loc. cit.*, Itinéraires, Sheet F.

FIG. 352.—Ghiaour-Kalessi. Sculptured Figures on Wall of Fortress. Plate X. Drawn by Guillaume.

sinister hand of the hill-fort entrance. In height they average
3 m. each. To judge from outward appearances, the one is a smooth-
faced youth, whilst the beard and spirited attitude of the other
indicate a man in the vigour of life. The figures are clad in short
tunics, fastened at the waist by a belt, in which is stuck a broadsword. They are apparently without leggings; but the feet are
encased in "tip-tilted boots." On the head is a tall pointed cap
or hood falling behind so as to cover the neck and shoulders. A
flat band runs round the tiara of the elder man, with an ornament
in front akin to the Egyptian uræus. The figures walk in the
same direction; the left arm is pressed against the body, as if to
keep in place some object, now indistinct. The dexter arm is
outstretched, as though indicating some point towards the horizon.
The right hand of the elder figure is broken.

The reader will long ere this have noticed that these figures
bear a striking resemblance to scores at Iasili-Kaïa. The slight
innovations which are observable in this instance, the hood for
example, may have been a country fashion introduced for convenience sake; but the shape of the tiara is not destroyed by it
nor by the uræus by which it is adorned; and all the difference
about the sword consists in its being carried at the side, in full
view, instead of falling behind. Last, not least, the execution of
these figures is precisely the same as that of cognate sculptures in
Pteria and the Kalaba lion; as reference to plan (Fig. 352), which
we were first in publishing, will show.

The differences which we have enumerated are of small moment,
and may be explained on the basis that the monuments at Iasili-
Kaïa and Ghiaour-Kalessi were due to different hands. Each
artist, whilst reproducing the main lines and character of the
national costume, superadded details of his own creation. Hence
these figures may be identified with the Hittite warriors in the
procession at Iasili-Kaïa, save that their demeanour is nobler and
such as would not disparage deities. But to what end and how
came these colossal figures to be carved in this lonely spot, spared
too and cared for by several generations of men which succeeded
each other in the country? To these questions we have no solution to give, and all we can offer is the following hypothesis,
which is plausible, if nothing more: these warriors, whose bold
outline is plainly seen from the road below, were the heroic leaders
of advancing irresistible bands, which first occupied the pass and

erected this remarkable fortress. This gave them the command
of the outlying country and the regions to the west, which they
seem to indicate with their outstretched hands. The uræus about
one of the figures is sufficient proof of his royal dignity ; the other
was the elder, or at all events a favourite son, wont to head the
young blood in quest of adventures and wild affrays. Their
sculptured image near the pass they had so often defended, whence
they had sallied forth to harry the land to the very edge of the
great sea, was intended as a memorial to subsequent generations,
and in part would account for their having been preserved.

The Hittite remains, stated to exist in the vicinity of the
tombs of the ancient kings of the Phrygians, somewhere between
Koutahiah and Sivri-Hissar, will be treated in a separate study.
For the present, suffice it to say, that in a valley of rocks, full of
tombs and catacombs, rises a stony hill, the summit of which was
levelled out, and apparently transformed into a vast high-place.
Structural fragments, perhaps of the sanctuary which once rose
here, may still be traced. Its approaches were covered by a
citadel, almost entirely excavated in the solid rock. Fortunately
for us there is no difficulty in tracing to their true owners the
monuments under notice, for they bear upon them inscriptions,
and the names of some of the Phrygian kings, written in characters
akin to the archaic Greek alphabet, and in a language closely
related to the Hellenic. But whether the Hittites were already
in possession on the arrival of the Phrygo emigrants, and whether
the place was dedicated by them to the great mother of the gods,
Cybele, the Matar Kubile of the Phrygian texts, is not so easy to
say. At all events, sculptured on a rocky wall, is a figure
apparently more ancient than the images carved on the neighbouring stones (Fig. 353).[1] It seems to be a priest standing
before an altar ; he holds up a primitive lituus or staff, surmounted
by a ball or globe, out of which issue twin horns. The position
of the arms, the short tunic, and round cap recall Pterian figures,
albeit the resemblance is not so striking as at Ghiaour-Kalessi.

The most curious point about this image is the staff, which is
quite unique of its kind, since, so far as we know, not one has been
met with of precisely the same pattern, either in Cappadocia or

[1] This figure has been described by Mr. Ramsay, in the *Journal of Hellenic Studies*,
tom. iii., in a paper entitled, "The Rock Necropolis of Phrygia," pp. 9, 10, Plate
XXI. B.

Syria. The surface of the stone is much defaced, so that characteristic details, which are so helpful in tracing the origin of any
decoration, are absent or at any rate nearly all obliterated. The
only data we have for connecting it with Cappadocian art are
the peculiar signs above the altar in front of the figure. One
of these is the representation of a bird, a hieroglyph which is

FIG. 353.—Carving at Doghanlou-Deresi. After Ramsay. Height, 71 c.

perhaps oftener repeated than any other in the inscribed stones
of Hamath, Ierabis, Aleppo, etc. The next character to which
I would draw attention is the cap, which it will be remembered
was likewise found upon the lintel of an old doorway in Cilicia
(Fig. 274).[1] Nor is this all; close to where this sculpture was
discovered is a tumulus, out of which Mr. Ramsay unearthed an
inscription with undeniable Hittite hieroglyphs.[2]

[1] See also last line of inscription, Fig. 256.
[2] Mr. Ramsay, in 1882 (*Journal*, etc., tom. iii. p. 10), had not made up his mind
as to the position of the sign under notice; but he is now in favour of a Hittite

The number and variety of the monuments left by the Phrygians in this district, which was transformed by them into a great religious and political centre, may be the reason why Hittite vestiges are so rarely encountered. For the Phrygians were well known for their fanaticism with regard to their great goddess Matar, and as the most unlikely people to tolerate alien shrines. Hence the old sanctuaries may have been destroyed to make room for the new. However that may be, the Kalaba lion, the figures at Ghiaour-Kalessi, and the hieroglyphs near the tomb of Midas suffice to prove that the Western Hittites crossed the Halys, and were long settled in the valley of the Sangarius or Sakkara.

§ 3.—*Hittite Monuments in Lycaonia.*

The Hittites of Cappadocia, whose capital was in Pteria, penetrated to the central plateau by the lower course of the Halys and the road which passes through Ancyra. But the flow of immigration was far more active from Cilicia, for on this side the highlands of the Taurus could be reached through the long defile known as Cilician Gates. The movement may also have been due to fresh arrivals, and consequent pressure for elbow-room. In fact, close to this pass at Tyana and Ibreez, and throughout the southern portion of the Anatolian plateau, Hittite monuments are more plentiful than in Phrygia ; and not a few are accompanied by characters of the nature of the Hamathite inscriptions. Dana, or Tyana, was an important place at a remote period. We find its name in Assyrian inscriptions, in the itinerary of Xenophon, and as the chief town of Cappadocia under the Roman empire.[1] It stands on the very border of Cappadocia, in a plain which is the prolongation of the broad Lycaonian level. Here Mr. Ramsay, in 1882, noticed in the house of a Greek merchant a slab, with a

origin. His opinion and the reasons he adduces may be read in a letter (January 4, 1886, to the same journal) of great interest— for no one better than he is qualified to speak on the subject. He would likewise range in the same category the colossal ram carved upon a rock near the bas-relief reproduced by us. We are reluctant, however, to commit ourselves to a decided opinion, in the absence of an inscription or even a good drawing, which would enable us to judge of the workmanship.

[1] The site is only a few miles from Bor, a town marked in Kiepert's map. It is also found in Hamilton's.—Editor.

seated bearded figure and high square cap carved upon it.[1] Above
the personage is an inscription of four lines in Hittite hieroglyphs,
but which differ from similar characters of the Naharaim in that
they are incised instead of being in relief.   The other monument
alluded to was discovered in the neighbourhood of Ibreez or Ivriz,
about three hours south-east of Eregli, ancient Kybistra, almost
on the borders of Lycaonia.   Ibreez stands at the foot of a hill, to
which it has given the name (Ibriz-Dagh), and is one of the spurs of
the Bulgar-Dagh, whose innumerable ridges are among the loftiest
of the mighty Taurus range.   Torrents, fed by copious springs,
descend from the woody heights, interspersed with patches of
green corn and herbage, gay with flowers, blue, red, and yellow ;
with fine walnuts, which grow wild ; with plum and fig and all
manner of fruitful trees ; whilst the slopes converging to the banks
of streams and rivulets are clad with vineyards.

The monument (Fig. 354), which in future will form the chief
attraction to the village, was noticed by Otter in 1736 ; but Fischer
was the first to make a drawing of it, which he communicated
to Dr. Kiepert, who has published it in Ritter's great work [2]
(*Erdkunde*, iii. 18 ; *Asia Minor*, vol. i.).   It has since been visited
by the Rev. E. J. Davis, who has published a circumstantial
description, together with a good drawing of it.[3]

The bas-relief was again visited by Ramsay in 1882, who, whilst
he acknowledged the excellence of Mr. Davis's sketch, pointed out
details in the costume which had been overlooked by the latter.
The omission was doubtless due in part to the visit of the reverend
gentleman having occurred in the rainy season, when the stream
which washes the base of the cliff on which the figures are carved
had risen much above its ordinary level, so that some of the signs
were invisible.   Hence the task of making a proper drawing is
not one easily accomplished ; for even in the dry season the feet
of the larger figure are only about 2 m. 50 c. above water-mark,

[1] Mr. Ramsay's hasty sketch has been published in WRIGHT's *Empire*, Plate
XV. See also Professor Sayce's letter to the *Academy* (Aug. 5, 1882), in which he
details the circumstances which prevented Mr. Ramsay from obtaining a careful copy
of the monument.

[2] RITTER, *Kleinasien*, tom. i. Plate III.

[3] DAVIS, "On a New Hamathite Inscription" (*Trans. Soc. Bibl. Arch.*, vol. iv.
p. 336). Mr. Davis is the author of two books on travel : *Anatolica*, published in
1874 ; and *Life in Asiatic Turkey*, which contains a drawing of the monument under
notice, but which I have not seen. The letterpress, notably on Pisidia, is far
superior to the drawings.

while the width of the canal interposes between the investigator and the sculptures. Consequently measurements must be achieved by guesses and dint of comparison.

FIG. 354.—Carving at Ibreez.   After Davis and Ramsay.

As at Iasili-Kaïa, that portion of the rock which was destined to receive the carving was alone prepared for the work; all the rest was suffered to remain in its natural state. The monument consists of two colossal figures of unequal size, cut in relief, not exceeding 10 c. The larger figure is about 6 m. 8 c., and the smaller 3 m. 60 c. The subject is not hard to grasp. It seems to portray a priest or king offering prayer or thanksgiving to a deity : a god it would seem combining the attributes of Ceres and Bacchus. As is well known, difference of height, in all primitive art, serves to indicate difference of station. The god is clad in a short tunic, turned up in front and behind in a kind of volute ornament ; in his outstretched left hand he holds some ears of bearded wheat, cultivated at the present day in the country. The stalks reach the ground behind his left foot, which is stepping forward, and a vine stem is between his feet, the tendrils of which are gracefully arranged about his waist, alternating with foliage and large clusters of grapes, his right hand holding the extreme end.

The " Baal of Tarsus," before the introduction of Grecian types, was similarly represented. On a coin of that city, surmounted by a Semitic legend, supposed to date from the Persian age, we find him figured in the attitude of a Greek Jove ; his sinister hand holds a sceptre, and the other carries a bunch of grapes (Fig. 355).

FIG. 355.—Silver Coin of Tarsus. HEUZEY, *Les Fragments de Tarse*, Fig. 2.

To return. "The expression of the face," writes Mr. Davis, "is jovial and benevolent, the features well indicated, especially the high aquiline nose, the lips are small and not projecting, the short moustache allows the mouth to be seen." Whether due to inadequate drawing or not we cannot say ; but we have failed to detect the joviality referred to. On the head of the god is the distinctive tiara ornamented with horns, the emblem of strength with the Assyrians and Greeks, and tip-tilted boots on the feet, bound round the leg and above the ankle by leather thongs. The legs from the thigh are bare, the muscles of the calf and knee well delineated. Around the waist is a richly ornamented girdle, probably of metal, with carved parallel lines, which form the " herring-bone " pattern. It will have been observed that the costume of the principal figure is exactly that of the Hittite heroes and deities at Ghiaour-Kalessi and Iasili-Kaia. The claim of the god to be distinguished above his fellows is not in gorgeous attire, but in his superhuman height ; compared to which

the next figure looks like a pigmy. To compensate for this, however, the artist has evidently taken great pains to reproduce on stone
every detail and minutiæ of the silken embroidery, the heavily
fringed robe, and rich apparel of an Eastern monarch.   On his
head is a low, rounded tiara, with an ornament in front of precious
stones, such as is still worn by sultans and rajahs.   A loose robe
reaches to the ankles, and over it is thrown an embroidered shawl
or κανάκης.   The whole costume is ornamented by designs
derived from squares, lozenges, stars, and so forth; which recall
similar forms about the tomb of Midas, intended to represent an
elaborate carpet.[1]

So far as profuse display of drapery and precious stones, in the
maze of which the artist lost the dominant lines, allows us to judge,
the embroidered mantle was secured round the waist by a massive
girdle set with precious stones, hidden at the side by the arm,
but well outlined in front.   A broad collar or necklace is about
the neck, apparently made of rings or bands of metal, through
which is passed a heavy triple chain; probably imitated from a
gold or more likely a silver ornament, since the silver mines
of the Bulgar Maden are in the neighbourhood of Ibreez.   The
arms are bare up to the elbow, above which is seen a plain armlet.
The figures, according to Mr. Davis, have no earrings; whilst Mr.
Ramsay's account is the other way.   The crescent-moon symbol
on the breast of the priest, if intended for a clasp is, to say the
least, very awkwardly placed.   Of the two, the figure of the priest
betrays greater inexperience on the part of the artist; who in
his endeavour to portray the hands folded in the act of prayer,
was unaware that when raised they would be parallel one to the
other; consequently that which is towards the spectator is alone
seen, if we except two fingers of the other hand.

Conflicting feelings are experienced in presence of a work in
which Assyrian influence is so much more distinct than in cognate
sculptures of Cappadocia; in that good design and great skill
in detail—be it in the articulations, the profile of the faces, showing
the hooked nose of the Semites, the beard and hair crisply
curled, which, more than aught else, remind us of Khorsabad and
Kujunjik—should be associated with so much that is rude and
archaic, and only encountered in the earliest manifestations of
Chaldæan art.   Nevertheless, no one versed in such matters will

[1] Téxier, *Asie Mincure*, tom. i. Plate LVI.

dream of attributing this bas-relief to Assyrian hands; not to
speak of distinct features of the national costume—conical cap,
short tunic, and curved boots—which have never been seen on
bas-reliefs or cylinders of the Tigris valley expressly, as it were
to remove doubt, if doubt were possible, characters are carved
in front of the god and behind the priest, of the same nature as
the inscribed stones at Hamath and Merash.   Besides the two
legends referred to, there is another text below the bas-relief, just
above the present water-mark.   A curious point about these
hieroglyphs is this: that in the last line of the inscription relating
to the god is the determinative prefix Φ of a deity.   Mr. Davis also
heard of another inscription carved upon the solid rock on the
summit of a hill, about midway between Bulgar Maden and
Tshifteh Khan, of which no detailed account has come to hand.
The inscription consists of five lines, much injured; some of the
characters however that have been copied show that it was
Hittite.[1]

Within the last few years, monuments of undeniable Hittite
origin have been signalled on the west of Lycaonia; where once
were important cities, such as Isauria, perched on the top of the
loftiest ridge of the Taurus range, with the plain of Konieh,
Iconium, extending away to other mountains; with Laodicea Com-
busta, Ladik, and Tryæon Ilgun, and others of ancient fame.   In
the middle of a plain, somewhere between Ilgum and Yaïla of
Kosli-Tolu, rises a small artificial mound, out of which a calcareous
tablet, 80 c. high, by 1 m. 79 c. in length, has been unearthed.[2]   One

[1] Bulgar Maden is west-south-west of Ibreez, high up in the mountains, where
the Ibiz Chai takes its rise.   These indications are taken from Professor Sayce, " A
Forgotten Empire" (*Fraser's Magazine*, August, 1880, pp. 223–233), where he
refers to another Hittite monument, stated to exist by M. Calvert at Frahtin, not
far from Ibreez.   It is rock-cut, and portrays a large figure in tip-curved shoes
and pointed cap, having on his left two worshippers much smaller, accompanied by
Hittite signs.

[2] I published this inscription in the *Revue Archéologique* (3ᵉ série, 1885, tom. v.
p. 262), from a copy of Dr. Maryan Sokolowski, Professor at the Cracow University.
He formed part of the scientific expedition twice sent out at the expense of Count
Charles Lanckoronski, for the express purpose of collecting materials towards an
exhaustive description of Pamphylia.   This having been achieved, the members
extended their journey to Pisidia and Lycaonia; though brief, the visit was not
barren of results.   They have added one more text to the Hittite collection ; together
with an excellent account and almost accurate drawing of the Eflatoun monument,
which had not been visited since Hamilton.   Mr. Ramsay repaired to the place in
1886.   He sent me a copy of his drawing of the stone, which seems superior to
Sokolowski's ; and it is to be hoped that it will ere long be given to the world.

side is covered by Hittite characters in cameo, divided by raised bars in three parallel lines. The plain is traversed by a bank, which may cover a stone wall foundation; the superstructure, undoubtedly of crude bricks, has long disappeared. Mr. Ramsay heard from the natives of multitudinous old ruins in the neighbourhood; his time, however, was too short to allow him to verify the report. But we may be sure that a general survey would yield fruitful results.

Nine miles on the north of Bey-Sheher (ancient Caralis, Caralitis) are the springs of Eflatoun, also called Plato's Fountain. Hamilton was the first to visit the monument, which he describes as "very curious and very ancient, built on the side of a circular hollow in the limestone, round which numerous fresh-water springs rise in great abundance, forming a small lake, from whence a considerable stream flows rapidly into the lake of Bey-Sheher" (Fig. 356). His views with respect to the monument precisely coincide with ours.[1] During my campaign in Galatia, I was unable to extend my investigations so far afield; but ever since I have lost no opportunity of calling the attention of travellers bound for Asia Minor, to Hamilton's remarkable passage. Unfortunately, Eflatoun lies outside the usual road taken by travellers; so that very few have sufficient time or money at their disposal to undertake so long a detour. Mr. Ramsay, with Sir Charles Wilson, paid a flying visit to the ruins; and his drawing, which he was good enough to communicate to me, bears visible signs of hurry, and is not more explicit than Hamilton's. I had well-nigh given up all hope of being able to procure efficient information on the subject, when I received a letter, accompanied by a number of capital drawings done in sepia, from Dr. Maryan Sokolowski, which I forthwith published in the *Revue Archéologique*.[2] Since then photographs of the monument have been most kindly forwarded to me by Mr. John Haynes, taken in 1884, during the "Wolfe Expedition to Asia Minor," of which he formed part.[3] In the

---

[1] Hamilton, *Researches*, tom. ii. pp. 350–351. Nobody seems to know, or have cared to inquire, how this spring came to be called "Plato's" Fountain.

[2] *Revue Arch.*, 3ᵉ série, tom. v. pp. 257–264; Plates XI., XII.

[3] See "Preliminary Report of an Archæological Journey made in Asia Minor, 1884," by M. Sterrett. The report has been published by the Archæ.-American Institute, which has recently founded the Archæ.-American School at Athens, of which M. Sterrett is a member. With regard to the "Wolfe Expedition to Babylonia," undertaken before that of 1884, read the account which appeared in the *Revue Arch.*, 3 série, tom. viii. by M. Ménant.

FIG. 356.—Eflatoun-Bounar. By Maryan Sokolowski.

summer of 1886, Mr. Ramsay returned to Eflatoun-Bounar, in order to examine at greater leisure the stone document afresh. In his opinion, the Polish explorer has not faithfully rendered what is written on the stones. He confesses, however, to the work being so worn and stained in many places of the façade—nearly all that now remains—that it is almost impossible to decipher what was really carved upon it; and we know that in doubtful cases, photography should be supplemented by "touch." Whilst we fully admit that M. Sokolowski's drawings may require emendation, we give them the preference as on the whole the more complete of the two sets.

The district in which these ruins occur is a dreary albeit undulating plain. The monument now only consists of two wall sections, built of gigantic blocks of trachyte, cut and bevelled at the edges with great nicety; the one forms an unpierced façade, whose base is washed by the flood; and the little that remains of the other is at right angles with the first (Fig. 357). This wall would be meaningless, unless we assume that it originally served to enclose the space behind the façade, where everything points to a rectangular chamber having formerly stood there. It was entered by a doorway let into the back wall. At this point a number of ancient blocks lie about the ground, as will be seen in our sketch; and Mr. Ramsay noticed one which was built in the dyke. The construction of the latter was in all probability effected with stones taken from the monument; which from this and other causes has been reduced to one-third of its original size. The rectangular chamber which interposed between the twin walls was roofed over. Among the stones strewing the ground is one which formed part of a window-case. An animal, probably a lion, was carved upon its lower portion; from which we may infer, says Mr. Ramsay, that a frieze composed of animals ran along the whole length of the wall above these openings, with outlook towards the hill.

Part of this decoration might be recovered, were search made among the blocks accumulated here or built in the dam. For the present, we must be content to study the best-preserved side, which faces the lake or south. The height is 3 m. 85 c. by 6 m. 83 c. in length.[1] The inner facing has still fourteen blocks turned to

---

[1] These are Mr. Ramsay's measurements, and they practically agree with Hamilton's. The seven metres specified by M. Sokolowski, are evidently due to some confusion in his notes.

a dark brown by age and exposure; they are of different size, but well dressed and admirably fitted together. One point to be noticed is the huge top monolith, on which is carved a globe, with outstretched wings, slightly bent at the extremities, as though the better to cover the figures sculptured underneath. The stone though gigantic (22 ft. 5 in. long), was not sufficiently large to receive the whole disc, so that it was carried on to a smaller stone now disappeared. A double-winged globe, necessarily smaller, was repeated under the topmost, but the wings, instead of being curled downwards, were slightly raised at the ends. The two sets of winged discs formed a kind of rude entablature, supported by a square pillar on either side. The space between the pillars was occupied by two other stones, and eight more completed the façade.

Each block is occupied by a figure in considerable relief, averaging even now from 25 c. to 50 c. The widest divergence of opinion exists in respect to the relative attitude of the pictures under discussion. For example, on the pillars, our drawing shows two full-length pictures with raised arms, whilst in Mr. Ramsay's they are seated. The sole detail to be made out in the photographs are the low, rounded cap and pointed tiara of these two figures, which recall the headdress of the Eyuk sphinxes, e.g. the characteristic head-gear of Hathor.[1] On the central stone, third from the right next to the water, our cut has a much defaced figure, and Mr. Ramsay sees in it an altar with base and cornice. The two upper corner blocks are the least injured, hence sepia drawings and photographs are for once agreed in their portraiture, and the costume they have given us corresponds in every particular with that of Boghaz-Keui (Plate VIII. D and E), and vividly brings to the memory Assyrian bas-reliefs. It is the same flowing mantle, which covers one leg and leaves the other bare from the middle of the thigh, allowing the short tunic to be seen. The heads are very indistinct, so that it is hard to say whether they were originally provided with caps or not, and the wildest supposition is possible. The detail on the top of the head (Fig. 358), for instance, may be taken for a round cap or modius, as specified by Mr. Ramsay, or, as we incline to think, for the hair of the personage, whose attitude, notably the uplifted arms and position at

[1] The detail seems to be pretty distinct, since M. Sokolowski describes it as a "rounded cap."

FIG. 357.—Side View of Eflatoun-Bounar. Drawn by Sokolowski.

the entrance of a sacred edifice, suggest the Iasili-Kaïa demons (Figs. 315, 316). In this hypothesis the figures of the façades would be repetitions of the same type.[1]

These portraits, like cognate examples in Egypt and Assyria, were drawn full face down to the middle, but imperfect skill in perspective caused the artist to chalk in the lower limbs in profile. The fact that we find here the same conventional treatment as in the Nile and Tigris valleys is no indication of its having been imported, but in this and other instances it was due to lack of knowledge. The points of resemblance, if any, are rather with the art productions of Pterium. Should our conjecture be confirmed and raised to the rank of established facts acquired to science, namely, that all the figures of the façades belong to the dæmonic type which guard the adytum entrance at Boghaz-Keui (Figs. 314, 321),[2]

the no less important fact would naturally follow of community of art between
Cappadocia and Lycaonia. If the imperfect state of our knowledge does not
permit a categorical answer, no one will
deny that the costume we find here is
practically the same as in Fig. 358, which
we described as a variant of the Hittite
national dress.

FIG.   358. — Eflatoun - Bounar.
Corner Figure. Drawn by Wallet,
from a photograph.

It everywhere consists of a short tunic,
with or without mantle ; a round or
pointed tiara, as seen on the colossal
figures of the façade, whose size and
position point them out as the chief local
deities. In fact, every part made familiar
to us by the sculptured and architectural remains at Eyuk and Boghaz-Keui is here reproduced, be it the well-dressed stones with bevelled edges, even to the characteristic turned-up shoes, a bit of which, on the testimony of Mr. Ramsay, is still perceptible on the stone (Fig. 358), but which our cut does not indicate.

---

[1] M. Sokolowski has placed about the waist of all these pictures the short sword made familiar to us by the bas-reliefs of Cappadocia, whilst no sign or mention occur in the photographs and detailed notes which were forwarded me by Mr. Ramsay. I am bound to say that some imagination is required to detect it in the photographs.

[2] Professor Sayce points out that the winged sphere at Eflatoun recalls that which surmounts the head of a figure, which we take to be a king, on one of the Birejik stelas.

This monument stands absolutely alone in that its construction throughout was effected with massive stones, some of gigantic size, hence we cannot compare it with analogous structures in Cappadocia in trying to determine its probable destination. Like the remarkable sculpture at Ibreez, this temple was raised on the very edge of the flood, to the god, it would seem, of fresh-water springs, who brings in his wake an abundance of corn and wine and all manner of good things. Was the corresponding figure of the tall god, made taller by his cap (61 c. high), a priest, as at Ibriz, or a goddess, the mother and wife of the god, as at Iasili-Kaïa? The altar, stated by Mr. Ramsay to intervene between the twin figures, would coincide in the most admirable way with our hypothesis. But the defaced state of the monument, whose decay is hastened by the wind beating on its face and its proximity to the water, renders it more than problematical whether we shall ever know more in respect thereto than we do at the present hour.

In support, too, of this conjecture is the discovery, made three years ago by M. Sterrett, of a huge stela on which four figures, in good preservation, are carved in very high relief, sometimes 70 c.[1] The stone lies prostrate on the ground near Fassiler, a village on the south-eastern boundaries of Lycaonia and the district of Isauria. The stela, whose top is rounded off, when standing, measured 7 m. 23 c. in height by 2 m. 75 c. at the base, and 1 m. 65 c. towards the top. The lower portion is sunk into the soil, but above ground its thickness is 82 c. It cannot be easily set up, by reason of its enormous weight; consequently no photograph was obtained; and as the mission was not provided with a draughtsman, apart from exact measurements, a rough sketch or rather diagram, showing the relative position and outline of the figures, was alone attempted.

The subject represented on the stela consists of twin lions, back to back, cut in low relief on the lower portion of the stone; whilst the front part projects beyond it, with a relief of 60 c. Between them are two colossal figures of different size, the taller standing on the head of the other. The personage who serves as living support or pedestal is clad in the usual long robe, the hands are folded high up on the breast and support the chin, and on the

---

[1] Fassiler is not marked in Kiepert's map. It is five hours east of Seidi Sheher, and seven south-west of Eflatoun, on the high-road taken by caravans to Konieh.

head is a mural crown.[1] The top figure, on the other hand, wears
a short tunic, conical tiara, and four raised bosses are carved in
front.   The right arm is raised as though in command ; the left
is bent, and carries some indistinct object.   The face is broad,
the eyes round and protruding, the ears large.   The feet were
omitted as a superfluous detail ; for when the stone was in place
they could not be seen from below.   Some idea may be formed
of the truly gigantic proportions of these portraits, when we state
that the cap of the upper figure is 1 m. 20 c. in height.

There is every reason to believe that the subject represented
on this stela was a divine couple, as that which moves at the head
of the procession at Boghaz-Keui, with this difference, that the
figures are superimposed, instead of standing side by side (an
arrangement imposed upon the artist by the narrow field at his
command) ; that the lions which generally support the goddess,
recognizable by the mural crown she wears, are on the same plane,
one on each side of her.[2]   But the dress and attributes which are
seen here are precisely the same as at Iasili-Kaïa.   It is much to
be wished that a good drawing or cast may soon be obtained
of this interesting monument ; or, better still, that the actual stone
may be conveyed to Europe and placed in one of our museums,
where it would be accessible to the whole world.

As will have been observed, Lycaonia seems to have had peculiar attractions for the Hittites ; and both in the neighbourhood
of the silver mines of the Bulgar-Dagh, as in the broad levels,
are found numerous instances of their presence.   These, as we
pointed out, sufficiently resemble Syrian and Cappadocian sculptures to warrant the theory of a common origin.   The inhabitants
of Lycaonia were removed from the Greeks of the coast by broad
masses of lofty mountains and deep morasses ; whilst the hilly
district to the south-east about Isauria was held by predatory
tribes, whose usual occupation was to harry the land of their

[1] Opinions are divided with regard to the head-gear under notice M. Sterrett
sees in it a helmet, and Mr. Ramsay, who visited Fassiler a few months ago, is
equally positive as to its being a mural crown, like that worn by the goddess and
her train at Boghaz-Keui. His letter (Aug. 8, 1886), which was accompanied by a
sketch of the same nature as M. Sterrett's, reached me too late to be reproduced,
had I wished to do so.

[2] Mr. Ramsay is at one with us in viewing difference of arrangement solely in the
light of a curious variant. Wholly improbable is the belief held by M. Sterrett, that
both were male figures.

neighbours. Hence it came to pass that the language, the customs, and culture of this region continued till a late age; and when St. Paul visited Derbe and Lystra, the inhabitants spoke a dialect which was unlike Greek.[1]   Profoundly affected though they may have been by Hellenic civilization, they never entirely relinquished their traditional methods, as reference to the annexed woodcut will show (Fig. 359).[2]   The monument, doubtless a funereal

stela, was found by Téxier some fifty years ago, built in the modern city wall of Konieh.   It is the portrait of a warrior with a Greek helmet, *e.g.* furnished with crest, nose-piece, and end at the back to protect the neck.   He holds a pitchfork in his sinister hand, and in his dexter a scimitar, which may be compared with the Boghaz-Keui example (Fig. 319).   A bronze coat of mail reaches to the middle of the thigh, leggings and knee-pieces protect his legs, and his feet are encased in tip-tilted shoes, laced in front.   A circular shield completes his armour.   In this presentment of the Lycaonian warrior are characteristics which at once recall the earliest sculptures of this region; nevertheless, if the modelling was faithfully rendered by Téxier, centuries divide it from those at Ibreez and Eflatoun.   The legend permits

Fig. 359.—Stela at Iconium.   Téxier, Plate CIII.

us to date this monument before the Macedonian conquest; for it contains letters of the syllabaries of Lycaonia, Lycia, and Caria, which had preserved a considerable number of characters of an older syllabary in order to express sounds not provided for in the simpler Greek alphabet.

[1] *Acts* xiv. 2.
[2] When Téxier (whose account is the only one we possess) saw the monument, it still preserved traces of colour, notably a red fringe under the shield.   It was doubtless destroyed soon after Téxier's visit, for it has been sought in vain by subsequent travellers.

Fig. 360.—General View of the Karabel Pass, showing Bas-Relief carved on the Rock. Le Bas, *Voyage Arch. Itinéraire*, Plate LIX.

§ 4.—*Hittite Monuments in Lydia.*

Lydian monuments have often been mentioned in these pages in connection with cognate examples encountered in Phrygia and Lycaonia. It was known that these provinces had long been under Hittite influence, hence remains of their art might be expected to exist here as in the other localities which had formerly owned their sway. Nor were the hopes of the learned world doomed to disappointment. In 1874, Mr. Davis was travelling in Asia Minor, and, in an out-of-the-way corner of Phrygia, he came to a village called " Karaatlu," hard by the lake Salda or " Salt," within a·short distance of the head springs of the Lycus. Whilst resting a few hours at this place, he had pointed out to him some stones, which on examination turned out to be an ancient bas-relief, consisting of two erect figures—very much worn, yet sufficiently clear to enable Mr. Davis to pronounce them "unlike Greek work, but closely resembling the rock-sculptures at Ghiaour-Kalessi."[1] Unfortunately, no drawing was made of the monument. Two other bas-reliefs, due to the Hittites or a people nearly related to them, are reported from a place near Smyrna ; and are supposed to be the so-called figures of Sesostris, specified by Herodotus.

One of these pseudo-Sesostris was discovered by Renouard so far back as 1834 ; and a copy by Téxier was presented to the Académie des Inscriptions in 1839.[2] It is indifferently called the Nimphi or Karabel warrior ; the former appellative is due to a village hard by, the Nimphæum of the Byzantines ; the latter, to an isolated house which gives the name to the important pass leading to the plains watered by the Hermus and the Cayster. It is the figure of a man carved upon a calcareous boulder of rock, which overhangs the ravine, some 50 m. or 60 m. deep (Fig. 360). The mass of greyish white stone forms a bold foreground, and agreeably contrasts with the dark green of the forest-clad range

---

[1] *Anotolica*, p. 135.

[2] Only to cite circumstantial studies consult TÉXIER, *Description*, tom. ii. pp. 302–308, Plate CXXXII. ; KIEPERT, *Archæ. Zeitung*, tom. i. p. 33 ; DE MOUSTIER, *Voyage de Constantinople à Ephèse* with the *Tour du Monde*, tom. ix. p. 266. The latter traveller was the first who photographed the monument ; but his figure is deformed, owing to his having placed his camera at the side instead of in front of it. The striking resemblance it bears to the Pterian sculptures was forthwith pointed out by Kiepert, as well as the error of attributing to it an Egyptian origin.

of the Mahmoud Dagh, against which it leans. The rock upon
which the carving occurs is perpendicular to the ravine; but as
the figure stands in a recess it cannot be seen from the path
immediately underlying it. To obtain the view of the annexed

Fig. 361.—The Karabel Bas-Relief. G. Perrot, *Mémoires d'Archéologie*, Plate I.

woodcut, it is necessary to walk to the southward until about to
turn the corner of the rock.

The niche, recalling a pylon, by which the warrior is framed,

measures 2 m. 50 c. by 1 m. 90 c. at the base, and 1 m. 50 c. towards the apex. In his left hand is carried a spear, a bow is slung at the back, and he wears the conical cap, the short tunic, and tip-curved boots with which we are familiar. He is in profile; the left foot well forward. On his head is an indistinct salience, probably the uræus as at Ghiaour-Kalessi (Fig. 352), and the semi-lunar hilt of a short dagger appears on the left side; nor should the horizontal stripes of the tunic be left unnoticed. The work is in mezzo-rilievo. No attempt was made to model the features, the relief of which is not above 5 c. Engraved symbols are

FIG. 362.—The Karabel Bas-Relief. TÉXIER, *Description*, Plate CXXXII.

seen between the head and spear (Figs. 361 and 362).[1] The

---

[1] The first of our two figures is the exact reproduction of a photograph by M. Svoboda. The fact that all the details specified by us are not visible in our cut is due to the necessity of having had to place the camera at a considerable distance from the object in order to obtain a front view. Notwithstanding its blurred aspect, we reproduce it because it gives a more correct idea of the real proportions of the figure than either of the drawings of Kiepert or Téxier. The latter makes it too thin and elegant, whilst the former errs in the opposite direction; for he has carried the lower portion of the bow on to the body, making that part thicker than reality. On the other hand, Téxier's copy will be found helpful, in that it shows the details enumerated by us. The visual error of the German explorer was pointed out by us twenty-five years ago (G. PERROT, "Le Bas-Relief de Nymphi," *Revue Arch.* nouvelle série, tom. xiii.).

rough uneven surface of the stone is due to the action of wind and rain.

We will now turn to Herodotus, and compare his description with that of modern travellers.

" By far the greater proportion of the stelas set up by Sesostris to commemorate his conquests in Asia Minor have been destroyed. Nevertheless, I found rock-cut carvings of this prince in Palestine and Syria; as well as two figures in Ionia chiselled on the hill-side. One may be seen on the road which runs from Ephesus to Phocœa, and the other on the shorter route from Smyrna to Sardes. These figures are four cubits and a half in height; they hold a javelin in the dexter hand, and a bow in the sinister; the rest of the equipment is partly Egyptian, partly Ethiopian. Across the breast are hieratic Egyptian characters, which read thus: '*This country I have subdued with the power of my arm.*' Some have thought that this figure was intended as a representation of Memnon, wherein they have greatly erred."[1] It should be noticed that Herodotus, as though he had doubts respecting the parentage and country of his hero, does not specify them; and is not so confident of the Egyptian origin of these bas-reliefs as he was at Nahr-el-Kelb. We may conclude from this that he had not seen the sculptures under notice, and that his account was from information he had received. On the other hand, it is possible that he may have seen them, but, owing to some cause or other, he had no time to take notes, and his narrative therefore was written from memory, which played him false. Hence the discrepancy between the figure as we find it and his description. True, there is the other bas-relief, but unfortunately its mutilated state will not allow us to compare it with the Greek text, and note in what respects it coincides or disagrees with it. This was not discovered until long after the first, which is far away the best preserved, or, to speak correctly, the least corroded of the two. It is that described by Téxier and visited by subsequent travellers. Like the Sesostris of Herodotus, he is armed with spear and bow; the measurement of four cubits and a half (equal to 2 m. 50 c.) may

---

[1] See note 2, p. 379, vol. i. of this work, and Herodotus, ii. 102, upon the proper reading of μέγεθος πέμπτης σπιθαμῆς. The stelas seen by the Greek writer in Syria are doubtless the rock-carvings at Nahr-el-Kelb, near Beyrouth, of which we gave an account in the earlier part of this work.

be said to correspond as nearly as possible with the actual size of our figure (2 m. 15 c.) ; but no engraved characters have been found across his breast.[1]   The small points of divergence with regard to the respective size of the figures and the non-existence of inscribed characters (for these may have been trumped up by Herodotus's informers) are as nothing compared with the bow and spear, which are absolutely unique of their kind, and peculiar to the race which had preceded the Greeks on the soil.   Hence it came to pass that when the contemporaries of Herodotus described these bas-reliefs, they might omit details known to everybody, as unimportant, and such as the imagination of their hearer would supply of itself ; but the spear and bow were too striking to be easily forgotten or passed over.   The Sesostris of Herodotus sufficiently resembles the Karabel picture to make it probable that we have here the figure which was to be seen on the main road between Ephesus and Phocœa.   At the outset, when this bas-relief began to be discussed, it was perhaps too hastily assumed that it was the one described as standing on the cross-road which runs from Smyrna to Sardes.   But reference to Kiepert's excellent map, or, better still, verification on the spot, proves that the path in question was five or six kilometres north of Karabel, leading through the narrow gorge of Bel-Kaye, the highest pass of this mountain range.   The waters, which are drained in the extensive plains of Bournabat and the Nif-Chai valley, have their watershed line a little below this point.

Remains of the old causeway are extant, and appear to be anterior to the Roman epoch.   The modern village of Nimphi is on the right bank of the Nif-Chai, which is spanned by a bridge constructed on the stout foundations of the former structure.

The second figure was discovered by M. K. Humann in 1876 ;[2] its conspicuous position near the ancient route marked it to the passer-by or the evilly disposed.   From some unexplained cause, this path was abandoned for a new one at the back of the mono- lith, a rich luxuriant vegetation soon sprang up on the disused track, and completely buried the carved face of the rock.   Hence

---

[1] Savants long ago contended that the position of the inscription said to accompany the figure was unprecedented in the bas-reliefs which strictly belong to the Nile valley.

[2] *Archæ. Zeitung,* tom. viii. p. 50 ; SAYCE, *The Monuments,* p. 267-269.

travellers in quest of the monument actually skirted it without suspecting its presence. The figure, which is somewhat smaller than the first,[1] was doubtless in the deplorable state in which it was discovered. The whole of the upper part seems to have been struck with a hammer, or some such implement, with the intention of destroying it.[2] The features are wholly obliterated; a bit of the cap however remains; the legs are intact, and the feet encased in tip-tilted boots much more accentuated than in Téxier's figure. Part of the bow, spear, and one inscribed symbol, as well as the rude frame by which it is surrounded, attest that they were identical, and the bow in precisely the same position as in cognate sculptures already described. The loss to archæology implied by the wanton mutilation of this figure, which, to judge from the legs, was finely modelled, cannot well be overestimated; for we may reasonably suppose that the care which had been lavished on the lower limbs was applied to the features and details about the dress.

This figure, although 200 or 250 m. nearer the head of the pass, has no better claim than Téxier's to be considered as that which was seen in ancient times on the Smyrna road, and which, if not destroyed, may yet be discovered, buried as the former amidst bushes. There is nothing surprising in the fact that a work that was destined to commemorate the victories of these tribes, along with the name of the captain who had led them through the pass, should have been twice repeated. As stated, the first bas-relief is high up above the road, and the second 12 or 15 m. below the old path, traces of which have been found; the former is on the

---

[1] The following are the principal dimensions of the second bas-relief: Height of monolith 3 m., breadth of sculptured face 4 m. 70 c., thickness 3 to 4 m.; height of niche 2 m. 30 c.; width towards the apex 1 m. 40 c. to 1 m. 20 c.; depth of niche at the base 90 c. As may be observed, it is not pyramidal in shape, being slightly broader at the top than at the base.

[2] The information contained in this and preceding pages in regard to this monument is taken from a report dated March 29, 1876, kindly forwarded me by M. A. Martin, then a lieutenant in the French navy. At my request, he carefully examined the twin pseudo-Sesostris, in order to test Humann's account. He believes that the mutilation of the second bas-relief was due to the well-known aversion of Mahommedans against images. On the other hand, Humann was told by a native that the sculpture was injured and reduced to its present state by a Kurdish shepherd, who used to pitch his tent against the monolith, and turned the niche into a convenient fireplace. Were this the case, however, we should find the legs most defaced, whereas they are the best preserved and almost intact.

right bank of the stream, and the latter on the left, 2 m. above water-level, on a calcareous boulder of rock which has fallen from the mountain (Fig. 363). The carved side of the stone faces east, and is parallel to the road; the figure being in profile, looks north, *i.e.* towards the land he was about to invade, the marvellously rich plains of Lydia.

It would be sheer loss of time at the present day to try and demonstrate that Herodotus made a mistake when he ascribed these two monuments to Egyptian influence. We know now that the most bellicose and enterprising Pharaohs, contrary to the statement of the Greeks, far from penetrating into Colchis, never crossed the Taurus range, nor the Mœander and Hermus streams. Rosellini long ago, and more recently Maspero, declared that the inscribed symbols were not

FIG. 363.—The second Bas-Relief in the Pass of Karabel, after A. H. Sayce, M.A.

Egyptian hieroglyphs; and the squeezes and careful copies of the inscription taken by Professor Sayce have revealed the fact that the characters are precisely similar to those of the monuments in Northern Syria (Fig. 364). These signs were the name of the king or personage for whom the monument had been raised; and although they cannot be deciphered, the sign-manual of the Hittite scribe is so clear and patent as to admit of no doubt that the symbols in question were as old as the monument itself. The close resemblance which we find between these and the emblems of the Merash stelas, or the rock-cut sculptures of Cappadocia and Lycaonia, equally applies to the pseudo-

FIG. 364.—Group of Signs in first Bas-Relief of the Karabel Pass. SAYCE, *The Monuments.*

Sesostris of Karabel, and the pictures of Boghaz-Keui and Ghiaour-Kalessi (Figs. 311, 313, 352). The only difference is in the weapons, which in the course of time would naturally be modified in some slight details, albeit the dominant lines fixed by tradition

would be preserved. To him who knows, however, minor accessories are of small importance, and scarcely to be weighed in the
balance when compared with identity of style.

Too much stress cannot well be laid on the important fact, that
the sculptures in Asia Minor, no matter where encountered, be it
in the heart of Cappadocia or Smyrna, *i.e.* at the very gates of
Europe, were all executed in flat relief, without modelling, or so
feeble that nothing of it remains in the centre of open spaces, or
niches hollowed out in the rock surface. The figures are everywhere distinguished by the same attitude, the same apportioning
of the various parts, the same treatment of the nude and drapery.
For centuries, from the Euphrates, or to speak more correctly,
from the Halys to the shores of the Ægean, one single type, the
only one created by an art whose resources were exceedingly
limited, satisfied the needs of this conquering race, which left
behind it the effigy of its kings and deities.

The rock-cut figure in the same district, known as the Niobe of
Mount Sipylus, may be added, albeit less confidently, to this series
of archaic monuments due to Hittite influence. The low range
called Sipylus, rises almost like a wall behind the bay of Smyrna.
It is ten leagues long by three or four broad, exquisite in shape
and colour. The highest peak, the Manissa Dagh, is on the east
side, which is also the most abrupt; the Iamanlar Dagh, to the
west, not reaching over 976 m., the gentle slopes of which are
covered with remains of ancient structures, connected by tradition
with the capital of Tantalus, of Pelops, and Niobe; names which
lingered in the popular fancy, perhaps as an imperfect remembrance
of a western Phrygian empire, which towards the twelfth or tenth
century B.C., was absorbed by the growing power of the Lydians
in the valley of the Hermus. The extent, number, and variety
of these remains bear witness that a flourishing community was
established here, long before the early Greek colonists settled on
this coast.

The inscription, in Hittite characters, which accompanies the
colossal statue, called by the Turks Buyuk Souret, "Great Image,"
indicates its priority of date over the sepulchral memorials, altars,
niches, and rock-excavated harbours, which render the western
slopes of Sipylus pre-eminent in world-wide interest. Hence we
may be permitted to consider this figure as a gigantic idol, sculptured on the side of the cliff by a people attracted here by the

exquisite blending of hill and dale, and the singular fertility of the alluvial plain extending to the sea.[1]

The cliff on which the great image is carved rises on the northern declivity of Sipylus, about half an hour's steep ascent from the plain, two leagues east of Manissa (ancient Magnesia). The rock, in which a deep recess has been excavated to receive

FIG. 365.—The so-called Niobe of Mount Sipylus.

[1] The latest work upon this district is due to M. G. Weber, entitled : *Le Sipylos et ses monuments, monographie historique et topographique, contenant une carte, quatre planches lithographies*, etc., in 8°, 1880, Ducher et Cᵉ. M. Weber's long residence at Smyrna, his thorough knowledge of the antiquities to be found in its neighbourhood, his wide reading and acumen, qualify him to give a critical account of them. Hence we shall freely borrow from him.

the statue, measures 15 m. 25 c. in height (Fig. 365).[1]   The figure is sculptured in high relief, almost in the round ; the back alone adhering to the rock.   The huge frame, 10 m. high, surrounding the niche properly so-called, is rounded off towards its apex.   The centre of this deep niche is occupied by a square base, upon which rises a high-backed arm-chair, with a rounded symmetrical salience on each side.   The archaic goddess is seated in this arm-chair, the feet apparently supported by a footstool ; the body bends forward, and the stumpy arms are raised towards her breasts, which are quite distinct.   The head, now only a round shapeless mass, is very salient and erect, and forms one body with the rock, upon which the rain which trickles down from the cliff above has left indelible and characteristic traces.[2]

The existence of this statue, whose features and costume are so corroded as to be hardly traceable, was noticed by ancient writers who busied themselves with the antiquities of this region. In the account of Pausanias—himself a native of Lydia—relating to the monuments of Mount Sipylus, we find a passage twice repeated, which if hardly pressed may seem applicable to the figure we are considering.   The first runs thus : " The Magnesians settled on the northern slopes of Mount Sipylus have a statue of the mother of the gods, the oldest goddess of all, on the Codine rock."[3]   And the second : " I myself beheld the Niobe of Mount Sipylus ; which is nothing but a steep cliff when seen close, with no resemblance to a woman, mourning or otherwise.   But at a short distance, there appears a womanly form which ' looks ' as if immersed in grief and dissolved in tears."[4]   Of all the citations, the first is the

---

[1] Our woodcut (Fig. 364), by M. St. Elme-Gautier, was partly drawn from a photograph of M. Svoboda, kindly forwarded to me by M. Dugit, and partly from Mr. Martin's sketches.

[2] We borrow Weber's description (*Le Sipylos*, p. 37), who has had ample opportunities to examine the monument under different aspects, induced by varying light. He has detected details therefore impossible to obtain by a single visit.   MM. Weber, Sayce, Simpson (*loc. cit.*) and Dennis (*loc. cit.*) are in accord that the goddess is seated ; contrary to MM. Van Lennep and Martin, who hold to a bust which rests upon a pedestal.   Without having seen the monument, but arguing from analogy, we are in favour of a seated goddess.   Our judgment is based on the fact that quarter or half figures are unknown in primitive art, and are only found in a comparatively late age.

[3] *Pausanias*, iii. 22 ; μητρὸς θεῶν ἀρχαιότατον ἁπάντων ἄγαλμα.

[4] *Pausanias*, i. 21 : δόξεις ὁρᾶν.   Sipylus, remarks M. Pappadopoulos Kerameus, (Ὁμηρός, tom. iv. p. 362), was called *Kousinas* by the Byzantines ; and he is of opinion that it is the same as Κοδδίνου πέτρα.

only one which fits our figure ; for the Niobe of Homer, Sophocles,
and Ovid is seated near the mountain springs, ever moist with rain
and snow.[1]　Needless to say that Sipylus is not in the region of
perpetual snow ; and far from being on the summit of a hill, the
image is sculptured on the rocky base of the cliff, with no spring
or stream in the immediate neighbourhood.　Then, too, the Buyuk
Souret is too regular and artificial to agree with the Niobe of
Pausanias.　Even now, in its defaced state, whether we view it
near or from afar, it is impossible to mistake its real nature ; and
in its pristine days this must have been even more so.　The very
words of the historian make it self-evident that a *lusus naturæ* was
intended, such as is to be found in almost every locality.[2]　There
was somewhere on Sipylus a rock which at a particular angle and
distance somewhat resembled a sorrowing human form, identified
by popular fancy with the tragic story of Niobe.　This particular rock has been sought in vain, and in all probability will
never be found ; a fact that does not invalidate the testimony
of classic writers with regard to its existence ; for the special
outline which gave it a far-off resemblance to a human form may
have been worn down since antiquity, or destroyed by the early
Christians on account of the cultus offered to it.　How and when
Niobe was destroyed is unknown ; but the name was too deeply
impressed in the popular fancy to disappear.　It was forthwith
transferred to the statue called by Pausanias the "oldest goddess,"
and its appellative was accepted by travellers without question-
ing until recent times.　Strickland, and after him Weber and
others, as well as ourselves, are confident that the statue on the
rocky base of Sipylus is the ancient Kubele of the Phrygians, the
Cybele of Pausanias, or by whatever other name Mother Earth,
the personification of fecundity, was addressed, whose worship
passed from Cappadocia into Phrygia.　To judge solely from its
fabrication, the statue might properly be ascribed to the Phrygians,
were it not for the group of Hittite characters in front of it.
Mr. Dennis, British consul at Smyrna, was the first to notice the
uneven surface of this portion of the stone ; but as this was on a

---

[1] HOMER, *Iliad*, xxiv. **615** ; SOPHOCLES, *Electra*, vv. 148–150, *Antigone*, vv. 821–
831.　OVID, *Metamorphoses*, vi. 310 ; Fixa cacumine montis.

[2] Pausanias, in this instance, uses the words πέτρα καὶ κρημνός, ἄγαλμα, statue in
reference to Cybele.

line with the head of the figure, *i.e.* at the height of 8 m., decipherment was impossible.   A ladder was therefore brought from Smyrna, placed against the rock, and a transcription of the signs made, which turned out to be Hittite.[1]   Professor Sayce, some weeks later, repaired to the spot, for the purpose of verifying this important discovery.   He made a careful copy of the inscription (Fig. 366), and pointed out details which had escaped his two predecessors.[2]   According to his version, around the head are traces of a circular ornament akin to the headdress of the sphinx at Eyuk (Fig. 327) and the goddess at Eflatoum (Fig. 357);[3] and behind the

FIG. 366.—Hittite Characters on rock near the Pseudo-Niobe.

head is an indistinct object, perhaps a lotus or urœus.   It is but fair to note that Professor Sayce is the only traveller who has perceived these appendages.   On the other hand, it will be readily admitted that indistinct objects are not made clearer by a distance of several yards interposed between them and the beholder ; but that when the latter is brought on a line with and close to them, dispositions may be *felt* and seen, although apparently non-existent and unsuspected before.[4]   Whatever the truth may be, the presence of Hittite characters is enough to

[1] Mr. Dennis published his transcription in a letter to M. Newton (*Proceedings Soc. B. and Archæ.*, January, 1881, p. 49). Gotlob, who also visited the monument, believes that on the same rock, besides characters which seem to be Hittite, is a cartouche of Ramses II. (WRIGHT, *The Empire*, Plate XXII.), which Mr. Dennis, despite vigilant search, has been unable to detect.

[2] SAYCE, *Academy*, October 18, 1879, and *Notes from Journeys in the Troad*, etc., p. 88.   *Journal of Hellenic Studies*, tom. i. pp. 75-93.

[3] Comparison with the Eyuk sphinx belongs to Professor Sayce, who also finds a close resemblance between the Buyuk Souret and the statue of Nofretari, wife of Ramses II., at Ipsamboul.   But he seems to me to have travelled very far when he ascribes similarity of date—or nearly so—to these bas-reliefs, the Niobe, according to him, having been executed by an artist who had seen the Egyptian sculpture.

[4] Thanks to the ladders with which they were provided, MM. Sayce and Dennis were able to walk round the statue and get a back view of it.   Professor Sayce thinks that he detected the tip-tilted shoes.   This however is stoutly denied by Mr. Dennis ; indeed it seems rather hard to believe in the presence of shoes, when most travellers have failed to see any legs.   On the other hand, Mr. Dennis maintains the existence of a shallow groove on either side of the face and neck, which, according to Professor Sayce, was caused by the action of the rain.   The whole controversy may be read in the *Academy*, August 28, 1880.

justify us in assigning a remote antiquity to the statue in question. If not the work of the warlike Khetas, it was executed by the Phrygians established around Sipylus. At any rate, it is much older than the tombs which another branch of the same stock excavated on the banks of the Sangarius, in the vicinity of Seid-el-Ghazi ; for the inscriptions which accompany them, as stated, were all written in letters taken from the Phœnician alphabet. The Buyuk Souret, rightly considered by Pausanias as the most ancient image of Cybele, dates from a time when the influence of Syro-Cappadocian culture was paramount in the peninsula. Compared with the bas-reliefs reviewed in this chapter, it testifies to greater effort, a higher standard, and decisive progress ; it is not a bas-relief, but a veritable statue ; the last and most important rupesque sculpture of Asia Minor.[1]

§ 5.—*Bronzes and Jewels.*

Wherever a sculptor exists who boldly cuts stone in the human or animal form, with its real dimensions—a sculptor who does not recoil before the execution of colossal figures—artificers, such as goldsmiths, stone engravers, smelters and potters, forthwith reproduce the types created by statuary, and reduce them to proportions in harmony with their special handicrafts, so as to satisfy diversity of needs, scattering countless exemplars broadcast among their customers at home and abroad.

The industrial artist of Syro-Cappadocia had an abundance of mineral ores, notably silver and copper; the latter he early learnt to mix with an alloy of tin, derived first from Chaldæa and subsequently from Phœnicia; and he worked it into instruments of peace and war, or representations of national heroes and deities (Fig. 367). This piece, presented to the Louvre by De Saulcy, is supposed to have been found near Angora (ancient Ancyra).[2] It is the figure of a man standing on a living animal, like the chief

---

[1] We may expect that fresh researches in that region will bring to light sculptures akin to the Karabel figures. M. Solomon Reinach reports a monument of the same nature, said to exist on the road which runs between Magnesia and Myrina. Although his efforts to find it proved abortive, he is none the less convinced of the correctness of the information received from the natives (POTTIER and REINACH, *La Nécropole de Myrina*, in 4°, Thorin, 1887, pp. 20, 21).

[2] The figure under notice was published and described by me in the *Revue Archéologique*, etc. ("Un bronze d'Asie Mineure," etc. pp. 25-41).

deity at Iasili-Kaïa.   The absence of hair about the neck of the quadruped makes it probable that in this instance the craftsman

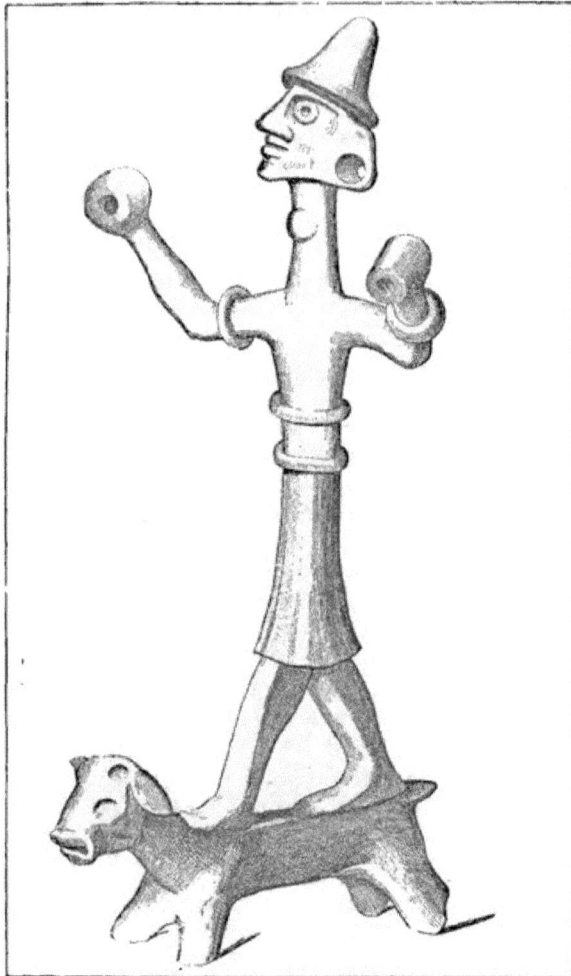

FIG. 367.—Bronze Statuette.   Height, 17 c.   Drawn by Dardel.

intended to portray a lioness, instead of the usual lion.   Nor does the resemblance with the rock-cut sculptures described by us stop here. Thus, the conical cap at once brings to mind the twin figures at Ghiaour-Kalessi (Fig. 352); and the abnormal widening of the lower portion of the head is held by some to designate a woollen or leather piece, such as we noticed in Fig. 351, which served to protect the back part of the neck; but it may with even greater probability have been intended for hair worn rather long. The circular hole, showing the position of the ear, was doubtless furnished with a ring, as in sundry figures at Boghaz-Keui and Eyuk. No ethnical deduction is to be drawn from the features, which are barely outlined; the eye is a mere circle, with a hole in the middle by way of pupil. The short tunic of the figure is fastened round the waist by a double circlet, like that on the arms. The legs and feet are bare. In his hands are held two indistinct objects—probably symbolical—which it is impossible to determine—but which we may suppose to have been a double-headed axe and spear or bow. Above the eye of the lioness is a small hole, into which may have been inserted a symbolic ornament.

The execution of this bronze is so rude and loose, it evinces so little effort to overcome the difficulties offered by the material, the general outline of the personage having but the faintest resemblance to the human form, that it cannot be regarded as an artistic production, even of the most elementary and barbarous kind. It is a mode of procedure encountered more or less throughout the range of this class of industrial objects, amulets, puppet-idols, and so forth. Primitive tribes, we know, are not exacting with regard to the outward forms of their cultus. All they ask is to be provided with a distinct divine type, accompanied by attributes which shall at once appeal to their imagination and evoke their hopes and fears. Our bronze belongs to this type; but despite its archaic nature we are inclined to think that it is not so old as at first appears. This may be inferred from the very satisfactory attitude of the figure on the back of the animal, with arms and feet wide apart, so as to ensure equilibrium and the utmost solidity. If the craftsman took so little pains with it, this was because he was obliged to furnish a copy of a well-known statue at the lowest possible cost. That the type (as that of Fig. 267), was widely diffused throughout the peninsula may be gathered from the numbers that even now are found in the country; and all as primitive as our exemplar, if not more so. I have stated elsewhere that out of some scores that were placed in my hands, I kept one 6 c. high.

Fig. 368, also in the Louvre, belongs to the same class. Like the preceding symbolic objects, now disappeared, were carried in the hands; a bracelet encircles the right arm; and the circular-hilted dagger of the Hittite warrior is about his waist. The salience on the legs shows how deep they entered the back of the animal which served as living support to the figure.[1]   Rough outline and rigid make are the character-istics of the next bronze (Fig. 369), representing a bull, doubtless an idol, akin to the Eyuk example (Fig. 330); for it is self-evident that he could never have stood on his bent-legs, and was not intended as a living animal; proved by the appendages below the hoofs which could only have been fixed on to a curved surface.

FIG. 368.—Bronze Statuette.   Actual size.
Louvre.   Drawn by St. Elme Gautier.

The want of artistic skill which distinguishes devotional objects was not extended to personal ornaments; such as armlets, rings for the ear and fingers, necklaces, or collars; such would be a gold bracelet from Aleppo; a city described in Assyrian and Egyp-tian documents as the capital of a Hittite principality (Fig. 370). Its vigorous workmanship and frankly Eastern ornamention forbid its being dated from the Seleucidæ, an epoch which more than any other has left abundant traces of its artistic activity, and which may be studied in all local collections.   If this piece of jewellery did not originate in the valley of the Euphrates, it certainly came out of a Hittite workshop.   As with the artist of Northern Syria and Cappadocia, here also, the form selected as a means of enrichment is the usual lion, the fore-parts being

[1] This figure was recovered at Kara-Sheher, near Koutahia, and presented to the Louvre, together with Figs. 369, 370, 371, 382, 386, from the same country, by M. Sorlin-Dorigny.

carved in the round, whilst the rest of the body is barely

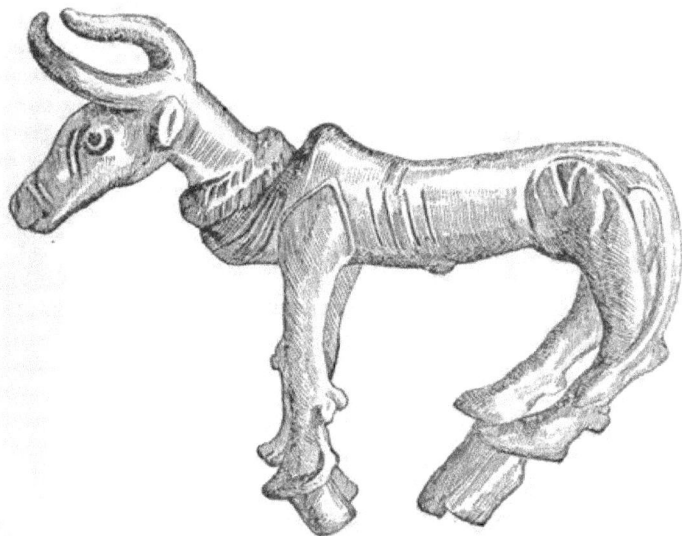

FIG. 369.—Bronze Statuette. Actual size. Louvre. St. Elme Gautier.

indicated ; as comparison with Figs. 297 and 340 will prove. If this be deemed somewhat conjectural by some, greater doubt and difficulty exist when we try to classify the charming pendant, stated to have been recovered in the same region, and which figures in the Appendix, No. 6. To judge from its fine granulated ornament,

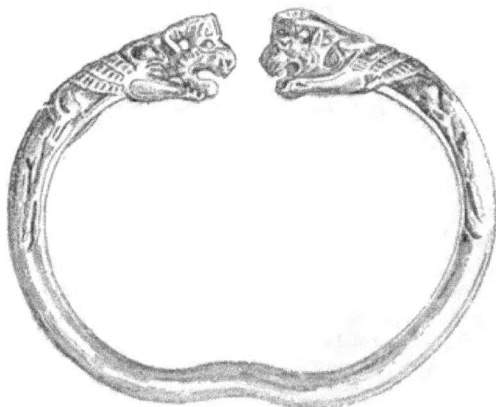

FIG. 370.—Gold Bracelet. Actual size. Louvre. St. Elme Gautier.

we are inclined to date it from a Phœnician or early Greek epoch.

§ 6.—*Glyptic Art.*

The elaborate system of writing possessed by the Hittites induces the belief, amounting almost to certainty, that they borrowed at a remote age the use of seals from the Assyrians and Egyptians, their nearest civilized neighbours. Consequently there is an inclination to credit the Hittites with the fabrication of not a few intaglios which have been recovered within recent years in the peninsula and Assyria. But no matter where such monuments are found, considerable difficulty is experienced in tracing their true origin.

The surest criterion is the presence in the field of the intaglio of characters such as we see in Fig. 371. It is a small calcareous grey stone, ovoid in shape, which was picked up by Sir H. Layard in the palace of Sennacherib, at Nineveh, and placed in the British Museum, where it lay forgotten, until the advent of the Hittite theory. The emblems, circle, lozenge,[1] and bird, are duplicates of those at Hamath and Carchemish,[2] except that here they are more distinct and sharply defined, and that the bird has assumed a cursive, abridged form.[3]

Fig. 371.—Intaglio. British Museum. Wright, *The Empire.* Plate XX. 4.

As will have been observed in the course of this work, as well as by reference to some typical specimens in the Appendix, all such intaglios have their field wholly taken up by the inscription, composed of characters repeated twice over, as in the seal of Tarkondemos. That exiguity of space was not the reason which obliged the engraver to limit himself to mere signs may be inferred from the annexed illustration, the largest example of the series (Fig. 372).[4] The impression is the base of a cone, with two outer concentric zones occupied by forms of a seemingly ornamental nature; which consist, for the border, of a tau

---

[1] This sign, of less frequent usage than the other two, will be found in the first line of Plate J. III. (Wright, *The Empire*).

[2] With regard to these seals, see section on the Glyptic art of the Hittites in this volume (Figs 287, 288, 289); and the whole series may be seen in Plate XIII. Wright's *Empire.*

[3] *Hist. of Art,* tom. iv. p. 493, note 1.

[4] Out of the eighteen seals published by M. E. Schlumberger and myself in the *Revue Archéo.*, are two (Figs. 3 and 4 in plate) where the signs, being equal in number to those of the annexed example, must represent the same text. Nevertheless there are differences of arrangement and design sufficiently distinct to permit us to affirm that each of the three impressions was obtained from a different block or matrix.

and straight stroke, and for the inner or second band, of inverted cones of different sizes. In the central disc are twelve signs, out of which four are stars, one set radiated and the other plain, besides two crescents. The general disposition recalls the boss of Tarkon-demos (Fig. 262), except that this, besides a short inscription, bears a human form. One is apt to ask whether the cones of the second band are not Assyrian "arrow-heads" conventionalized into a pleasing design, like the false "cartouches" of countless Punic bowls, which were se-lected to fill up a bare surface.[1]

In the same series are signs which represent the human figure, and are but reduced copies of carved ones. Thus, in Fig. 373 we have a worshipping priest,

FIG. 372.—Clay Seal. Original size. WRIGHT, *The Empire*. Plate XX. 2.

dressed in the chasuble of Fig. 333 at Eyuk, Plate VIII. D. at Boghaz-Keui, and Fig. 358, at Eflatoun Bounar. Another in-taglio, likewise accompanied by characters, bears the familiar type of a hero or deity standing upon a lion (Fig. 374). The head is gone ; but his tunic and the bow slung on his back are distinct.

These are all of fine compact creamy impasto ; and most are

FIG. 373.—Clay Seal. Original size. WRIGHT, *The Empire*, Plate XX. 7.

FIG. 374.—Clay Seal. Original size. WRIGHT, *The Empire*, Plate XX. 7.

FIG. 375.—Two-sided Seal. Original size. St. Elme Gautier.

circular in form. The impressions were probably obtained from a stone matrix, on which figures and emblems were incised ; and when passed through the kiln were of sufficient hardness to serve as seals. Our next intaglio (Fig. 375), was found by M. Sterrett at Chanah, near Fassiler, in Lycaonia.[2] It is a stone, but so soft as to lack the consistency of well-baked clay. One side is wholly

---

[1] *Hist. of Art*, tom. iii. pp. **800–802**. A collection of these seals is in the possession of M. Greville Chester.

[2] The drawing was made from a wax impression kindly communicated to me by M. Sterrett. Hence our figures are raised, whilst in the original they are sunk.

obliterated; on the other is the figure of a man with the national curved shoes, surrounded by characters. A bull's horns are about his head, and he carries a bow like the Karabel (Fig. 362). Fig. 376 is another seal (in the Bibliothèque Nationale) of certain Hittite origin. One face shows a winged disc, with a deity in the centre, which, as in cognate monuments of Assyria, is only indicated by the headdress seen above it.[1] Observation should be drawn to the characters, which are remarkably well defined and executed. The barred oval, lozenge, and bird in its abridged form, are duplicates of those which occur on the stone documents of Northern Syria. On the reverse is a winged steed, the prototype of the Greek Pegasus. The Luynes Collection possesses a hematite

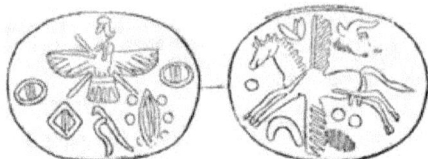

FIG. 376.—Two-sided Intaglio in Agate. LAJARD, *Culte de Mithra.* Plate XLIV. 3, 3ª.

cylinder, which may confidently be referred to a Hittite origin; for it bears the emblem denoting a "king." The composition represents a chariot drawn by two lions, in which is seated a beardless personage,

perhaps a king. Behind are two figures of singular aspect. A simple band is around their loins; their headdress is most strange, and simulates a bull's head; the folds of skin which fall on the neck are quite distinct, and look as if taken from the living animal. The general character and attitude of these figures recall the Boghaz-Keui demons (Figs. 315, 316), save that here the human features are preserved.

As will have been noticed, the glyptic monuments which we have called Hittite were all distinguished by figures of well-known rupesque types, and characters having the value of trades' marks. This test—not to be contested by the most captious—is absent from a series of hematite cylinders which will next engage our attention, and which are of a nature to tax critical acumen to the utmost. They are found, it is true, in public and notable collections; but, respecting a certain number, nobody knows whence or how they came there; whilst the well-authenticated fact that not a few were recovered in Asia Minor, is no sure indication of their having been executed in that part of the globe. If

[1] *Hist. of Art,* tom. ii. Fig. 19.

forms and details of costume bring to memory the rock-cut carvings of Cappadocia, and intaglios with Hittite characters; that which invests monuments with their special physiognomy, namely, treatment and workmanship, point to Chaldæa as the country of their birth.   In dealing with this group of documents, therefore, it behoves us to exercise extreme caution, and pause before we venture to pass an opinion.   Thus, for instance, M. Ménant has no hesitation in ascribing the cylinder (Fig. 378) [1] in the Louvre, to Syro-Cappadocian art; "because," he observes, "of the four small figures, which move like those at Boghaz-Keui, and the characteristic bull's head." [2]   But the quick walking pace of the lads, far from being peculiar to Hittite art, is encountered all over the world;

FIG. 377.—Cylinder. J. MÉNANT, Les Pierres gravés de la Haute Asie, Fig. 114.

FIG. 378.—Cylinder. MÉNANT, Les Pierres gravés, Fig. 3.

whilst the flounced petticoats and wide-brimmed hats of the principal figures betray Chaldæan technique; nor is the outline of the conical caps like the Pterian tiara.   The practice of introducing into a large composition subordinate forms, whether human, animal, or symbolic, was common to Assyrian and Chaldæan artists; and arose from their disinclination to leave any part

---

[1] M. Imhoof Blumner has a cylinder which in general disposition closely resembles Fig. 378.   Like ours, four small figures stand beneath an interlaced band carried right across the seal; two large figures face each other, with a bull's head between them.   But the main scene is occupied by four pictures, instead of three, as in our cylinder; two of which wear the long Assyrian robe, and the remaining two the characteristic flounced petticoat of Chaldæa.   The birds above the interlacing are replaced by crouching winged sphinxes, and the frogs by a "crux ansata" and a crescent moon.   Nobody can dream for a moment of ascribing a Hittite origin to this seal; its resemblance to the Louvre exemplar is so striking that we incline to view them both as Assyrian.   M. Imhoof Blumner writes that the cylinder under notice came from the collection of the late Dr. Barnsby, of Aleppo, which he had recruited from Bagdad, Damas, and the environs; but it is doubtful whether many pieces came from Anatolia.

[2] MÉNANT, Les Pierres gravées de la Haute Asie, tom. ii. pp. 117-118.

uncovered,[1] hence it has no claim to be considered as a Hittite peculiarity. On the other hand, the frog does not occur in the inscribed stones of Northern Syria, whilst the attitude of the bull and bird is foreign to Hittite art, wherein lack of skill is manifest, in that the figures, without exception, are drawn in profile, and quiescent; whereas here the bull is full face, and the bird is flapping its wings preparatory to flying away.[2] Representations of human and animal forms, when transferred to a system of writing, must of necessity undergo simplification to suit their new surroundings, albeit preserving their natural characteristics; when these are absent, we have no right to assume that the sign we have before us is the portraiture of the original form.

The same doubts are felt with regard to Fig 379. It shows three figures of widely different aspect; whom M. Ménant identi-

FIG. 379.—Cylinder. Hemat. MÉNANT, *Les Pierres Gravées*, Fig. 112.   FIG. 380.—Cylinder. Hemat. MÉNANT, *Les Pierres Gravées*, ii. Fig. 113.

fies as Egyptian, Chaldæan, and Hittite; the latter carrying a standard surmounted by a winged disc. They move towards two kings or gods, standing in a bower or cella, framed by a wide interlaced border. One of the personages holds the crux ansata, and is distinguished by an Egyptian headdress. "A most fascinating theory," writes M. Ménant," would be to recognize in the figures of the bower Hittite and Egyptian kings, brought together for the purpose of concluding an alliance, which Egyptians, Chaldæans, and Hittites are to witness." Against this hypothesis is the overwhelming objection, that if one of the figures is an Egyptian god or hero, the long robe and peculiar headdress of the other recall the mitred bulls of Nineveh, and point to Chaldæa as their original home. Again, the artistic way with which the

---

[1] *Hist. of Art*, tom. ii. Fig. 327. LAJARD, *Culte de Mithra*, Plate XXIX. 1, Plate XLIX. 1.

[2] WRIGHT, *The Empire*, Plate IV. H. V., fourth line on the left. See also LAJARD (*Culte de Mithra*, Plates XXXI. 7, and XL. 3), where, amongst others, are two intaglios of marked Chaldæan character.

cloak is draped about the right shoulder is far beyond the ken of the Hittite engraver; and his skill would have been utterly inadequate to handle several figures with diversified costume and attributes. So elaborate a piece of workmanship testifies to an eclectic art which knows what to choose and what to reject; and the place of its fabrication, therefore, must be ascribed to Assyria or Phœnicia.

It is more difficult to pronounce upon a cylinder in the national collection at the Hague (Fig. 380), which portrays a god standing on a mountain, receiving the homage of two worshippers, clad in Chaldæan robe and Assyrian mantle; a crescent with central globe intervenes between them, which it is needless to say is of frequent occurrence in Mesopotamia. The posture, headdress, and short tunic of the deity closely resemble those of the Iasili-Kaïa figures (Plate VIII. E), whilst the costume of the warrior behind the god, includiug his sword and spear, recall Fig. 262, with this difference, that Tarkondemos carries a sheathed sword, whilst it is drawn in this instance. But the wild goat, often encountered in Syro-Cappadocian inscriptions, on the silver boss of Tarkondemos, also occurs here. We may venture to ask the question as to whether the artist intended to commemorate the victory of a Hittite chief, who is seen by the side of his national deity,

FIG. 381.—Cylinder. Hemat. Drawn by St. Elme Gautier.

equipped in the armour with which he successfully overcame his adversaries, the latter offering costly gifts to the local god or prince, perhaps both, save that the skill and technique displayed in this composition tell against such a theory.

The same hesitation is felt in trying to classify cylinders which have been recently acquired for the Louvre. The first in the series (Fig. 381) comes from Aïdin in Lydia. Its apex, now chipped off, had a hole for the purpose of suspension. The second figure, counting from the left, is the only one which presents some analogy with our rupesque carvings. He wears the usual short tunic and tip-tilted shoes; but his dress and that of the other pictures are treated in true Chaldæan style. The peculiar contrivance of investing the central figure with a double profile, that he may address the multitude on each side without having to turn round, is of frequent occurrence in the valley of the Euphrates.[1] The whole subject represents an adoration scene, interspersed with

FIG. 382.—Cylinder, drawn out lengthwise. By St. Elme Gautier.

strange figures of winged genii, having birds' heads. Their gracility brings to the mind the Egyptian mode of procedure. Fig. 382 shows the same cylinder enlarged.[2]

The four-sided seal, conical in shape (Fig. 383), reported to come from Asia Minor, calls for special mention, in that the subject is sufficiently simple to justify the Cappadocian origin which is claimed for it. Fig. 384 shows the same cylinder,

FIG. 383.—Four-faced Seal. Hemat. St. Elme Gautier.

its four faces drawn out. In the first compartment or face are two bulls, with a tree interposing between them ; in the second is a lion, then a stag, and finally a horse. The tip-tilted shoes of the two figures standing on the horse and the stag are distinctly seen. In the field are stars and an emblem which bears a far-off likeness to the symbol at Boghaz-Keui, formerly held by us to be a mandragora. We are somewhat perplexed in

assigning a proper place to the next cylinder (Fig. 385), enlarged in Fig. 386 to show the animals which occupy the lower portion,

FIG. 384.—Showing four sides of Seal. St. Elme Gautier.

but which no imagination, however vivid, can connect with alphabetical signs. It is self-evident that they were introduced in the composition to fill a bare corner, as in sundry Chaldæan cylinders.[3] The chief part of

[1] *Hist. of Art*, tom. ii. Fig. 17 ; Ménant, *Pierres gravées*, i. pp. 111–120.
[2] Similarly on a Chaldæan cylinder (Lajard, *Culte de Mithra*, Plate XXXVI. Fig. 13) will be found slender-winged figures, with a human body, ending in a goat's head.
[3] Ménant, *Pierres*, etc., i. Fig. 114.

the field is occupied by a worshipping scene.   On the left is a
winged genie, with a human body and the head of a bull ; he holds
in his right hand a fish, which does not seem to be intended as an
offering, but apparently introduced that it might take part in the
religious performance.   The central figure holds a palm ; then
comes a second genie, with a human face, and two
other personages, turned away from the scene, with
flowers in their hands.   There is not a single instance
of a fish or a bull-headed genie in the Eyuk and
Boghaz-Keui carvings ; the physiognomy they bear
here at once recalls the extreme East.[1]   The three
principal figures, however, are clad in short tunics,
and the central one, the king, perhaps, has a cap
which closely resembles the Cappadocian tiara.   The
shoes are not curved.

FIG. 385.
Cylinder. Hemat.
St. Elme Gautier.

Our last specimen was seen at Aïdin by M. Sorlin-Dorigny.
Its owner, however, would not part with it, but he allowed an
impression to be taken, which for the purposes of science is as good
as the original.   It is a seal of the
nature of scores of our clay intaglios ; and consists of a central
disc surrounded by a broad zone
or border, and both divisions are
occupied by characters badly
drawn, several of which, however,
may be identified with those
which occur in the inscriptions at
Carchemish, Hamath, etc.

FIG. 386.—Showing the whole Decoration of
the Cylinder. St. Elme Gautier.

It would have been an easy matter to give greater extension to
the list of cylinders, cones, and seals which may be referred to
Hittite influence.   That Syro-Cappadocia had engravers is proved
by numbers of intaglios bearing upon them the stamp of its
peculiar art, along with characters which are now acknowledged as
proper to the early tribes that occupied the soil.[2]   Nevertheless,

[1] MÉNANT, ii. pp. 49–54 ; Le Mythe de Dagon.
[2] We have purposely omitted from the list of Hittite monuments of Western Asia
Minor a stone found at Ak Hissar, ancient Thyatira, by M. A. Fontrier.   It is
pyramidal in form, and serves as pediment to a wooden pillar of the local khan.   Like
Professor Sayce, I fail to recognize as Hittite the characters of the inscription in the
photograph sent me by the discoverer.   On the other hand, M. Oppert has identi-

there are, as stated, scores of monuments which it is exceedingly difficult to localize; either because the place of their birth is more or less doubtful, or because characteristics recalling our rock-cut sculptures bear a very small proportion to the large number of those that are evident reminiscences of Assyria, Chaldæa, or Phœnicia. Hence a new departure is beset with almost insuperable difficulties, albeit useful in that it yields ample scope for discussion and the free exchange of ideas. And as each fresh discovery increases the points of comparison, we may confidently expect to reap a rich harvest.

The number of the monuments we have selected in order to subject them to analysis is of necessity very small; but it will suffice to give an idea of the method we propose to adopt with regard to a future work bearing on the same subject. As in this instance, we shall first present all the known intaglios, with or without figures, having upon them Hittite characters. These we will take as subject-types of Syro-Cappadocian art; carefully tabulating their peculiarities of make, inasmuch as they are the sign-manual of the nation that executed them. We will compare them with seals of doubtful origin, notably those unaccompanied by signs, and where forms and style harmonize with signed intaglios, we shall not deem the absence of written characters as a disqualification to their being classed among Hittite art-productions. In all instances where faint resemblances alone exist, rejection will be the rule; and when differences preponderate over points of touch, comparisons will be instituted with local workshops scattered up and down Asia Minor, in which for centuries the art of the engraver was sedulously carried on.

Adopting prudence as our motto, we hope to add, in a near future a fresh chapter to the history of glyptic art; which will form a fit pendant to a volume on statuary, towards which abundant materials have already been amassed.

fied with the utmost certainty Hittite symbols in a copy made by Father Ryllo, of the Society of the Jesuits, of a monument which he discovered in Mesopotamia, and which is preserved in the Vatican.

The present pope has ordered all the Hittite documents in the library of the Vatican to be published.—Editor.

CHAPTER V.

THE journey which we have accomplished from the banks of the great river to the shores of the Ægean, on the track of the people we have called Hittites, was a long one. On the way, we have assigned, as their handicraft, all such monuments as were accompanied by signs which they seem to have been the first to use, as well as bas-reliefs with or without inscriptions, but characterized by their peculiarities of style, dress, and manipulation. These we were careful to note and dwell upon, inasmuch as they permit us to recognize the monuments under discussion as due to one civilization; and we were equally mindful to draw attention to differences existing here and there. Albeit they are all distinguished by a strong family likeness, and points of touch are multitudinous between them, we are far from assuming that they were brought to light in one period or the creation of a single people.

The art, the broad outlines of which we have essayed to define, had attained its greatest degree of perfection a thousand years, before the enterprising sons of Hellas became the dominant race in the peninsula. It will be readily admitted, therefore, that, in that long interval, diversities, which have been likened to art-dialects, were unfolded; and tribes and principalities sprung up and adopted the themes and forms created by the vigorous race which had preceded them, modifying them in the borrowing.

Within these limits we persist in the belief that we did not err, when on our return from Asia Minor, some twenty-five years ago, we collated these monuments and ranged them into one group, although divided by enormous distances of time and space one from the other. The comparison which we then instituted was taken up and prosecuted by others, and, thanks to recent discoveries, the

field of their observations has been greatly enlarged.[1]   Critical
inquiry has likewise thrown side-lights on the obscure chapter of
history relating to the tribes which the early Greek colonists found
everywhere established in the land; with whom they gradually
entered into intercourse, be it with the occupiers of the plains or
the dwellers of the central plateau.   If it is little to have discovered, we may lay this unction to our hearts, that at one time
nobody dreamt we should achieve as much.   Consequently, we
may hope that the thick curtain which conceals mysteries which
it would be interesting to unravel may yet at some future time
be rolled aside.   Was the Hittite system of writing elaborated
west of the Taurus range, and was it of such a nature as to entitle
its inventors to be considered as a civilized and civilizing race ?
Did the princes of Carchemish and Kadesh extend their dominion
as far as the bay of Smyrna, as numberless small objects seem
to imply, especially the rupesque sculptures on Mount Tmolus,
and the no less remarkable specimens encountered in the stretches
of Lycaonia, one and all accompanied by the peculiar characters
which occur on the monuments of their ancient centres ?   Do the
carved rocks of Anatolia, cylinders and puppet-gods, bear witness
to a successful invasion, or are they the natural result of a great
military power firmly implanted on either side of the Taurus range,
whose influence was felt by semi-barbarous tribes at distances
greatly removed from the seat of government ?   Finally, did the
civilization of Northern Syria and Pteria, directly or indirectly,
through the Lycians, Carians, Phrygians, and Lydians, furnish
elements to Greece which the latter, with her usual readiness,
transfused into her myths, religious rites, and forms of expression,
be it in her plastic art or mode of thought ?

Such are some of the questions which present themselves to the
mind, but to which it is not easy to give positive answers ; we will
therefore restrict ourselves to pointing out solutions which seem to
coincide with the mass of evidence which lies before us.

Among modern scholars who have interested themselves about
the Hittites, the first place should be assigned to Professor Sayce,
for the degree of energy, acumen, and enthusiasm which he has
carried into the question.   He inclines to the belief that the
Hittites did not belong to the Semitic stock ; but were one of

---

[1] We take this opportunity to acknowledge our indebtedness to M. Lenormant's
work, entitled, "Les Inscriptions Hittiques" (*Journal des Savants*, 1883, pp. 400-417).

the numerous tribes in possession of the Armenian plateau, and which for convenience sake are sometimes called Proto-Armenian. Narrowness of space, or some other cause, induced them to forsake their lofty mountains, following the banks of the Euphrates and the Halys, when they spread throughout Syria and Asia Minor.[1] Hence they were related to the Muskai and Tublai of the Assyrian monuments, the Meshek and Tubal of the Bible, the Moschai and Tibareni of the classical writers.[2] The instances adduced in favour of this hypothesis rest on insecure foundations. Too much, we think, has been made to depend on the tip-curled shoes, designated by Professor Sayce as "snow boots," which, he argues, could only have originated in a hilly country, where for many months snow lies on the ground; but could never have been invented in a flat region, since their usage amidst tall grass and bushes would have been extremely inconvenient.[3] The habit once formed was retained; perhaps because the peculiar shoe was regarded as part of the national costume, that which distinguished them from their neighbours; one, too, which had descended to them from their rude mountaineer ancestors. I have not handled the "curled boot;" but I have seen it throughout the Levant. Is the fact to be explained by persistency of habits contracted in some northern country at a remote age? May not fashion account for its adoption by those primitive tribes, as in other parts of the world?

Decipherment of Hittite inscriptions would doubtless and may some day lead to more conclusive results. For the present, however, our knowledge is confined to the proper names to be found in the Bible, and in Assyrian and Egyptian inscriptions; respecting

---

[1] SAYCE, *The Monuments*, p. 253. The language of the Vannic inscriptions seems to belong to the Alarodian family of speech, of which modern Georgian is the best-known example.

[2] The form Τίβαροι is found in Hecateus of Miletus, who wrote about the fifth century before Christ. The Assyrian inscriptions show that the Tublai were in close alliance with the Cilicians and Muschai on the north, about the twelfth century before Christ. Between this period and the time when the Greeks began to busy themselves with the affairs of their Asiatic neighbours, these tribes seem to have been obliged to fall back towards the Euxine, perhaps before the invading Hittites. They were on the march of the Ten Thousand, and Xenophon alludes to them as veritable Barbarians. Remains of these primitive clans were to be found in the fastnesses of Cilicia as late as Cicero (*Ad familiares*, XV., iv. 10).

[3] SAYCE, *loc. cit.*, p. 252.

the derivation of which scholars are not agreed.[1] For, if a certain number cannot be reduced by means of a Semitic vocabulary, others are indubitably possessed of elements common to the family of speech used by the Semites; on the other hand, it is urged that although such names may be compounded with Assyrian or Hebrew words, they do not follow the rules of the Semitic grammar. Names, however, as Khiti-sar, Kilip-sar, etc., are not made up of organic compounds, as in Greek and Latin, but are formed by simple agglutination, wherein the affirmative verb is understood. Thus, we should not read *Khitisar*, "the king of the Kheta," but " Khiti (is) king."

It should be noted, on the one hand, that among the names of individuals and localities, preserved in the inscriptions of Nineveh and Thebes, few only can be traced to Semitic roots; and on the other, that in the rare instances where passing allusion is made to Hittites in the Old Testament, their names have a strong family likeness to Hebrew appellatives. Nor is this all; the gods specified in the treaty between Ramses II. and Khitisar, such as Sutekh, and Ashtoreth of the land of the Kheta, belong to the pantheon of the Western Semites. Then, too, the author of Genesis (x. 15) calls Heth, a son of Canaan, the younger offspring of Sidon; and we have seen that Kadesh, their great fortress on Orontes, is a Semitic name, signifying "holy."[2] Hence it may be apprehended that the study of Hittite onomatology is beset with difficulties and contradictory evidence, from which final conclusions cannot be drawn at the present hour.

The best documents to be examined are undoubtedly the sculptures, wherein their own image is portrayed. Unfortunately they have been too often made to bear false witness on the one hand, and on the other nothing proves that the Hittite sculptor was sufficiently master of his craft to reproduce with fidelity the

---

[1] A complete list of Hittite proper names will be found in *The Monuments of the Hittites* (Sayce); where it is formally stated that "Hittite names preserved in the Assyrian and Egyptian inscriptions, prove that the Hittites did not speak a Semitic language;" whilst Brugsch (*Egypt under the Pharaohs*) was content to remark that "Hittite names, found in Egyptian inscriptions, do not bear a Semitic, or at any rate, a pure Semitic stamp."

[2] On the coins of the Asmonæan age, Jerusalem is called *codsha haccadesh*, "holy;" a name which it preserved as Hierosolyma, Jerusalem. Again, in the Old Testament, Mount Zion is often designated *harshodsha, harcodshi*, "the holy hill," "the hill of holiness."

special characteristics of the national type ; whilst the greater proportion of the rock-carvings in Pteria and Eyuk, is found in such
a deplorable state as to preclude features or profile being properly
made out. If from these we pass to the Merash stelas (Figs. 280,
281), which are among the best preserved, we shall find in full
common place conventionality and monotonous treatment, betray-
ing inexperience and poverty of invention on the part of the artist,
who created but one type of humanity, which he reproduced *ad
nauseam*, without attempting to accentuate those lines which define
and stamp an individual or a nation. In every instance where the
contour of the face has been carefully outlined, the result has been
an Assyrian—or, if preferred, Semitic type ; witness the hook-
nosed figure in the Birejik stela (Fig. 278) and the bearded head
at Ghiaour-Kalessi (Fig. 352).

Nor is the problem which perplexes us more easily solved by
calling to our aid Egyptian and Assyrian monuments, where
Hittites are occasionally represented. As we have abundantly
proved, the art of Chaldæa, except at rare intervals, never
troubled itself with a faithful portraiture of ethnical types.[1] Thus,
on the gates of the temple at Balawat, the inhabitants of Carchemish are seen, along with the various peoples subdued by Shalmaneser, bringing costly gifts in token of their obedience.[2] But,
save the low-pointed tiara, akin to the Hittite sign (Figs. 274, 353),
there is nothing in their features or style of dress to denote their
nationality. The more ambitious aims of the Egyptian artist, who
took special pains to apportion to each race its peculiar physiognomy, have been adduced in proof that the Khiti were not Semites.
In the painting at Medinet Abou, to record the victories of Ramses
III., they are represented light in colour and slightly red, and as
having straight noses, in marked contrast with the swarthy, beaked
profile of the Amou, or Semites.[3] We have not seen the originals ;
but we must own that we have failed to detect any such difference
in the best copies of these bas-reliefs. This may be due to the
size of the figures, necessarily small in great battle-scenes, where

---

[1] *Hist. of Art*, tom. ii. pp. 351–354.

[2] Upon the Balawat gates, see *Hist. of Art*, tom. ii. pp. 202, 203, 253, 254. The
homage scene under notice will be found on sheets Nos. 1—4, of Plate E.
Fragments only of these bronze plates were recovered. A full account, with trans-
literation of the text of the bronze edging, and illustration by M. Pinches, will be
found in *Soc. Bibl. Archæ.*, 1878, pp. 83, 118.—EDITOR.

[3] LENORMANT, *Les Inscriptions Hittiques*, pp. 404, 405.

broad outlines are alone aimed at, to the neglect of small details. But we may expect to find the real Hittite physiognomy in the single figures of the same series, always on a large scale, yielding therefore ampler opportunity for characteristic outline. Such would be Fig. 388, with inscription: "This is the vile chief of the Khetas; him I made prisoner." With regard to the comparatively light colour, which distinguished the dwellers of the Amanus and Taurus range as against those of the plains, Palestine,

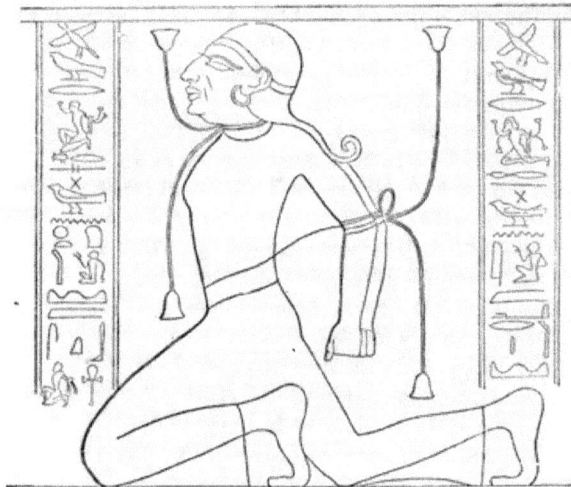

Fig. 388.—Hittite Prisoner. Lepsius, *Denkmaeler*, Plate CCIX.

and Phœnicia, we have stated, in another part of this work, that it was of a nature to strike the people from the delta, as it did the wide-awake Greeks at a subsequent period. At first, the term "Syrian" was applied by the latter to all the people they found established in the vast region between the river Halys and the Taurus Mountains (500 B.C.). But when their intercourse with the various populations became more intimate, they called the Cappadocians Leuco-Syri, [1] "White Syrians," to distinguish them

---

[1] We read in *Herodotus* (i. 6. 72, 76; ii. 104; iii. 90; v. 49; vii. 72;) that the Asiatic Greeks "call Syrian the people whom the Persians designate as Cappadocians." Σύρος is used in the same sense by his contemporary Xanthos (Nicholas of Damascus, frag. 49), whilst Pindarus, cited by Strabo (XII. iii. 9), speaks of the

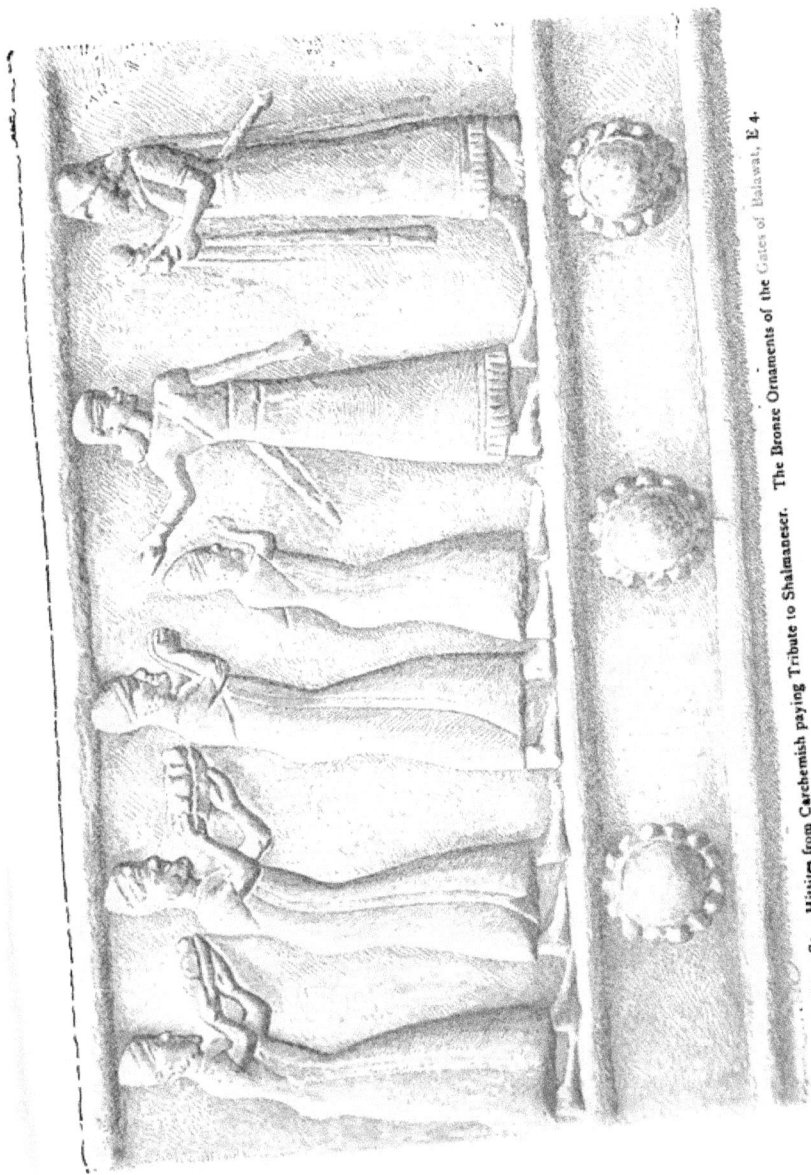

Fig. 387.—Hittites from Carchemish paying Tribute to Shalmaneser. The Bronze Ornaments of the Gates of Balawat, E 4.

from the inhabitants of Palestine. The opinions of classic writers, so freely expressed, has been impugned on the plea that nice ethnical differentiation was unknown to antiquity. But, even so, the fact remains that the Greeks in very early days penetrated into Cappadocia through Sinope and Tarsus; nor was their testimony left to take care of itself, as it is abundantly confirmed by the inscriptions on coins, which, until Alexander, were written in Aramaic. Now, a Semitic dialect would not have persisted so long in the eastern portion of the peninsula, amid unfavourable surroundings, had it not been introduced at a remote age, perhaps as far back as when the Hittites crossed the Taurus and became the dominant race in Asia Minor. Their empire fell to the Assyrians, the Medes, and the Persians in turn; but the bulk of the population, which they had found in possession of the soil on their arrival, remained appreciably the same. On the other hand, by excluding the Hittites from the world of the Semites, we increase the difficulties tenfold; for the feeble rays yielded by the history of this region are wholly inadequate in helping us to ascertain when the Semites spread in the peninsula and rose uppermost. Had such displacement been effected by other than peaceful means, traces of the inward conflict which reduced the Hittites to a subordinate place or entire extinction would have

---

Amazons established on the Thermôdôn as "Syrian;" and Stephanus Byzantinus (s. v. Χαλδαῖοι) writes that the appellative was to be found in Sophocles. The coast of the Euxine, between the Thermôdôn stream and the town of Harmene, was called Ασσυρια by Sylax, the author of the "Periplus," who lived about 550 B.C. (§ 89). The first time we hear of the Leuco Syri is in Strabo, who explains the expression on the ground of difference of colour (XII. iii. 5, 9, 12, 25). He may however have borrowed it from earlier writers, perhaps Hecateus of Miletus. These citations might be further extended, but they suffice for our thesis, whilst any one interested in the subject will find an able account of it in Noeldcke's paper, entitled: Ασσύριος, Σύρος, Σύριος, (Hermes, tom. v. 1871, pp. 443–468). In classical times the name of Assyrian or Syrian was indifferently applied to all the populations which were supposed to have lived under Assyrian rule (Ninus, Semiramis), and at first it had but a politico-geographical value for Noeldcke himself. It was only under the successors of Alexander that it came to denote people speaking the Aramaic language. Although fully admitting that a long space of time was requisite to elucidate the somewhat vague notion the Greeks attached to the appellative— even now as clear as murky water—no one will deny that community of blood and speech were the real cause why the name was given to Cappadocians and the natives of Palestine. Decipherment of Hittite inscriptions, or a bilingual tablet by means of which the character of the language spoken on the right bank of the Halys at the time of Crœsus, Xenophon, etc., would alone solve the question.

lived in the remembrance of their descendants, at any rate in the form of myths.

Such are some of the doubts and perplexities which beset this vexed question. Of all the hypotheses put forth hitherto, that to which we most incline as the least open to criticism is the following: The Hittites, who at one time could treat on even terms with Egypt, and arm against her all the tribes of Asia Minor, were a mixed race. In the estimation of Assyriologists, Semitic tribes at a very early date crept in everywhere in Mesopotamia, and settled among the older inhabitants. These, until further notice, have been connected with the large but ill-defined Turanian family. In the course of time, the two elements blended together, the younger and stronger imposing its language and traditions upon the older and weaker. Something like this, it is supposed, took place in Syria; Aramæan tribes, from the south, met cognate or other tribes descending from the upper valleys of the Taurus range, with whom they at first fiercely disputed the possession of the soil; but finally agreed to take their share and live in amity. This happy result may perhaps have been induced by fear of a common danger; when the need was felt of rallying under one chief, instead of a loose precarious federation.

Hence arose a strong military power which lasted one or two hundred years. During this period, diversity of language and appellatives still served to demonstrate diversity of origin, whether of individuals or localities. But military service, in bringing together clans from every part of the peninsula, aided, too, by the persistent action of a central government, created a state and a nation properly so called, as it had in Assyria and Chaldæa. The ideas and habits thus engendered were preserved after the splitting up of the empire into small divisions, which led to loss of independence. It was not in the nature of things that the rude mountaineers of Armenia, in their conflict with the Semitic tribes in possession of the vast district which interposes between the Amanus range and the Euphrates, should have come out with the honours of war. For affinity of blood connected these Semites with the powerful tribes established on the middle and lower course of the great river, whose superiority, resulting from a long period of settled life and consequent civilization, was fully acknowledged by semi-nomadic races. A brisk intercourse was kept up between the two cognate groups, and in their straits the distant settlers could always rely on their brethren. Knowledge of this powerful ally in the background enabled the Semites of Asia Minor to get the upper hand and lord it over their neighbours, albeit they probably were their inferiors in point of numbers and warlike energy.[1]

It was about the fifteenth or sixteenth (some authorities carry it back to the nineteenth) century B.C., that the Khetas constituted themselves into a nation in Syria, when they elaborated the art and system of writing, which bear unmistakable proofs of having been suggested by the art of ancient Babylon, Assyria, and Egypt; born, too, of the desire to possess means which would enable them to transmit their thoughts and deeds to a late posterity. Such a theory harmonizes with the nature of the monuments they have left behind them. If, as a rule, their subjects are modelled after the bas-reliefs of Egypt or Babylonia, their symbols and mode of execution, both in their national costume and representation of the human and animal forms, prove the strong individuality of the people which fabricated them. At the outset, the aim of the artist, whether on the banks of the Nile, the Euphrates, or the Halys, had been a faithful and realistic rendering of the actual objects; difference between them was shown in the selection and forms of the signs. These, among the Hittites, with the single exception of the stela of Tyana, in Cappadocia, were always in "cameo." The original pictorial characters were found too unwieldly for the purposes of daily life, and in due course of time they were modified into purely determinative or phonetic values.

According to Professor Sayce, Hittite hieroglyphs were first made use of in Cappadocia, where the most striking manifestations of the art of the people which invented them are to be found.[2] His theory is based upon the fact that the ideograph for "king" and

---

[1] Decipherment of a statistical table and inscription to record the campaigns of Anemenhid, discovered at Karnac, have led M. Maspero to the following conclusions: (1) In the reign of Thothmes I. the position occupied by the Khiti in Northern Syria was essentially the same as that which they had in the nineteenth dynasty. (2) The conquests of Thothmes I. extended as far as Carchemish, where "*at the crossing of the Euphrates, he planted a stela of victory* (to record his invasion) *which Thothmes II., found in place in one of his campaigns.*" (3) The Khiti were then in full possession of the Naharana, proved by towns whose names may still be identified, such as Dour Baniti, Deir-el-Banath; Tounipa, Tinnab, in the vicinity of Aleppo; Tourmana, Tourmanin, Khazaza, Azas, Ourima, Οὐριμᾶ γέγαντος, etc. (4) Although not formally stated, the context of this same inscription permits us to infer that in the time of Thothmes III. the suzerainty of Kadesh was still in the hands of the Khiti.

[2] Sayce. WRIGHT, *The Empire*, p. 177.

"country" represented by an elongated cone or pyramid repeated once for "king" and twice or more for "country," seems to have been suggested by the conical rocks which rise from the ground, near Urgub, and Utch Hissar, in Southern Cappadocia[1] (Fig. 256, 1, 2, 262; tailpiece, ch. i., and Fig. 389,[2] as well as Figs. 2, 3, Appendix). The reason adduced in favour of priority of date in regard to this district does not carry conviction with it; for conical hills of the same nature have been observed by Puchstein midway between Kaja-Dagh and Kurd-Dagh, south of Merash, which, all things considered, have superior claims to be looked upon as having served as prototypes to the ideograph for king and country. The character, it will be remembered, is but an abridged form of these peculiar rocks.[3] To make Cappadocia the cradle of Hittite culture is equivalent to saying that civilization, contrary to all precedent, travelled from West to East; but we contend that the accumulated experience of ages points the other way. Isolated instances, more or less numerous, might doubtless be cited against the theory we advocate; were they thoroughly inquired into, however, they would be found to have been due to special or accidental instances. As Hittite writing was but a form of sculpture, we may assume that it was as old as the latter. At any rate, we have proofs that it was in full swing at the time of Khitisar, from the fact that the treaty made with Ramses II. was engraved on a plate of silver. Before this struggle, so happily put an end to by this alliance, no Egyptian army had appeared beyond the passes of the Amanus and Taurus; whilst the Assyrians never penetrated westward of the Euphrates until long afterwards. Trade, properly so-called, can scarcely have existed in those early days between the barbarous semi-nomadic tribes of the central plateau and the more civilized populations that lived in towns or occupied the adjacent alluvial plains with outlook

---

[1] In the several valleys, writes Hamilton (*Asia Minor*, p. 251), many thousand conical hills, or rather pointed pinnacles, varying in height from fifty to two hundred feet, rose up in all directions, so closely arranged that their bases touched each other, leaving only a narrow path between them, and presenting a most strange and inexplicable phenomenon. In many places they were so slender and close together, that they resembled a forest of lofty fir-trees.—Editor.

[2] The drawing was made from a photograph kindly forwarded to us by Mr. John Henry Haynes. Consult also Reclus, *Géographic Universelle*, tom. ix. pp. 562–564.

[3] The rocks under notice, are styled "Basalt-kuppen," in the map of the German Expedition. "The soil where they occur," says the report, p. 2, "is of volcanic formation; numerous cones rise from the ground, sometimes to considerable heights, and invest the landscape with a strange aspect."

FIG. 389. Conical Rocks near Utch Hissar. St. Elme Gautier.

towards the sea; whose more fastidious needs were satisfied in full by Punic traders.   Hence the uplands of central Asia Minor nor Cappadocia were interpenetrated by the ferment and spiritual life which obtained in regions in almost daily contact with the outer world.   The Naharana was more favourably placed; for on the Mediterranean the narrow strip of Cœlo-Syria was the only barrier between it and the delta or at least the Egyptian possessions; whilst, on the other side, Chaldæa could be reached through the Euphrates.   No matter the way the Hittites took, or the purpose for which they left their homes, they everywhere met inscriptions, strongholds, palaces, temples, and sculptures.   Some of these, the statue of Ramses, for example, may have been carried off in one of their expeditions in Southern Syria, and set up as a trophy of their successful arms.[1]   Nor was this all; trading caravans brought them high-class industrial productions in vogue among neighbouring peoples; be it textiles, clay and metal vessels, jewellery, weapons, and objects of all kinds.   Thus enframed, stimulated and aided by the innumerable instances they beheld around them, the Hittites, in undisputed possession of a vast country, traversed by great and countless streams, in the full consciousness of their power, awoke to the need, with all the eagerness of a young vigorous nation, of procuring those outward signs of refined life, the value and importance of which were brought home to them by easy and frequent comparison.   As a matter of course, they never reached the high level which had been attained by their more favoured neighbours, whose civilization and richer past had placed them on a widely different platform.   Nevertheless, they may be said to have succeeded in all essentials; in that they formed themselves into a powerful federation, with such means of defence as to compel the great Eastern world to treat with them on a footing of parity.

It was on the Orontes, therefore, and not on the Halys, that the Hittites gathered themselves together into a first nucleus, and ere long developed into a mighty nation.   Their system of writing, peculiar style of dress, mode of warfare, in fact, all those habits which distinguish one people from another were then elaborated. Then, too, were aroused the restless spirit and need for action which seem to be inseparable from young blood, whether of individuals or communities, at that supreme moment of their life when budding youth suddenly awakes to the full strength of manhood, impel-

[1] MASPERO, Hist. Anc. des Peuples de l'Orient, 4ᵉ edition, p. 224

ling the hero or nation beyond the narrow limits of the home that
up to that time had seemed all sufficient. As stated, the roadway
on the south and east was almost impassable ; but no obstacles
existed towards the west. From this side they spread, therefore,
throughout Asia Minor ; they subdued all the tribes they met in the
country ; some few clans in the fastnesses of the Olympus range
being alone left unmolested. When this migration took place, the
Khiti had this immense advantage over the aborigines, that they
were acquainted with the art of working metals. Whether the
knowledge they thus carried with them was learnt of the Chalybes,
a northern Hittite tribe (which in early Greek tradition are described as the Cyclops of Asia Minor), or from Chaldæa and Egypt,
it is impossible to say. That the oldest Hittite inscriptions were
upon plates of metal may be inferred, says Professor Sayce, from
the nature of their written characters.[1] Nor is this mere conjecture,
for we know that the copy of the treaty made with Ramses II. of
Egypt was engraved on a plate of silver, and that the boss of
Tarkôndemôs was of the same precious metal (Fig. 262). Silver
was supplied to the Hittites from the rich mines of the Bulgar-
Dagh, which are worked at the present day under the name of
Gumush-Maden.[2] The use of bronze, as might be expected, was
far more general, for Hittite bas-reliefs, and Egyptian monuments
representing the battles around Kadesh and Carchemish, show us
bronze vases and bronze chariots. We may assume, therefore,
that the Hittites, in their first encounters with the inland tribes,
were already possessed of those swords, stout clubs ending in a
huge ball, double-headed axes, and scimitars, which we find at
Boghaz-Keui ; whilst the cutlasses, arrow-heads, and axes of the
latter were flint. Superiority of arms, it is needless to say, was
a primary cause in their obtaining a foothold among the semi-
barbarous aborigines, whose secluded position had enabled them to
preserve their independence. Though they had lived away from
all outward movement, they were shrewd enough to understand
that they could never hope to withstand soldiers who had held

---

[1] Sayce, *The Monuments*, p. 251.
[2] Upon the silver mines of the Bulgar-Dagh, consult Reclus, *Géographie
Universelle*, tom. i. p. 475 ; as well as Hamilton, *Researches*, tom. i. pp. 234–238.
Professor Sayce (*The Monuments*, p. 307) likewise mentions having discovered
old mines in the Gumush-Dagh, or Silver Mountains, on the north side of the
Mæandrian plain, which were probably worked by the Hittites.

their own against the best-disciplined troops then known.   They
may also have considered that the advantages which would accrue
to them, in accepting Hittite supremacy, would far outweigh the
disadvantages attached thereto.   As their allies, nothing would be
easier than to carry their predatory expeditions into the very heart
of the delta, whose wealth rumour had brought to them swelled
into fabulous proportions.   Then, too, through Hittite agency they
would be able to procure objects of a useful or ornamental character,
the need of which becomes indispensable to the merest savage, as
soon as he has learnt their use.

On the other hand, the country, from its size and newness, was
too valuable a prize to be easily relinquished by the invaders.[1]
And what better means could be devised than to settle in the land
where their interests could be watched over without intermission ?
Multitudinous villages, be it on rising ground or hill-tops, were
doubtless erected during this early period in Lycaonia and Cappadocia, which they generally strengthened with cyclopæan walls.
The district in which the Hittites seem to have thrown out the
deepest roots was certainly Pteria, evidenced in the number and
character of the monuments they have left behind them; for nowhere
did their constructive and artistic skill soar higher than at Boghaz-
Keui and Iasili-Kaïa.   The natural conditions of the country
enabled the Pterians or Western Hittites almost from the outset
to assume an independent attitude.   Broad masses of snow-capped
mountains interposed between them and their Syrian kinsmen ;
hence, during several months of the year, help was not to be looked
for, nor interference apprehended from that quarter.   Nevertheless,
friendly relations of the most intimate kind were kept up between
the two groups in the long period of their struggle with Egypt.
When the hands of the latter, however, were engaged in quelling
inward turmoils, which obliged her to renounce distant conquests,
each tribe, relieved of the fear of sudden attacks, fell away from
the mutual bond which had kept them together, in pursuance of
a policy as selfish as it was short-sighted.   Although this is mere
inference, it seems to be confirmed from the fact that we only find
the name of the Hittites of the Naharana in the inscriptions of
Nineveh recording the victories of the Assyrians, the remaining
tribes having apparently kept aloof from the general strife.   The

---

[1] The same hypothesis is set forth in a very able paper by E. Meyer, entitled,
"Kappadokien," published in Ersch and Grüber's Encyclopædia.

auxiliaries of former days, that had done such excellent service against Ramses and Sargon, around Kadesh and Carchemish, being conspicuous by their absence.

The study of the sculptured remains confirms inductions to be drawn from written records ; such monuments in Cappadocia as seem older, are invariably those which come nearer the Syrian carvings. Compare, for example, the Eyuk stones (Figs. 328, 344) with the Merash stelas (Figs. 280, 281) and with Fig. 283 at Roum-Kale. On the other hand, the resemblance is much less marked between the two series, which appear to be of a later date. From the hour when the rulers of Nineveh caused their influence to be felt on the banks of the lower stream of the Euphrates, the Eastern Hittite looked to Assyria for his models. Many a bas-relief (Fig. 279), many a fragment (Fig. 290), might almost pass for work executed for a Babylonian palace.[1] Meanwhile, in Asia Minor, the native artist adhered to the forms and symbols which long usage had endeared to him, albeit in his hands they underwent considerable modification, notably at Boghaz-Keui, where the figures in the passage exhibit so marked a degree of sober elegance, as to suggest the idea that they were the prototypes of Grecian art. Again, rock-cut sculptures are far more numerous in Asia Minor than in Syria. At the outset, this was doubtless due to difference of material, which in Northern Syria was hard and of a volcanic nature, whilst the prevailing stone in the central plateau is calcareous and comparatively soft. All deductions made, the fact remains that, except in Egypt, the ancient world has no parallel instance that can at all compare, in magnitude at least, with these rupesque carvings, affording another proof of the profound originality of the people which executed them. Even had such criteria been wanting, almost

---

[1] The Hittites borrowed the custom of wearing a beard arranged in rows of curls from Mesopotamian sculptures. Among Hittite characters are many which represent the human head with various attributes, but always smoothly shaved (Fig. 256). This peculiarity was reproduced by the Egyptian artist, in his portraiture of the Kheta and their Asiatic allies (Fig. 257, 259, 260, 349, 388). The same applies to the Merash stelas (Fig. 282), and the bas-reliefs at Eyuk, which we incline to regard among the oldest Hittite carvings. On the other hand, we find the beard on bas-reliefs which betray unmistakable signs of Assyrian influence (Figs. 276, 279, 290). If we except a few bearded figures (Plate VIII. E., heading the left procession, Figs. 352, 354), it may be said that closely shaven faces obtained throughout Asia Minor. The Assyrian model nowhere ran more imminent risk of being equalled than in Fig. 254, from Ibreez.

as much would have been learnt by a single glance at the map.[1]

The Hittites, during the time of their closest union with each other, were but a federation, and never grew into a state firmly knitted together. Hence it is not easy to conceive the possibility that the kings of Kadesh and Carchemish were ever in a position to march their armies across Asia Minor, their hands being at all times fully busy in trying to keep their neighbours in check. Nevertheless, the warriors carved on the cliffs of mountain passes would seem to be reminiscences of a successful invasion, in imitation, it may be, of Assyrian and Egyptian captains who left their names and effigies to mark their passage, at Nahr-el-Kelb (ancient Lycus), for example.[2] Everything is easy of explanation, if we suppose strongholds, such as Ghiaour-Kalessi, to have been erected by Western Hittites during their distant expeditions, which extended over a considerable period.[3] The broad masses of the Amanus and the Taurus range were formidable obstacles to claims being put forth at Kadesh or Carchemish to rule Asia Minor. The attempt, if made, would have been frustrated by mere distance. Nor would Tarsus have had a much better chance, for its natural means of communication with the outer world are towards Syria, rather than the central plateau. Criteria, as well as common sense, point to Pterium as having been an important centre—the only one deserving the name—for the space of two or three hundred years. Hissarlik, the Troy of Schliemann, is but an insignificant hamlet compared with Boghaz-Keui, and its stupendous, massive walls, extending over several kilometres, on which are depicted poliote deities, priests, warriors, and princes in turn. From thence, Hittite leaders, with every returning spring, started on those raids which we find vividly pictured on Egyptian and Assyrian monuments. On such occasions, garrisons beyond

---

[1] Sculptures chiselled in the solid rock are stated to exist in the neighbourhood of Antioch, and the mountains east of Alexandretta, with characters which seem to indicate a Hittite origin (SAYCE, *The Monuments, and Bilingual Inscriptions*, etc., pp. 269 and 306).

[2] *Hist. of Art*, tom. ii. p. 651, Fig. 312 ; tom. iii. pp. 6–8, Figs. 2 and 3.

[3] Egyptian monuments show us the Hittites fighting before Kadesh from chariots in which they scour the plain ; the foot-soldiers, with long spears and daggers, form as compact and well-ordered a phalanx as the Egyptian *tuhiru*, "picked men." It is worthy of remark, that the title of *ad in tuhiru* should have served to designate a high functionary at the court of the kings of the Khiti, answering to our field-marshal, generalissimo, etc. (LENORMANT, *Les Inscriptions Hittiques*.)

the Halys were revictualed, the walls of the strongholds were repaired, insubordinate subjects punished, boundaries enlarged, tribute and deputations received, and the autumn saw them turn back loaded with spoils, driving before them herds, flocks, and prisoners.   These, recruited perhaps from the very edge of the Ægean Sea, may have been the builders of the cyclopæan walls of Pterium.   We incline to the belief that the Greek tradition, which told of conquerors from the East who swept over the land, and carried their arms as far as the Mediterranean, was an echo of the Hittite invasion.   But these reminiscences have reached us in the garb and form given them by the Greeks, whose minds were deeply impressed by the recent events connected with the great empires of Assyria and Chaldæa, whose glory had filled the Eastern world, and which, like brilliant meteors, had showed themselves above the horizon, to sink without scarcely leaving a trace.   Hence, whatever of old traditions was still afloat among the people was all referred to the founders of the Assyrian monarchy, Belus, Ninus, and Semiramis.   We know now that the Assyrians never carried their arms westward of the Taurus range before the reign of Assur-nat-sirpal (700 B.C.).   Consequently, the events which took place in Asia Minor before the advent of the Sargonides should be ascribed to the Hittites.   Thus the myth recounted by Herodotus [1] as fabulous, to the effect that the Ionians saw in the warriors carved on rocky walls by the roadside, representations of Memnon, son of Dawn, were doubtless Hittite creations in honour of Hittite heroes.   It would coincide with another myth, which told of Memnon as having been despatched in aid of Priam with two hundred war-chariots by Tentamos, king of Assyria. [2]   Similarly, under the Roman empire, Hierapolis of Comagena was still popu-larly known by its ancient name—Ninus Vetus, the old Nineveh, an appellation which had been borne by the old Hittite capital, Carchemish. [3]   Again, a Lydian tradition derived the Heraclid dynasty from Ninus, son of Belus (Herodotus, i. 7).   This family was superseded by Gyges, the Gog of the Bible, and the Gugu of the Assyrian monuments, where he is figured paying tribute to Assur-nat-sirpal, with whom the history of Lydia may be said to commence.   The three epochs, under three generations of rulers, reckoned by the Lydians, were not drawn up until the reign of

[1] ii. 106.   [2] Diodorus, ii. 22.
[3] *Ammianus Marcellinus*, xiv. 8. 7.

Alyattes and Crœsus; the names of the dynasties thus preserved are important, nevertheless, as reminiscences of their remote past. One curious point should be noted, namely, that if any reliance is to be placed on the chronology of Herodotus, the duration of five hundred years, or thereabouts, assigned to the dynasty of the Heraclidæ, would carry us back to the end of the thirteenth century B.C. Now, the evidence yielded by Assyrian monuments proves that about this time the power of the Hittites was at its highest, and extended to the border of the Ægean.[1] In the preceding period, the Hittites of Cappadocia had engaged in all the wars against Egypt, so that leisure was denied them to spread towards the peninsula. In the meanwhile Thracian tribes had stolen a march on them, and, under the name of Phrygians, free men, had taken firm footing of the country between the Halys and about the head springs of the Sangarius and Hermus. The downfall of the Hittites may be dated from the day when this living barrier interposed in central Anatolia. Like the Assyrians, their action had been one of conquest; they had traversed vast provinces, but without settling in them. The Phrygians compelled them to recross the Halys, and renounce expeditions in the far west; nevertheless, they remained the intermediaries of a brisk commerce carried on by means of caravans, whose pathway between Mesopotamia and Asia Minor led across their territory. They retained, moreover, the moral advantage of having been the first (in that part of the world) to possess an art and a system of writing, together with public rites in keeping with "the majesty divine" of their great local deities. It was not for long, however, for they had to give way before the Carians, Lycians, Phrygians, and Lydians, whose experience and knowledge were enlarged by intercourse with Punic traders and Greek colonists settled on the coasts. Hence towards the eighth century B.C., civilization changed hands, and migrated from the eastern to the western bank of the Halys. Henceforward we only hear of the Hittites as vassals of the Assyrians. It is probable that to avoid being transplanted, or put to death as Pisiris had been by Sargon (717 B.C.), the kings of Cappadocia acknowledged the suzerainty of Assyria, Media, and Persia in turn. They were attacked by Crœsus, as the vassals of the latter power, towards the fifth century B.C.; and although the foolish invasion was swiftly arrested by the Eastern monarch, it

[1] SAYCE, *The Monuments*, p. 273.

had this permanent effect, that it broke up for ever the remaining Hittite group, whose chief centre, Boghaz-Keui, may then have been besieged and destroyed.   At any rate, we have proved that if Hittite arts were still in force towards the middle of the sixth century, it was in this district, where their monuments are found in abundance.   Tradition was cut asunder by this catastrophe, never to be resumed.   What was left of the old stock was fused in the remnants of the Moschian and Tibarenian tribes, which had perhaps preceded them in the country.   From this mixture of nationalities the emasculated Cappadocians were formed, whose very name became a term of reproach, whether under Persian or Greek rule, and whose feeble efforts to regain their independence under native princes, Ariarathes and Ariobarzanes, were effectually crushed by the iron rule of Rome.[1]

Thus it came to pass that, when the Greeks took upon themselves to write the history of the civilized world, the name of the Hittites was already forgotten.   If, in order to reinstate them on their proper level, modern scholars have recoiled before no obstacles, it was because they from the outset gauged the importance of adding another chapter to the history of the Asianic peninsula, which, from various causes, has ever been a main point of interest and attraction.   The civilization which the Hittites introduced in central Anatolia cannot wholly have perished.   To them may be attributed the peculiar pantheistic cultus which prevailed throughout Asia Minor ; and which at Comana, Zela, Pessinus, etc., was presided over by priest-kings, sometimes eunuch-priests, surrounded by thousands of self-mutilated hierodules, and other officials of either sex.[2]   It is possible that Atys, but more especially the great goddess who appears under the various names of Mâ, Kybêbê, Kybelê, Cybele, the Ephesian Artemis, Diana, may have been imported from Cappadocia into Phrygia.   Of the

---

[1] E. Meyer, *Kappadokien*, etc., believes that in historical times the Aryan element was dominant in Cappadocia. He bases his hypothesis on the fact that a number of local names end in -ασσος and -μνη, but, as we only know these names through Greek transliterations, his reason cannot be said to carry weight with it.   It received its name of Cappadocia (Kappatuka) from the Persians, as we learn from their inscriptions, as well as from Herodotus.

[2] Upon the origin of the worship at Ephesus, and the Asiatic elements which largely obtained down to the beginning of our era, see Curtius, *Beiträge zür Geschichte, etc. (Ephesos, Pergamon, Smyrna, Sardes)*, in 4to, 1872 ; Denkmäler, Berlin.

essentially Phrygian character of the worship evidenced on the
bas-reliefs at Boghaz-Keui, we have spoken elsewhere, when we
pointed out that the female deity wears the mural crown, and is
supported by lions, whilst at Pessinus they draw her chariot.   At
Merash (Fig. 281), she holds a pomegranate, the emblem of life
and fecundity throughout Asia Minor, a symbol likewise adopted
by Grecian art.   Is this to be taken as a fortuitous resemblance and
a mere coincidence?   We shall not dwell upon another striking
resemblance between the two arts ; namely, that the pretty custom
of placing flowers in the hands of goddesses, as at Boghaz-Keui
(Fig. 337) and Eyuk, is likewise found in the early manifestations
of Hellenic art ; for it may have been derived in both instances
from Egypt and Phœnicia, where its usage was universal, be it as
an emblem or simple and graceful means of ornament.

To Cappadocia also should be ascribed those war-chariots which
obtained throughout the peninsula, and which are so lovingly
dwelt upon by Homer, when he describes the encounters of his
two favourite heroes, Hector, the stay of Troy, and the divine
Achilles.   Curious enough, when archæologists tried to restore
the ancient Greek chariot from the Homeric text, it was found
to correspond in every particular with the Hittite examples
depicted in the monuments of Egypt.[1]   The helmet,[2] shield, and
leggings, which made of the Greek hoplite a "bronze man," cannot be set down as Hittite inventions ; for their defensive armour,

---

[1] HELBIG, *Das Homerische Epos, etc.*, 1884, in 8vo, pp. 88-95.   We learn from
Pentaour, the court poet, that in the memorable battle fought around Kadesh 2500
chariots were left in the hands of the Egyptians.   Some authorities incline to the
belief that war-chariots originated in Anterior Asia, whence they passed into Egypt
(BRUGSCH, *Geschichte Ægyptens*, p. 273 and following.   EBERS, *Ægypten, und die
Bücher Moses*, i. p. 221).

[2] HERODOTUS, iii. 152.   Professor Sayce brings nothing in support of his opinion
that "the Greeks borrowed their helmets from the Hittites, through the medium of
the Carians" (*Transactions Soc. Bibl. Archæ.*, tom. vii. p. 303).   For my part, I
cannot see a bronze helmet in the Hittite cap.

It may not be irrelevant to cite the passage in which the opinion of Professor
Sayce is expressed : "We have only to glance at the costume and arms of the
natives of Van as depicted on the Balawat bronzes to see that they were cousins of
the Hittites, and the striking resemblance between the helmets worn by the latter
and those of the early Greeks probably results from the fact that the Greek helmet
was really of Hittite origin.   Herodotus (i. 171) expressly states that the Greeks
had borrowed their helmets, as well as the 'emblems' on their shields, from the
Carians, and the Carians, as we know, were once subject to Hittite influence."   The
"Greek helmet" is distinctly seen by others besides Professor Sayce.—ED.

whether we see it on Pterian or Egyptian bas-reliefs, invariably consists of an indented shield, club, and single or double-headed axe, weapons which the Greeks identified with the Amazons. The fact that the axe was the attribute of "Jupiter Labranda," and the special weapon of the Carians, that some letters of their alphabet were clearly borrowed from Hittite hieroglyphs, must be ascribed to physical causes, which rendered Caria accessible to her neighbours, and consequently to the free circulation of ideas.

Hittite art to the last remained poor and crude; such as it was, however, it furnished, during the space of five or six hundred years, the main types and subjects in vogue among the populations of central Anatolia; whence, by easy stages, they penetrated among the Greeks of the seaboard. Thus, to name but an instance, the bas-reliefs in the temple at Assos, in Mysia, one of the earliest examples of the Doric order, vividly recall the Eyuk sculpture, representing a lion in deadly conflict with a ram. The Ionic order, as the name implies, had its birth in the Greek cities of Asia Minor. Now, it will be remembered that we called attention to the fluted pillar and the double volute, both distinct features of the order, in the œdicula at Boghaz-Keui. We do not deny that both may have been suggested by ivories and art-objects of Punic make; but we submit that the possibility of their having found their way through land routes, is every bit as good as through the "watery ways." If this be deemed conjectural by some, nobody will deny the Hittite origin of the noble type of the Amazons, which has yielded the loftiest and purest themes to the sister arts of sculpture, poetry, and painting. Tradition ascribed to them the foundation of the temple at Ephesus, and we think we recognize them at Boghaz-Keui, where they perform a military dance in honour of the deity. At any rate, their chief seat on the banks of the Thermôdôn was in this neighbourhood.

The Greeks, as the heirs of all the useful activity of primitive civilization, translated their concepts of the part played by the great nations who had preceded them on the soil in writing their history; wherein the name of the Hittites does not once occur. Some have thought to see it in the κήτειοι[1] of Homer (Od. xi. 521), who figure among the auxiliaries of the Trojans; whilst others have tried to prove that the name belonged to a tribe in the immediate neighbourhood of Ilium (Mysia). But in all the

[1] Gladstone, *Homeric Synchronisms*, pp. 174–182.

transcriptions which have been obtained from the various languages, the initial letter of the word "Hittite" is always a strong guttural aspirate, equivalent to the Hebrew ח, *ch;* now, as we know, the kappa cannot yield an aspirate of any kind. More than this, there is nothing to prove that κήτειοι was a proper name; the theory, therefore, must be set aside as untenable. The stir and commotion which formerly surrounded the Hittites in the Eastern world is only borne to us through the faint echo of the Memnon legend. The neglect which had fallen upon them when the inquisitive mind of the Greeks awoke to consciousness, we have explained as due to the fact that at that time they had ceased to be of any account in Syria, and had been obliged to concentrate themselves in Cappadocia, a number of tribes, the Mysians, Lydians, and Phrygians, interposing between them and the sea.

Nevertheless, Homer may have alluded to Hittite hieroglyphs, when he relates of Prœtos, king of Argos, who, wishing to rid himself of Bellerophon, sent him to Lycia with a folded (sealed) tablet, upon which he had written "many murderous signs." As soon as the king of Lycia beheld the characters, he understood the message, and spared nothing to put it in execution.[1] It has been sought to prove from this passage, that writing was known and practised when Homer sang his heroic tales in the halls of Ionian chiefs; but, if so, we should find multitudinous allusions thereto in his immortal poems, in which the life and customs of his time are mirrored. On the other hand, it is clear that the tablet contained more than a "single" sign; for this would imply a personal interview between the two kings, when the "deadly token" had been agreed upon. Improbable as this would be at the present hour, it would have been utterly impossible in those early days, when the distance between Asia Minor and Hellas was to be measured by days and weeks of perilous voyage. Nevertheless, we may be sure that if the poet used a similar expression, it was because he knew that his audience would understand that a death-warrant could be conveyed through painted or inscribed characters.[2] Now, what system of epigraphy was likely to meet their gaze, except the

---

[1] HOMER, *Iliad,* vi. 168, 169.

Πέμπε δέ μιν Λυκίηνδί, πόρεν δ' ὄγε σήματα λυγρά,
Γράψας ἐν πίνακιῳ πτυκτ θυμοφθόρα πολλά.

Aristarcus seems to have formed a shrewd guess with regard to the nature of the signs inscribed on the tablet by Prœtos, for in writing of them he uses the term εἴδωλα, images, and not γράμματα, letters.

Hittite hieroglyphs which they beheld everywhere in the monuments erected by the Hittites, and which even now we can read, after so many centuries of exposure to the elements? To these may be added small objects with Hittite emblems, brought by trading caravans from the table-land, be it hematite cylinders, plaques, bowls, or seals applied to bales of merchandise. A vessel covered all over with Hittite symbols was lately found at Babylon;[1] others have been exhumed in various parts of Asia Minor, warranting the inference that they were of common occurrence some centuries before Homer. A certain degree of attention was thus forcibly directed to this peculiar system of signs, by means of which interchange of thought could be carried on.

An ardent desire was thus aroused in those young communities, full of ferment and eager for progress, to possess themselves of so precious a boon. In which of these were Phœnician letters first applied to the Greek language? We shall probably never know; but this is certain, that they came in after an older writing, which prevailed throughout Asia Minor. Had the Cadmæan alphabet been first in date, no other would have been sought; since it is not conceivable that a scheme, almost perfect in its simplicity, would have been abandoned for a clumsy unwieldy one. To the Hittites, therefore, must be ascribed the singular honour of having been the inventors of a system of signs from which were derived the Lycian, Carian, Cappadocian, and Cypriote alphabets. In their modified form they served to create the language known to us in the immortal works of the great Greek writers. This of itself is sufficient claim to our gratitude, and justifies in full our having essayed to revive the memory of their name, and rescue them from oblivion.

[1] Wright, *The Empire*, Plate XXV.

ADDITIONS AND CORRECTIONS.

Vol. i. page 266, 1, 5, and 6. Our view is based upon M. Clermont-Ganneau's able paper entitled, "The Veil of the Temple at Olympia and Jerusalem," *Quarterly Statements, Palestine Exploration Fund*, April 1876, pp. 79–81.

FIG. 390.—Sculptures brought to light at Jerabis. *Graphic*, December 11th, 1880.

Vol. i. page 285. In support of our hypothesis as to the probable site of the royal tombs, see also "Notes" by the Rev. W. F. Birch, *Quarterly Statements*, 1886, pp. 26–34; 151–154.

Vol. i. page 327, note 3, add Schick.   The aqueducts at Siloam, with map, *Quarterly Statements*, 1886, pp. 88–91.

Vol. i. Page 357, Fig. 250.   De Saulcy ("Note sur les projectiles à main creux et en terre cuite." *Mémoires de la Société des Antiquaires de France*, vol. xxxv.) points out the mistake made by M. Greville Chester, in ascribing a remote Egyptian origin to the small clay vases which were described by him in the *Recovery*.   De Saulcy lighted upon precisely similar vessels at Tripoli, in Syria, each decorated by four trade-marks which run round the body of the vessel, and each surrounded by an Arabic legend, to the following effect : "*Bi Hama*, at Hama," *i.e.* manufactured at

Fig. 391.—Sculptures discovered at Jerabis.   *Graphic*, December 11th, 1880.

Hama.   The legend is important, inasmuch as it enables us to fix the date of these peculiarly shaped flagons, and this cannot be protracted beyond the middle ages.   He thinks, moreover, that they were caps, or fulminates, used in letting off Greek fire, the mercury found in them having been set free by the decomposing action of time.

Vol. ii. page 30, Fig. 262.   The latest account which reaches us in regard to the boss of Tarkondemôs is from the pen of M. Amiaud, entitled, *Simple coup d'œil sur la bulle de M. Jovanoff sur les Inscriptions Hétéennes*   M. Amiaud is of opinion that the genuineness of the piece is beyond cavil, and older than was at first supposed

by Professor Sayce; perhaps 1100 B.C.   He questions the reading of one or two
of the cuneiform characters, as well as the value of the Hittite signs proposed by the
Professor, and asks for fresh examination of the cast.   He further asks whether it
were not possible to institute a comparison between Phœnician letters and Hittite
hieroglyphs, as was done for the Cypriote syllabary, with the not improbable result
that, like the latter, the Punic alphabet would be found to have been derived from
Hittite signs.   The issue involved in the points raised by M. Amiaud was noticed
by Ed. Meyer, *Geschichte des Alterthüms*, tom. i. p. 238, as tending to upset the long-
established theory that the Phœnicians borrowed their letters from Egypt.

FIG. 392.—View of the Mound, or Tell.   Jerabis.

Vol. ii. page 49.   Here is a summary of the account of the Jerablus (or Jerabis)
monuments which M. Boscowen sent to the *Graphic*.   Facing the entrance, at the
extremity of the trench, are two imperfect tablets which formed part of an adoration scene, each occupied by a figure, or rather the upper part of a figure, for the
legs of the goddess, described in another place, are broken from above the knees;
whilst of the second figure, or priestess, the whole of the under-part up to the hips
has disappeared.   She is wrapped in loose drapery, which doubtless covered her
from head to foot; the fore-arms alone are exposed.   The curious band about her
waist should be noticed; it consists of twin cords looped behind; which seem to
have been in the prophet's mind when he wrote, " The women, having cords around
their body, sit by the wayside; and one says to her companion, why was I not
chosen, and my cord broken?" (Baruch vi. 42).   An inscription of four lines, in
Hittite characters, occupies the upper part of this stone.   A little further were three
figures clearly moving in a procession—a priest, recognizable by his long Assyrian
robe, and two warriors, with the usual short tunic, fringed border, and curled shoes.
An interlaced band enframed the stone, but the lowermost is alone extant.   The
manipulation of the dress and general character of these figures, notably the hieroglyphs, make it self-evident that they were executed for and by Hittites before
Carchemish fell to Sargon, and were part of a religious pomp, like the sculptures at
Eyuk and Iasili-Kaia.   The hooded mantle of the priestess, albeit somewhat differently arranged, recalls the Merash stelas (Figs. 280, 281); and the long garment
of the central figure in the next stone is akin to the Pterian chasuble (Figs. 314,
328); whilst the short tunic is common to Boghaz-Keui, Lydia, and Phrygia.

It is much to be regretted that these interesting bas-reliefs have been left behind, and that no good drawings were made. The rough sketches at our disposal do not permit us to judge of the fabrication, except that they seem to belong to the period preceding the downfall of the Hittites, when their art was dependent upon Assyrian art, exemplified in the sculptured stones at Saktchegheuksou (Fig. 279).

The remaining sketches are of minor interest. Figure 392 shows that the tell,

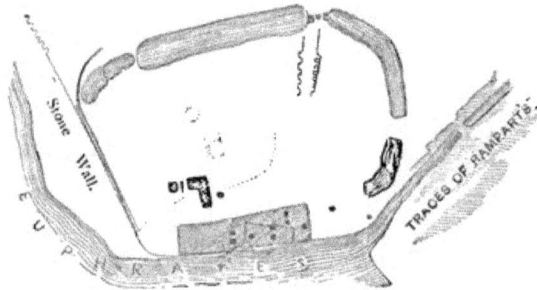

FIG. 393.—Plan of Ruins. Jerabis.

with a few huts at the base, occupies the same position as ancient Carchemish on the Balawat bronzes, to record the victories of Shalmanezer III. The city was built on the eastern bank of the Euphrates, and the plan (Fig. 393) reveals the fact that the mountain, where formerly stood the castle, or acropolis, was about the centre of the area, on the very margin of the river, as at Babylon and other ancient cities. Excavations have disclosed traces of the wall of enclosure, which ran north and south and

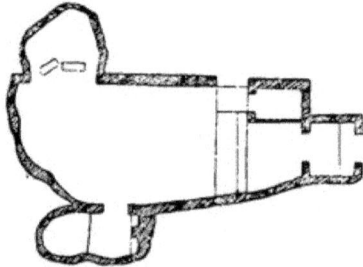

FIG. 394.—Plan of Excavations. Jerabis.

probably on the east side also; as well as traces of ditches, which followed the direction of the rampart inside, and were connected with the river. Fig. 394 shows three small chambers on the dexter hand, followed by a long passage which gave access to the main section of the structure.

Vol. ii. page 120. M. Radet, of the French School at Athens, visited Eflatoun Bounar in the spring of 1885. His critical account was submitted to the Académie des

Inscriptions, under the title *Voyage en Karamanie*. He was the first to observe that the façade is slightly pyramidal in shape, measuring 7 m. at the base, and 6 m. 80 c. towards the apex. Like M. Ramsay, he fails to detect " raised" arms in the colossal figures of the twin pillars, or the attitude of the caryatides figured in our woodcut. Like him, he believes that the said figures were intended for a divine couple, the goddess on the dexter hand being recognizable by a disc or halo around her face, *i.e.* the characteristic headdress of Hathor, which we long ago said ought to be there. He shares our opinion that the top block of the façade had formerly a crowning member, part of which he identifies in a stone 5 m. 25 c., the upper face of which is rounded off, forming a rude frame for three niches underneath, which may have been occupied by idols. It is to be regretted that no measurement or drawing was taken. His words seem to imply that the space interposing between the façade and the talus is not large enough for a chamber, the structure having been all front. Such an opinion, however, is belied by the stones heaped about the walls of the structure, portions of which are still standing. Moreover, a stone discovered by M. Ramsay was evidently a window-frame, and this could only have belonged to the side walls, since the façade was unpierced.

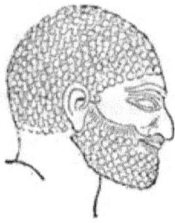

FIG. 1.

FIG. 2.

FIG. 3.

FIG. 4.

FIG. 5.

FIG. 6.

INDEX.

A.

Clermont-Ganneau discovers the Mesa stone, i. 119n., 305, 309n. ; his opinion on masons' marks of stones, i. 185 ; tombs, i. 278n. ; monolith of Siloam, on tree-worship, i. 138, 296n., 330 ; exposes the fraudulent author of the Moabite pottery, i. 349 ; a so-called MS., i. 350, 351 ; conjecture respecting the veil of the temple, i. 265, n. 1.
Club at Boghaz-Keui, ii. 129.
Cœre, i. 14, 263, 264.
Collignon, drawings of, Deunuk-Tach, ii. 42, 49–51.
Columns, isolated in Phœnicia, i. 235 ; in the temple of Jerusalem, i. 236 ; restoration of the twin columns, i. 235 ; Proto-Ionic at Gherdek Kaiassi in Pteria, ii. 179, 180.
Comagena, ii. 272.
Conder, views of, on the Royal Tombs at Jerusalem, i. 284, 288n ; dolmens in Moab, i. 294 ; Siloam canal, i. 326, 327 ; the site of Kadesh, ii. 17, n. 1, 2.
Cones, cylinders ending in, holed, ii. 246, 251 ; conical rocks in Cappadocia, ii. 264, 265.
Copper at Teti, i. 89, 98.
Cord, on Sardinian statuettes, i. 66–68 ; around "kuffeyehs," i. 361 ; as sashes for women, ii. 279.
Corsi, i. 20.
Costume, among the Jews, i. 360–362 ; Hittite, ii. 60–62, 65, 69, 71, 128, 129, 135, 136, 139, 143, 145, 160, 168, 203, 233, 240 ; female, ditto, ii. 67, 68.
Court of the people, i. 206, 212, 213 ; of the priests, i. 206 ; the gentiles, i. 218.
Crespi, i. 20, 77.
Crœsus, invasion of Cappadocia by, ii. 103.
Cubit, i. 201, 202n.
Curtius (Ernest), what he says of the cultus at Ephesus, ii. 274n.
Cybele in Pteria, ii. 146–148 ; in Phrygia, ii. 206–208.
Cypress wood at Jerusalem, i. 128, 131, 266.
Cypriote alphabet, ii. 33, 35.

D.

Dæmonic figures at Iasili-Kaïa, ii. 137.
Damascus, i. 132, 350.
Dardani, i. 17, ii. 23.
David, character and reign of, i. 127n., 128 ; purchases the threshing-floor of

Araunah the Jebusite, i. 145, 177, n. 3 ; his house on Mount Zion, i. 129 ; his tomb and that of his successors, i. 284, 288 ; teraphim, i. 334, 335n., 336.
Davis, discoveries of, ii. 209–211.
Debir, i. 217, n. 3, 218.
Deïd, i. 17.
Deir Ghuzaleh, ii. 292, 293.
Delbet, photographs of, ii. 101.
Dennis, views of, on the pseudo-Niobe, ii. 236, n. 2, 238, n. 1.
Deunuk-Tach, ii. 50, 51.
Dikili-Tach, ii. 182, n. 1.
Diminutive wheels or castors, i. 263, 264.
Diodorus, opinion of, respecting núraghs, i. 45 ; ii. 291.
Direkli-Tach, ii. 58.
Doghanlou Deresi, ii. 206, 207.
Dolmens (holed), i. 294 ; altars, i. 294, 295.
Doughty (Charles), discoveries of, in Arabia, ii. 271, n. 1.
Drafted stones at Jerusalem, i. 165, 169.
Drake, first copies of Hamathite inscriptions, ii. 5.
Dromos in front of palace at Eyuk, ii. 157.

E.

Edomites, i. 119.
Eflatoun-Bounar, ii. 215–221.
Egypt, sojourn of the Israelites in, i. 123, n. 1.
El Aksa, i. 159.
El Manasseh, i. 182.
El Marcighâth, i. 293.
Embattled edge, in our restoration of the temple, i. 241 ; no traces in the fortification wall at Boghaz-Keui, ii. 122.
Ephod, i. 336, 337.
Es Sakhra, i. 159.
Eunuch priest in Pteria, ii. 147, 274, n. 1.
Eye of Osiris on Jewish intaglio, i. 341.
Eyes, multiplicity of eyes on Sardinian statuettes, i. 60, 80.
Ezekiel, chapters of, xl.–xliii., i. 191, 197, 203, 224.

F.

Fairs, ii. 142, 143.
Fassler, ii. 222, n. 1.

www.ingramcontent.com/pod-product-compliance
Lightning Source LLC
Chambersburg PA
CBHW031404270326
41929CB00010BA/1314